Pearson Education Limited
Edinburgh Gate, Harlow,
Essex CM20 2JE, England
and Associated Companies throughout the World

www.longman-elt.com

© Richard Side 1994

First published by Nelson ELT 1994,
This edition published by Addison Wesley Longman Ltd 1995
Fifth impression 2001

ISBN 0-17-556433-7

Printed in China
GCC/05

Acknowledgements

The author would like to thank John Eckersley and the staff and
students of The Eckersley School of English, Oxford, for their help
and support during the writing of this book.

The publishers would like to thank the following for their kind
permission to use material in this book:

ACIS; Basil Blackwell, *Sweet Freedom* by Anne Coote and Beatrix
Campbell; British Railways Board; Cambridge University Press,
Language Habits of the Japanese by Kinosita Koreo;
Consumers' Association and Hodder and Stoughton, *Preventing
Heart Disease*; Deutsche Grammaphon; Dorling Kindersley, *The
British Medical Association Complete Family Health Encyclopedia*;
Faber and Faber Ltd., *I'm sorry I'll write that again* by Keith
Waterhouse/ *The Inheritors* by William Golding/ *The Wimbledon
Poisoner* by Nigel Williams/ *The Whitsun Weddings* by Philip Larkin;
Hamish Hamilton Publishers, *Arrow in the Blue* by Arthur Koestler/
The Black and White Medicine Show by Donald Gould; Heinemann
Publishers, *Teaching Reading Skills in a Foreign Language* by C.
Nuttall Collins; Hodder and Stoughton Ltd., *The New Naked
Manager* by Robert Heller; HarperCollins Publishers, *Goodbye
Tarzan (Men After Feminism)*, *"Stereotypic man"*, by Helen Franks;
In a Free State by V.S. Naipaul; John Murray Publishers, *Oxford
Observed* by Peter Snow; Judy Piatkus Ltd., *How to collect the money
you are owed*, by Malcolm Bird; Jonathon Cape Publishers, *The
Cement Garden* by Ian McEwan; Kate Adie, BBC, *The Listener*
(21/9/89); Macmillan London Ltd., *Service of All the Dead* by Colin
Dexter; Michael Joseph, *The Grass is Singing* by Doris Lessing/ *Ask
Me Tomorrow* by Stan Barstow; Milldon and Co Ltd.; National
Enquirer, *I'll Go to Jail Before I Let My Runaway Son Set Foot in My
House Again* by Karen Capuano; Nicholas Brearly Publishing, *Mind
Your Manners* by John Mole; Penguin Books Ltd., *For Whom the Bell
Tolls* by Ernest Hemingway/ *Advertising* by Michael Pollard; The
Daily Mail, *The Wretched Rabbit and me* by Julian Champkin; The
Hogarth Press, *In a Province* by Laurens van der Post; The
Observer, *Strife in the Fast Lane Takes Its Toll* by Tim Walker/
article from World Magazine *David Taylor, Zoo Vet*; The Readers
Digest Association Ltd; The Telegraph, *Sister's hopes rise for
Bentley's pardon*; Victor Gollanz Ltd., *The Green Business Guide* by
John Elkington and Peter Knight; The Guardian, *Family Awaits
Pardon For Bentley* by Duncan Campbell; Times Newspapers Ltd.,
Move to bury London's traffic crisis by Nick Rufford/ *Language Class
Gives Lesson in Sexual Harmony* by Caroline St Brooks/ *Gatwick
Stopover* by John Diamond; World Magazine/ *Camel Milking* by
Hamish Hamilton.

The publishers have made every effort to contact owners of
copyright, but this has not been possible in all cases. They
apologise for any omissions, and if details are sent, will be glad to
rectify these when the title is reprinted.

Cover Illustration: Dulce Tobin.

Cartoons and Illustrations:
Doug Baker, pages 7 and 24; Noel Ford, page 38 ; Sophie Grillet,
pages 15, 89 and 142; Rachel Ross, page 146; Mel Calman, pages
18 and 63; Julian Mosedale, *Penant*, page 25; Frank Nichols, *Linda
Rodgers Associates* page 44; John Brennan, *The Inkshed*, pages 51
and 77; Phil Green and John Lawson, *The Sunday Times*, page 54;
Rob Glynn, *Private Eye*, page 69; David Kaluba, page 73; Gary
Embury, *Penant*, page 114; Mathew Pritchett, *The Telegraph*, page
145; David Austin, pages 39, 156 and 158.

Photographs:
Allsport: 12.2a, 12.2c, 12.5; Arcaid: 4.2d; Armani: 9.5a; Audi: 9.1a;
BBC: 3.1; The Body Shop: 14.4; Stuart Boreham Photography: 10.2;
Allan Cash Photo Library: 4.2b, 4.2c; The Copthorne Effingham
Park: 4.1b; The Daily Mail: 12.4a, 12.4b; Mary Evans Picture Library:
1.1; Henley Management College: 14.2: Keble College, Oxford by
permission of the Wards and Fellows of Keble College: 4.1a;
NHPA: 3.2; Network: 13.3; Network/Abrahams: 8.1b; Network/
Doran: 13.3; Network/Lowe: 8.1d; Network/Sturrock: 8.1c; Panos
Pictures:10.4; 10.4b; Perrier: 9.5b; Pictor International: 2.1, 9.1d;
Proctor and Gamble: 9.3a, 9.3b; John Radcliffe Hospital: 11.2; Rex
Features: 4.2a, 5.5, 7.3, 8.1a, 11.6, 12.1a, 12.1d; The Science Photo
Library: 11.3; Scott Limited: 9.1c; Still Pictures: 5.1, 5.3a, 5.3b, 5.3c;
The Sunday Times: 5.2; The Telegraph: 6.3; Tony Stone
Worldwide: 2.3, 8.3, 9.4, 10.1, 14.6; John Walmsey Photography:
8.2; Ken Wells Photography: 9.1b; Michael Williams Photography:
6.1, 7.1; Zefa: 9.2a, 9.2b, 10.1a, 13.4, 13.5, 13.6, 14.1.

The author would also like to thank the following people for their
co-operation in allowing us to interview them:

Helen Andrews, page 11; Catriona Davidson, pages 20 and 149;
Bernard Davis, pages 20, 80, 113 and 149; Pat Halliday, page 35;
Susannah Newman, ACIS, page 38; Colin Dexter, pages 50 and 83;
Noel Newson, Oxford City Planning Department, page 56; Sharon
Watson, page 62; Dominic Bullock, pages 62 and 80; David Hearst,
The Guardian, page 68; Fox FM news, page 70; Jenny Pearce, page
91; Mark Roberts, The Belou Group, page 99; Fox FM, page 105;
OGV, page 105; Pedigree Petfoods, page 105; The Suite Shop, page
105; Johnsons, page 105; Banbury Cycle Centre, page 105; Pizza
Piazza, page 105; Simon Mollison, page 110; Amanda Thurston,
Acupuncture Centre, Oxford, page 125; Ian Barker, page 128;
Amanda Jenkins, page 134; Helen Elkington, page 138; Mary Piggot,
Oxford Social Services, page 144; Mark Pear, page 149; Bill Simon,
Henley Management College, page 154; John Eckersley, page 160.

In Advance

RICHARD SIDE

	1 The Tricks of the Trade	2 Putting Your Foot in It	3 Jobs and Giraffes	4 Creating an Atmosphere	5 In a Jam	6 Not Like in the Movies	7 A Monstrous Machine
UNIT							
TOPIC	Language learning skills at advanced level	Cross-cultural behaviour	Work and animals	Describing places	Traffic problems	Reporting	Narrative writing
LISTENING 1	Advanced students: learning English	Greetings in different countries	Stable owner talking about horses	People describing places	Oxford's traffic problems	Journalist: war reporting in Yugoslavia	Discussion on opening sentences of novels
LISTENING 2	Teacher of students in LISTENING 1: learning English	6 short dialogues/ register	Interview with job interviewer	Interview with Colin Dexter: literary description	Conversation about commuting	Radio news broadcast	Interview with Colin Dexter: writing technique
READING 1	Variety of discourse types: appropriacy	Japanese and Western linguistic behaviour	Job advertisements	Newspaper review of hotels: *Gatwick Stopover*	*Move to bury London's traffic crisis*	Kate Adie reporting Tiananmen Square massacre	*A Monstrous Machine* by Arthur Koestler
READING 2	Discourse analysis: cohesion/ coherence	*The Way We Do Things Round Here*	Magazine article about a zoo vet	Extracts from two novels	*Strife in the fast lane takes its toll*	*Sister's hopes rise for Bentley pardon*	First pages of novels
SPEAKING	Skills needed when speaking	Short role-plays: register	Role-play: job interview	Describing a place: spontaneous and considered speaking	Role-plays: • City council meeting • A road accident	Reading a news broadcast	Eliciting others' opinions First paragraphs of novels
WRITING	Different types of written text	Formal letter of apology/register	A job advertisement Formal job rejection letter	Paragraph describing a place LITERARY EXTENSION: 'The Whitsun Weddings'	Report of role-play in SPEAKING 1	Writing a newspaper report	Narrative: continuing a given extract
LEXIS	Study skills: learning vocabulary Collocation: introduction; *make + have* Connotation: introduction	Appropriacy Dictionary skills Collocation *give, take* and *have*	Animal idioms Adjectives: personal and job qualities Adjectives/noun collocation: *work* Phrasal verbs: meaning of 'on'	Adverbs describing place Adjectives for atmosphere Describing smell	Vocabulary and collocation from READING 1 Verbs of movement Adjectives followed by prepositions Phrasal verbs : 'up'	Newspaper vocabulary and headlines Reporting verbs	Onomatopoeia Adverbs of manner
GRAMMAR	Grammar: what is it and do we need it?	Articles	Participle and verbless clauses Cleft sentences	Adjectives: attributive and predicative	Relative clauses and participle clauses	Grammar of headlines Infinitive future The passive	Continuous aspect

P r a c t i c e   S e c t i o n

8	9	10	11	12	13	14
quality of opportunity	Too Smart to be Taken in	The Kindness of Strangers	Kill or Cure?	Just not Cricket!	Parents and Children	Getting Down to Business
Education, ringing, sexual tereotypes	Advertising	Travelling, experiencing alien cultures	Medicine	The nature and fairness of sport	Parental authority, adolescence	Business
olchildren: ng with school the opposite	Marketing consultant on advertising	Travelling overland from India to England	Interview with an acupuncturist	Discussion on use of drugs in sport	Interview with social worker on READING 1	Interview with tutor from Henley Management College
ol teacher ussing sexual otyping	6 radio advertisements	Experiences on a lorry in Brazil	Argument about the effectiveness of modern medicine	Olympic swimming coach: synchronised swimming	Discussion: dealing with a child who behaves badly	John Eckersley: running a language school
education	4 advertisements for cosmetic aids	Travelling in Japan	Description of a modern hospital	News reports on Seoul Olympics	I'll go to jail before I let my son set foot in my house again	The Harvard Business School
otypic man	Advertising: arguments for and against	Camel milking in Somalia	Nonconformists, mystics, charlatans and cranks	The Wretched Rabbit and me – article on caving	Parents who are authoritarian	The Body Shop International
ussing ation – sing your mistakes	Giving opinions on advertising	Negotiating: planning a journey	Arguing skills Pronunciation of unstressed words	Informal argument	Role-play: parent/ child/social worker meeting (READING 1)	Telephoning Giving a presentation
nary (from ING 1)	Appropriacy and linking – writing an advertisement Presenting a formal written argument	Describing a journey	Re-writing: style, organisation, register and sentence structure (fronting)	Report/humorous article on synchronised swimming	Summary (from READING 1)	Dealing with the late payment of an invoice Standard phrases for business letters
sal verbs with sm in language	Formal and informal discourse Advertising vocabulary Nouns referring back to spoken or written texts	Collocation: submodifiers Collocation: types of travelling Connotation: misfit, loner, etc.	Disease and treatment Idioms on health Discourse markers	Sporting idioms Collocating prepositions Collocation: run and get	Slang Synonymy	Business vocabulary Collocation
ditional clauses	Pronouns	Perfect aspect	Fronting	Using modals to express the past	Complex sentences and discourse	Future forms

P r a c t i c e   S e c t i o n

The Tricks of the Trade

'I wonder why those foreign
students walked out.'

'I looked up the absolute participle
phrase and you'll be pleased to know
you were right after all, dear.'

F O C U S

1 In small groups, discuss the following questions.

a Below is a list of difficulties that some people encounter when they reach an advanced level in English. Which of them apply to you?

- ☐ feeling you aren't learning fast enough
- ☐ boredom with being in a classroom
- ☐ coping with large amounts of vocabulary
- ☐ frustration: you'll never be as good as you want to be
- ☐ too many exams
- ☐ not getting sufficient opportunity to speak English
- ☐ still making elementary mistakes
- ☐ not being able to understand English/American people in films

b What are the advantages of being advanced? Write a similar list to that in **a**.

2 a How long does it take to reach an advanced level?

b How necessary is it for you to learn English to such a standard?

c In what situations will you use English in the future?

d Which aspects of your English would you particularly like to improve? Be as specific as possible.

LISTENING 1

1 a Most units in this book contain two listening sections. They will include activities for **extensive** listening and for **intensive** listening. What do you think these two terms mean?

b Look at the following examples of listening activities which you will find in this book. Which do you think are intensive, which are extensive, and which are a mixture?

1 listening for gist
2 note taking
3 short extracts
4 focusing on general meaning
5 focusing on stress and intonation patterns
6 listening for specific words
7 listening for specific information
8 concentrating on very fast sentences
9 long extracts

2 In the following recording, you will hear three students talking about learning English.

a Do they mention anything you talked about in exercise 1 of the FOCUS section? Make brief notes on the problems which each student mentions.

| 1 **Ewa** (Swedish): .... |
| .... |
| .... |
| .... |
| 2 **Jan** (German): .... |
| .... |
| .... |
| .... |
| 3 **Maria** (Venezuelan): .... |
| .... |
| .... |
| .... |

b Do any of the students say anything you disagree or sympathise with? What?

3 a Are there any aspects of their speech that you found difficult to understand, such as *accent, speed, vocabulary, long sentences* or *context*?

b Do you need to listen to any of the extracts again? Why?

4 Has this LISTENING section been focused on intensive or extensive listening or both?

READING 1

Text types

1 In pairs, briefly list all the things you have read recently. Include things like:

- flight departure boards
- road signs
- telephone directory

2 Look at the texts (1–11) to decide where they are from. Give reasons for your decision.

1   To be more precise we should really say that the heart is *two* pumps working side by side, separated by the atrial septum (Latin for wall) and the ventricular septum.

2   "In the eight short stories in Black Venus, Angela Carter resembles an expert show-man, pulling up the curtain on a series of players tumbling about the stage to amaze, shock and entertain. Earthy, bawdy and bizarre in turn, there is a fine intelligence at work here."

THE DAILY TELEGRAPH

3

BRITISH RAILWAYS BOARD

This ticket is issued subject to the conditions shown in the Board's current Passenger Conditions of Carriage and also in any other of the Board's publications and notices appropriate to its use.

It is not transferable and must be given up on expiry or renewal.

4   You must allow 4 working days for payments through the banking system and 7 working days for postal payments.

Do not mail cash.

5 *In order to receive the maximum benefit from the policy you must maintain the sum insured at a level which represents the full cost of rebuilding your property. Indexation will ensure that for most properties the sum insured remains adequate. However, you should review the amount of cover at regular intervals in case the rebuilding cost of your property has not altered in line with changes in the index, and when you make changes or improvements to your home. A leaflet is available from this branch to help you.*

6

We're giving away
THOUSANDS OF POUNDS
in this **Prize Draw**
and this key could help you win a Special Prize worth
THOUSANDS MORE!

See inside for details…

7

Take-Off
CHEAP FLIGHTS WORLDWIDE
business or pleasure.
Haymarket Travel
071-930-2455

8 Gone to lunch. Back about 2.

9 To Richard and Sue
Happy Christmas love
Keith and Julia

10 Dear Richard
Thanks for your card. Sorry I haven't been in touch but you know how things are over Christmas. We had a pile of relations over as well so you can imagine the chaos.

11 Morris, William, artist, 44, 231
Morris, W.R. (Lord Nuffield), 45, 72, 90, 106, 111, 113, 173, 203-4
Mosley, Oswald, 123
Mowbray's, publishers, 186
Mozley, James, 242
Müller, Max, 252
Mumford, Lewis, 78, 152
Murray, Gilbert, 189
Museum, Ashmolean, 113, 133, 206, 209, 211, 216, 218, 220, 222, 226, 229

3 Which of these types of text would you normally:

a read carefully, paying attention to every word?

b skim over quickly to get the general idea?

c scan through to find the information you are looking for?

d read only if you were bored and had nothing else to do?

e understand at a glance?

f never generally bother to read at all?

4 Which of the texts featured in exercise **2**, if any, present difficulties in understanding?

Which of the following reasons would you use to explain the difficulties?

a Much of the vocabulary is unknown.

b The words are familiar but they do not seem to make much sense here.

c The context is difficult to understand.

d It is difficult to see the relationships between phrases because of the use of complex sentences.

e The text contains a lot of idioms.

How can you overcome these problems?

APPROPRIACY

5 **Appropriacy** is a word often used to talk about language. What do you think it means?

6 a Compare these two extracts to text 4 of the reading passages on page 8.

If I were you I'd give it four working days if you're paying through a bank and seven if you're posting it. For heaven's sake don't post cash.

If you are paying this through a bank, please make sure you allow four working days. Allow seven if you are posting it. You should write a cheque in the latter case.

b Read the information in the box below, then discuss with a partner in which situation each of the two texts on the previous page might be appropriate.

There are three main criteria for deciding whether or not language is appropriate.

a The relationship between the person who receives the message and the person who sends it. Do they know each other? How well? Is there any difference in status? This will affect **register** – for example, how **formal** or **informal** the message is, whether it is polite, friendly, personal or businesslike.

b The **format**. Is it a letter, a notice, a telegram? Is it spoken or written, hand-written or printed?

c The **purpose**. What is the main purpose of the text? To give information (what sort?), to be friendly, to show how clever the author is?

7 Look at the texts in Reading 1 again and answer these questions.

a Which are formal in register, which informal, and which are neither formal nor informal?

b Which are personal messages to a specific person?

c Why does text 1 use 'we' when presumably only one person is writing?

d What sort of reader is text 1 written for?

e Why doesn't text 8 read 'I have gone out to lunch. I will be back at about two o'clock'?

f Would any of them sound natural if spoken?

8 Read this note from a man to his wife. Rewrite it to make it more appropriate, considering the register, format and purpose.

Dear Mrs Macintosh
I regret to inform you that owing to circumstances beyond my control I will be unable to return this evening until approximately 10 o'clock. Please accept my apologies for any inconvenience this may cause.
Yours sincerely
P. A. Macintosh

SPEAKING

1 How many different types of speaking activity can you think of? With a partner, add to the following list:

- conversations
- interviews
- talking to yourself
- leaving telephone messages

2 Look at the list you have just written and answer these questions.

a Which types of activity are **interactive** (involve listening and responding) and which are **non-interactive**?

b Which types allow you to think about what you say before you say it?

c Which are more formal?

d Which are more informal?

e Choose two or three different types. Why are they so different?

f What sort of speaking activity have you been involved in when answering these questions?

3 a Below is a list of speaking skills. In pairs, decide what each one involves.

Non-interactive	Interactive
• fluency	• turn-taking
• accuracy	• appropriacy
• clarity	• asking for clarification
• organisation	• encouragement/ acknowledgement

b Which do you have the most difficulty with when speaking in English?

4 Speaking activities

a Work in groups of three or four. One of you will need a watch, preferably a stop watch.

Select a topic which one student in each group must talk about for one minute. The other members of the group will stop the speaker if they:

- hesitate for a long time
- make serious mistakes in their English
- repeat themselves
- talk about a different topic

The person who interrupted must then talk on the same topic for the rest of the minute. The person talking at the end of the minute scores three points.

b Working in the same groups again, one student should try to sell something of theirs, (for example, their jacket) to the others. The seller should ask for a very high price, and try to persuade the other students that it is worth it.

The other students are sceptical and will question every statement.

Example

Why is it worth £89? Why is it so special?

Stop when the seller can't think of any more answers to the questions, or when they manage to sell the item.

c Which skills did you practise in these two activities? Choose from the list in exercise **3**.

5 How can you improve your spoken English? Look at the following statements and tick those which you consider to be the most useful and practical. Compare your list with a partner and add any further suggestions you can think of.

a The teacher should correct me immediately every time I make a mistake. ☐

b The teacher should correct me immediately only if I make serious mistakes. ☐

c The teacher should let me finish what I want to say and then point out the mistakes I have made. ☐

d I should talk in English with other students as much as possible. ☐

e I should only speak English to the teacher. ☐

f I should try and repeat everything I hear. ☐

g If I listen to English as much as possible, for example on the radio, my spoken English will automatically improve. ☐

h I should try to meet English people and talk to them. ☐

i I should learn common spoken phrases and use them. ☐

j I should always think carefully before I speak so that I don't make any mistakes. ☐

k It doesn't matter if I make mistakes when I am talking because I can always repeat what I want to say another way if people don't understand. ☐

LISTENING 2

In this recording you will hear Helen, the teacher of the students interviewed in LISTENING 1.

1 Listen to the recording once. Which of these statements is the best summary of the conversation?

a Grammar and intonation are of great importance in conveying meaning and attitude.

b Scandinavians tend to be better at learning English than other nationalities.

c The way you have learned the language affects your strengths and weaknesses at advanced level.

2 a Listen to the first three questions Helen is asked. How clearly are they expressed? Does Helen have any problems understanding them?

b Write down all three questions exactly as they are said on the recording. What difficulties are there in doing this?

c Re-write the second and third questions so that they are clearer.

3 Listen to the section where Helen talks about the Scandinavians' problems with grammar. If Helen wrote her answer, how would it be different?

4 Phonology

a What is said about the importance of pronunciation and intonation?

b What generally do you notice about the difference in intonation patterns between the speaker in this recording and Maria in LISTENING 1? What effect do those differences have?

c Listen carefully to how Helen says *'Er no. It's not a big problem.'* Which word does she stress? Why? Say this sentence with as many stress and intonation patterns as you can. How does the meaning or attitude change with the intonation?

5 Has this section been more concerned with intensive or extensive listening?

READING 2

I Skim the following text and answer these questions:

  a Where do you think the text is from?

  b Is there anything to indicate that the text is an extract from a much longer text?

  c Who was it written for/by?

2 Now read the text more carefully.

  a Can you explain what is meant by **coherence** and **cohesion**?

  b Do you think these are common words in everyday English? Give reasons for your answer.

Text and non-text

1 The text is the core of the reading process, the means by which the message is transmitted from writer to reader. So we need to study its characteristics and find out what other features, besides presupposition, make a text easy or difficult to follow. We might start by examining this sample:

5   There was no possibility of a walk that day. Income tax rates for 1984 have already been announced. What is the defining characteristic of the ungulates? Surely you did not tell her how it happened?

What is wrong with <u>this</u>? The lack of relationship between <u>the sentences</u> is obvious. <u>They</u> go together only in the accidental sense of being together on the same page, misleadingly laid out as if 10 <u>they</u> were part of a text. <u>It</u> is difficult to imagine any context in which <u>they</u> might occur together like <u>this</u>, and we cannot work out what <u>their</u> value, relative to <u>one another</u>, might be. <u>They</u> do not constitute a text at all.

However, a common context is not by itself enough to define a text, as the following example will show:

15   A man put some perfume into a drawer.

        James Brown forgot about some perfume.

        A man bought some perfume for Mrs Brown.

We can detect that these sentences might all relate to the same situation, but if so, in a number of ways the situation is not clearly expressed. For one thing the sequencing is unclear. A 20 rearrangement may help; at the same time we will set out the sentences to show another feature that makes them unlike a text (*layout based on an article by Gerry Abbott*).

A man	bought	some perfume	for Mrs Brown.
A man	put	some perfume	into a drawer.
James Brown	forgot about	some perfume.	

25 Now the sentences are ordered in a way that suggests they are telling a story; but no reader would accept this as a normally coherent text. What is lacking? The best way to find out would be to rewrite the sentences yourself to produce an acceptable text. As you do this, notice what you have to do to achieve the result you want. If you have completed this task you will have realised that the sentences can most easily be interpreted as a story if we assume that the 'James Brown' and 'a man' 30 refer to the same individual in each case, and that the perfume is also the same each time. You will probably have changed the sentences to show this, but you may have made other changes too. Perhaps you have produced something along these lines:

One day,	James Brown	bought	some perfume	for his wife.
However,	he	put	the present	into a drawer
35 and	–	forgot about	it.	

Coherence and cohesion

This now reads like a normal text; we can see that it is *coherent* because we have made use of *cohesion* to indicate the relationships between the various elements.

3 Which of these two examples lacks coherence and which lacks cohesion?

a It was raining. James got wet.

b It was raining so James didn't get wet.

4 The text includes a number of cohesive devices. What can you say about the following?

a Paragraphs

Why does the author start a new paragraph on line 13 (*However, a common context. . .*)?

b References

Look at the words underlined between lines 8 and 12. What does each word refer to? Is it possible to rewrite the paragraph without using pronouns?

c Lexical choice

In the sentence which begins on line 2, how does the author avoid repetition of the word *characteristics?*

In lines 27 to 30, how does the author avoid repetition of the word *coherent?*

d Connectives

What is the function of these words and phrases in linking and signposting the text?

So (line 2)   *at the same time* (line 20)

this (line 4)   *Now* (line 25)

but if so (line 18)   *the semi colon (;)* (line 36)

5 Working with a partner, rewrite the paragraph below so that it is easier to understand. Use suitable cohesive devices and change the punctuation where necessary.

> A particular kind of cohesive device is the **discourse marker**, for example *however*, *although*, *furthermore*, *namely*. Discourse markers mark the functional value of a sentence. Discourse markers tell you what the writer intends when he writes a sentence. If the writer uses *although*, he is conceding something. If the writer uses *namely*, he is specifying something and so on.

L E X I S

1 What does *knowing* a word mean? With a partner, make a list of all the things you need to understand about a word before you feel confident that you know it. Add to this list.

- basic meaning
- spelling

2 Here are a number of techniques used by students to learn a word. Which of them do you use?

Discuss the advantages and disadvantages of these methods and any others that you use.

a I just hope I'll remember it.

b I write the word down with a translation.

c I repeat it to myself several times until I remember it.

d I write the word with the meaning in English.

e I write the word and copy the meaning from the dictionary.

f I write an example sentence using the word.

g I highlight the word in the text.

h I don't bother to learn it unless I think it's going to be useful.

i I write it down and then see if I can remember the meaning on the way home.

j I use pictures to help me remember.

3 In small groups, design a vocabulary notebook. Think about the following:

> • Should the book be divided into sections? What sort of sections?
>
> • How many words should there be to a page?
>
> • How much space should be left between words? (Think how difficult it is to learn a long list.)
>
> • Should you write an example sentence? If so, where?
>
> • Should you use different coloured pens or is this impractical?
>
> • How can you make the book comprehensive without spending too much time over each word?
>
> • Should you mark parts of speech, intonation, stress and pronunciation?

Collocation

The phrase *achieve the result* is an example of **verb/noun collocation**. **Collocation** means that two or more words are commonly found together in an established partnership. There are no good reasons, grammatical or lexical, why they go together, they just do. Try to learn such words in their partnership, rather than separately.

Example:

$\left.\begin{array}{l} \text{obtain} \\ \text{produce} \\ \text{achieve} \\ \text{gain *} \\ \text{win} \end{array}\right\}$ a result

The first three verbs often collocate with *result*. *Gain* is possible but unusual. *Win* does not collocate with it at all.

4 Here are some examples of collocation from the reading texts. Put a tick next to each of the five verb/noun collocations.

☐ to follow a text   ☐ clearly expressed

☐ easily interpreted   ☐ telling a story

☐ connections are made   ☐ subject to the conditions

☐ make changes

☐ maximum benefit   ☐ maintain the sum

                        ☐ normally coherent

Verb/noun collocation

5 Two of the most common verbs found in collocations are *make* and *have*.

a Look at the following words. Decide which collocate with *have* and which collocate with *make*.

a bath	a holiday	a good sleep
a mistake	a promise	one's mind up
decisions	progress	desperate need of
an offer	a remark	a connection
a look	a talk with	

b Which verb collocates with these phrases?

.... somebody happy

.... yourself understood

.... our position clear

6 a Look up the word *decision* in a good monolingual dictionary. Apart from *make*, how many verbs can you find that collocate with *decision*?

b Now do the same with the noun *promise*.

7 With a partner discuss the best way to learn and remember these collocations.

8 Connotation

The **connotations** of a word are the ideas and qualities that are associated with it beyond its basic meaning.

a *Slim* and *thin* have practically the same meaning when describing a person but have different connotations. What are those connotations?

b Explain the difference in connotation between these pairs of words:

1 a lean/skinny (person)

2 to use (someone's) skills/to exploit (someone)

3 to be in love/infatuated (with someone)

4 irrational/illogical (behaviour)

5 jump/leap

6 a(n) magisterial/authoritative (voice)

7 a nationalistic/patriotic (person)

GRAMMAR

Section A

1 What is grammar? In pairs, write a short, one-sentence definition. Compare it with sentences written by other pairs.

2 Do you need to study grammar in order to learn a language? Why? Discuss your opinions with a partner.

3 Look at the following comments made about grammar. Do you think they were made by:
- a teacher?
- language students?
- a native speaker of English?

a *Students tend to think of grammar only as doing exercises. That's why they find it so boring.*

b *I hate it because you can spend hours studying something like the present perfect, and the next time it comes up in normal conversation, you still get it wrong.*

c The only thing I know is that you can't end a sentence with a preposition.

d *You don't really need grammar. If you know enough vocabulary you can usually make yourself understood.*

e Students think of grammar in terms of right or wrong, whereas in fact, it is more a question of choosing the best structure to make your meaning as clear as possible. So the structures are just clearer than others in certain contexts.

f *Some people spend hours studying grammar books and doing exercises. It seems to be useful for some people and a complete waste of time for others.*

g *The trouble is you understand it all on Monday evening, but on Tuesday morning you've forgotten it all again.*

h I know nothing about grammar.

i I think it's very important to know the rules so that you don't break them.

4 In small groups, discuss the following.

a Do you disagree with any of the above statements made by students?

b Does the teacher's comment in statement e above seem sensible or idealistic?

c Do you find studying grammar useful or agree with statement f that it is a *waste of time*?

d What do you think of the native speaker's comments?

e Can you think of any reasons for the opinion expressed in sentence *b*?

f Suggest some ways in which grammar can be learnt effectively.

Section B

The following grammatical terms a–n will be used frequently in this book.
Find at least one example of each from the sentences on the right.

a Present perfect	h Passive
b Past perfect	i Indefinite article
c Present continuous	j Adverb
d Modal verb	k Present participle
e Relative clause	l Personal pronoun
f Conditional clause	m Relative pronoun
g Verbless clause	n Transitive verb

1 She knew the meaning because she'd already looked it up.

2 Confident and smiling, he opened a grammar book.

3 If you haven't understood, ask the teacher to explain.

4 Will those who haven't a clue what the teacher's talking about, please raise their hands.

5 Revision sessions should be arranged at fairly frequent intervals.

6 Doing grammar exercises is useless unless you know when to use the structure.

Which areas of grammar do you feel you need to improve on?

WRITING

1 Look at these different types of writing. Think of an example of each one.

- Creative writing
- Personal writing
- Institutional writing
- Social writing
- Study writing
- Public writing

2 Now use these types as headings for the lists below.

	Public writing	

diaries
journals
shopping lists
reminders for oneself
packing lists
addresses
recipes
	letters of – enquiry
	            – complaint
	            – request
	form filling
	applications (for memberships)
		poems
		stories
		rhymes
		drama
		songs
		autobiography

letters
invitations
notes – of condolence
        – of thanks
        – of congratulations
telephone messages
instructions – to friends
               – to family
	making notes while reading
	taking notes from lectures
	making a card index
	summaries
	synopses
	reviews
	reports of – experiments
	              – workshops
	              – visits
	essays
	bibliographies
		agendas posters
		minutes instructions
		memoranda speeches
		reports applications
		reviews curriculum vitae
		contracts specifications
		business letters note-making (by
		public notices doctors and other
		advertisements professionals)

3 In small groups, discuss the following questions.

  a What are the different purposes of each type of writing listed in the table above (to remind yourself, to publicise something, etc.)?

  b Which types are the most formal?

  c Which types require the most planning and revising?

4 Many types of writing follow certain conventions. Most letters for example, begin 'Dear. . . ' and end with the writer's name. Which conventions do the types of writing listed below follow?

- faxes
- advertisements
- C Vs
- poetry
- essays
- memos
- lectures
- notes of thanks
- notes

5 In the same groups, write a list of all the things you dislike about writing and another list of all the things you find useful and interesting about it. Refer to specific types of writing from the list above. Compare your lists with those of other groups.

6 **Writing task**

Write about your reasons for learning English and what you hope to do with the language when you've finished the course. You can also refer to your experience of learning English so far and any specific difficulties with the language which you hope to overcome during this course.

Write this in two different formats:

a As part of a letter to a good friend telling them your latest news.

b As part of a report to your employer justifying your request for time off work to study.

Think about the different register you will use in each case. Limit each part to about 100 words.

GRAMMAR

Complex sentences

A **complex** sentence contains two or more clauses or parts.

1 a Of the following three sentences, which is not a complex sentence?

   1 Last night I watched a film on TV.

   2 Last night I telephoned my mother and watched a film on TV.

   3 Although I should have been doing some work last night, I watched a film on TV.

   Clauses can be added to the simple sentence using a **co-ordinating conjunction** like 'and', 'but', etc. . This means that the added (**co-ordinate**) clause is as important as the main clause.

   Clauses can also be added using a **subordinating conjunction** like 'if', 'so', 'who', 'although', etc. . This means the added (**subordinate**) clause is not as important as the main clause and cannot be used on its own.

   b In the three sentences in part **a** above, identify the co-ordinate clause and the subordinate clause.

2 Underline the subordinate clause in the sentences below.

   a I met a guy once who read grammar books for fun.

   b People often don't like grammar because it is full of long words like *co-ordinating conjunctions*.

   c The trouble is that the phrase *linking words* is not always precise enough.

   d While it may look easier, it may actually be more confusing in the long run.

   e Grammar fascinates some people such a lot that they spend hours studying details.

   f There is a danger of losing a sense of proportion unless we are careful.

   g Many people don't understand the rules of grammar for their own language until they study them.

   h If we can already speak the language well, there is little point in looking at the rules.

3 In the sentences above, identify:

   1 a reason clause

   2 a relative clause

   3 two conditional clauses

   4 a *that* clause

   5 a result clause

   6 a time clause

Verb forms

How much do you know about English verbs?

Decide if the following statements are true or false.

		True	False
a	There is no future tense in English.	☐	☐
b	*The train leaves at 7.00 p.m.* is an acceptable sentence referring to the future.	☐	☐
c	You are visiting a friend's house. Your host says, *'Will you stay for lunch?'* This means he or she is asking about your plans for the future.	☐	☐
d	*Will, must, may, might, would,* and *shall* are all examples of modal verbs.	☐	☐
e	Modal verbs can never be followed by an infinitive with *to*.	☐	☐
f	*I'm going* is an example of the present continuous.	☐	☐
g	*I've gone* is an example of the past continuous.	☐	☐
h	In the sentence *Sharon kicked the dog*, **kicked** is a transitive verb.	☐	☐
i	In the sentence *The sun set in the west*, **set** is an intransitive verb.	☐	☐
j	The sentences below all contain examples of the passive.	☐	☐

This garment should be dry-cleaned.

I wasn't told about the meeting until this morning.

They would have been hurt if they'd been going any faster.

I could have gone to the play but I didn't want to.

L E X I S

Strength of adjectives

In the following sentences, choose the strongest adjective from the two given. Decide if there is a difference in register.

Example
She is completely *in love*/(*infatuated*) with Paul.

a I *hate/dislike* getting up early.

b She was *in agony/in pain* before she went to the dentist.

c I'm not drinking out of that glass: it's *dirty/filthy*.

d There's a(n) *disgusting/unpleasant* smell in the basement.

e His latest book won considerable *praise/acclaim*.

f I *approve of/admire* her principles.

g I thought the film was *hilarious/funny*.

h There is a *huge/large* gap between rich and poor in this country.

i It's *cold/freezing* outside.

Think of some similar pairs of adjectives to add to this list.

Vocabulary differentiation

Choose the best word from the given alternatives to fill the gaps in the sentences below.

Decide why your choice is best. Is it because of collocation, connotation or something else?

1 He's been .... depressed since he heard the news.
a) deeply b) highly c) absolutely

2 I need to buy another .... of cigarettes.
a) box b) packet c) container

3 She sneered at him ....
a) smilingly b) encouragingly c) contemptuously

4 Men and women should always be given ....
opportunities.
a) equal b) equivalent c) comparable

5 The car .... slowly round the corner.
a) raced b) crawled c) roared

6 I should like to make this point .... clear.
a) glass b) ice c) crystal

7 The film kept us in .... right to the end.
a) suspense b) anticipation c) expectation

8 There's a .... affairs programme on at nine o'clock.
a) present b) news c) current

9 He .... a fortune in business before he was thirty.
a) made b) took c) did

10 Did you .... a good holiday?
a) take b) have c) do

Dictionary skills

1 Look up the word *descend* in an English/English dictionary and answer the following questions.

a How many meanings are given?

b What grammatical information is given?

c What is the pronunciation?

d Does the word have any particularly formal or informal connotations?

e Is it commonly followed by any particular prepositions?

f Is it used in any common phrases or idioms?

g What is the meaning of **descend** in the following sentence: *How can you descend to such a cheap trick?*

h Are any other derivatives (nouns, etc. .) of *descend* given?

2 Look up the word *fleece*.
How many abbreviations are used in the definition and what do they mean?

3 Look up the phrase *green fingers* and the phrasal verb *take on*.

How did you find these words? Is there a system for the layout of *green* and *take* in the dictionary?

Collocation

Match the verbs on the left with a collocating noun from the list on the right. More than one may be possible.

achieve	a story
tell	a look
make	time
have	a result
break	changes
spend	an apology
accept	a break
take	a cold
run	a promise
catch	a risk

19

FOCUS

I Look at the following questions. In your country, what would you do in each of these situations? If none of the answers is suitable, write what you feel would be the best answer. Discuss your answers with a partner.

a You go into a shop to buy a carton of milk. Which of these do you <u>not</u> say?

1) A carton of milk, please.
2) Give me a carton of milk.
3) Could I please have a carton of milk?
4) A carton of milk.

b You arrive at a bus stop just as a very full bus pulls up. There is a long queue of people waiting. What do you do?

1) Go to the back of the queue.
2) Stand near the front of the queue and wait until you can get on.
3) Push your way on to the bus.
4) Go and buy a newspaper to read until the next bus arrives.

c You have been invited to the house of an important business contact whom you have not met before. He/she offers you a cup of coffee. Which of these would you <u>not</u> say?

1) Thank you, that would be very nice.
2) Yes, please.
3) Only if you're making one.
4) I don't mind.

d In a restaurant, the waiter brings you a different meal from the one you ordered. What do you do?

1) Complain quietly.
2) Complain loudly.
3) Keep quiet and eat it anyway.
4) Set fire to the restaurant.

e On a crowded tube train, do you give up your seat. . .

1) to old ladies only?
2) to anyone who is older than about 60?
3) to any female (if you are male)?
4) only if forced to do so?

2 Go through your answers again and decide if they are typical of your own nationality/culture or whether they are more a reflection of your own personality.
Are there any answers where you feel you are personally in conflict with your national stereotype?

3 How do you think a British or American person would react in these situations?
In what ways are these reactions different to your own?

4 Put the questions in exercise **I** above into categories according to whether they deal with:

a language
b gesture
c general behaviour

5 In small groups, write another question on an aspect of language or behaviour. Here are some ideas: *giving or receiving presents, greeting friends, relatives or members of the opposite sex, inviting someone to your house, etc.* .

LISTENING 1

I You will hear two people talking about different kinds of greeting. What different ways of greeting people are mentioned and what countries are they used in?

2 Both speakers say that there are some aspects of these greetings that they do not fully understand.
What are they?

3 Listen again to the sections where Bernard talks about the way people greet each other in Thailand and Peru. With a partner, demonstrate exactly what happens.

4 What other ways are there of greeting somebody? In your culture, what differences are there in how you greet people of different social status? Do women use the same ritual greetings as men?

READING 1

The following extracts are from an article by a Japanese professor.

1 Work in pairs. One person should read extracts 1 and 2, and the other, extracts 3 and 4 on page 164. Aim to understand the main points the author is making and not the meaning of every word in each text.

1 I am sitting talking with an overnight house guest when my wife comes in and announces, 'Ofuro ga wakimashita. Oshokuji no yōi mo mō sugu dekimasu. Dochira o saki ni nasaimasu ka?' (The bath is ready, and supper will be ready shortly. Would you prefer to bathe first, or eat?)

The guest replies, 'Dochira de mo gotsugō no yoroshii hō ni' (Whichever is more convenient).

My wife then counters with 'Osuki na yō ni' (Whatever you prefer).

Finally the guest says, 'Sā, dō shiyō ka nā. . . Jā, moshi osashitsukae nakanara saki ni ofuro o itadakimashō ka' (H'mm, what shall I do?. . . Well then, if it's all right with you, perhaps I'll take a bath first).

This is a perfectly ordinary dialogue in Japan. But change the setting to a foreign airliner. After the meal, the flight attendants come around asking, 'Coffee or tea?' Occasionally Japanese passengers will be sitting next to me and will ask me to say, 'Either is fine,' in English. If I comply, though, the attendant will first look suspicious, then bewildered, and may even repeat the question in a different form: 'Which do you prefer?'

2 Japanese make frequent, even excessive, use of polite language, including terms of respect in regard to others, terms of humility in regard to themselves, and formal language that elevates the tone of discourse, as in the above 'Osore irimasu ga, ozaseki ni omodori ni natte . . .' (We are sorry to trouble you, but would you kindly return to your seats). While polite forms exist in Western languages as well, they are much more sparingly used. A Western flight attendant would never begin an announcement with a phrase like: 'We are sorry to trouble you.' Because Japanese speech makes such extensive use of polite forms, it tends to sound long-winded to Western listeners, while Western speech, from the Japanese viewpoint, is concise to the point of abruptness.

a Find out from your partner what the other extracts tell us about the following points. Ask your partner questions if you do not fully understand what he/she is saying.

Extracts 1 and 2
• expressing preferences
• polite language
• Western listeners
• Western speech

Extracts 3 and 4
• debating
• being specific/accurate
• Japanese ink painting

b With your partner decide whether the four texts make any similar points.

c Can you think of any cultural or geographical reasons why the Japanese language should work in this way?

2 With your partner read the following passage and suggest a suitable heading for it.

1 I believe that the Japanese linguistic habits described above are basically a result of the geographical environment. Until around the middle of the nineteenth century, Japan was almost
5 completely isolated from the rest of the world, and the vast majority of its inhabitants never spoke to anyone but other Japanese. While the nation may have started out as an assemblage of different peoples, it was homogenised into virtually a single
10 tribe at a very early date. As a result, until a little over a century ago we Japanese were living in a tribal society effectively cut off from outside contact. I believe that this exerted a decisive influence on our language habits.

15 It is only natural that a homogeneous people crowded onto four smallish islands should value the ability to avoid confrontation – the knack, one might say, of getting along with everybody. This sort of environment naturally fostered such
20 language habits as deferring to others' viewpoints, avoiding giving offence, and softening the impact of one's speech. In negotiations, for example, the ideal procedure would be to speak vaguely at first in order to elicit the other party's views, then
25 gradually bring the matter to a conclusion that appeared to come from the other side but that actually gave one most of what one had wanted in the first place.

A single ethnic group is much like one big
30 family. As such, the Japanese do not feel it necessary to go into great detail when speaking with one another; they merely sketch the outlines and expect the listener to be able to fill in

the gaps. The situation is just the opposite in
35 Europe, where numerous linguistically distinct countries are connected by land, making it easy for people to travel back and forth. It is only a slight exaggeration to say that in many European cities one cannot be sure what language the man
40 coming down the street will use until he opens his mouth.

When people from different cultures and educated in different tongues try to communicate, indirect or roundabout expressions can easily lead
45 to misunderstandings. One cannot, as within a single tribe, expect the other party to fill in the meaning from a sketchy statement. In negotiations the inevitable result is that the details are clarified almost to the point of tedium
50 as each side does its utmost to get its way.

Now answer these questions on the final passage.

3 What is the function of each paragraph?

4 Say as accurately as you can what the function of the following words and phrases are within the text.
Example
for example, in line 22, introduces a practical illustration of the language habits listed in the previous sentence.
a *While* (line 7)
b *As a result* (line 10)
c *As such* (line 30)
d *as* (line 45)

5 What exactly do the following pronouns refer to in the text?
a *this* (line 13)
b *This* (line 18)
c *where* (line 35)
d *he/his* (line 40)
e *its* (line 50)

6 Look at the text again and use the context to work out the meaning of the following words and phrases.

    a *homogenised* (line 9)
    b *knack* (line 17)
    c *getting along with* (line 18)
    d *fostered* (line 19)
    e *deferring* (line 20)
    f *elicit* (line 24)
    g *sketch the outlines* (lines 32–33)
    h *get its way* (line 50)

7 a Find one verb and one adjective which collocate with *influence* (lines 13–14).

   b Which adjective collocates with *majority* (line 6)?

   c Which verb pattern collocates with *detail* (line 31)?

8 Find words or phrases which mean the following:

    a *isolated*
    b *argument or conflict*
    c *doing something so often that it becomes boring*
    d *tries its best*

SPEAKING

Using the right register when talking to someone is important in order to avoid giving offence or being misunderstood.

1 For each of these situations, decide what degree of formality would be used in the language. Are there any situations where the two speakers would use different registers?

   a Two friends discussing what to do together at the weekend.

   b Complaining to a shop assistant about faulty goods.

   c Asking an air hostess for another cup of coffee.

   d Explaining to a friend that you have accidentally broken her Walkman.

   e Explaining to your bank manager that you want to borrow £1000 for a holiday.

   f Flattering your employer about his new suit.

2 Look at the phrases below and decide whether they could be used in any of the situations above.

   a Please accept my apologies.
   b Sorry to trouble you.
   c That's very kind of you.
   d Certainly sir/madam.
   e I'm sorry to say that seems unlikely.
   f You must be joking!
   g I'll see what I can do.
   h Don't worry about it.
   i What do you reckon?
   j May I suggest an alternative?

3 Working in pairs, act out the following conversations which relate to the situations in exercise 1.

   a *Two friends*
     A: You want to go out somewhere at the weekend, for example to see a film.
     B: You haven't got any money. You want to stay in and watch TV.

   b *Customer and shop assistant*
     A: The suitcase you bought has a broken lock. You want the case replaced or your money back. You don't have a receipt. If the assistant refuses, ask to see the manager.
     B: You can't replace or refund goods without a receipt: this is company policy. Call the manager only if you have no alternative.

   c *Passenger and air steward(ess)*
     A: You are travelling on a ten hour flight and want some coffee.
     You don't like tea. Don't get angry.
     B: Unfortunately, you've run out of coffee. Offer something else.

   d *Two friends*
     A: You dropped your friend's Walkman and it is now broken and cannot be repaired. You feel awful.
     B: It was an old Walkman and you have another. You don't really mind.

   e *Customer and bank manager*
     A: You want to borrow £1000 to spend on a holiday with your family who live abroad. You can repay the loan in six months.
     B: You are not convinced of the financial security of this customer. You can only offer £500 for two months.

   f *Employee and employer*
     A: You want a promotion so you have to be pleasant to your boss (who is quite reserved). Compliment him on his new suit. You shouldn't be too enthusiastic or your boss might think you are being sarcastic.
     B: You are really pleased that this employee likes your new suit, which cost you a lot of money. Thank him/her and say where you bought it.

LEXIS

APPROPRIACY

1 Look at this cartoon. What point does it illustrate about language register?

'You can tell he's had the benefit of a classical education.'

2 Here are some broad linguistic guidelines that can be used when deciding whether language is formal or informal:

> a **Vocabulary**. *Derive*, for example, is a more formal word than *come from*.
>
> b **Grammatical forms**. Some grammatical forms are more common in formal language, for example, non-defining relative clauses and some modal verbs ('*Would you mind. . .* ').
>
> c **Sentence structure**. Generally, a more complex sentence structure indicates more formal language.
>
> d **Contractions**. Contracted forms such as '*I've*' instead of '*I have*' are more common in informal language.
>
> e **Ellipsis**. This practice of omitting words is common in informal language, for example, '*You all right?*' instead of '*Are you all right?*'
>
> f **Idioms** and **colloquialisms**. These are generally used in more informal language.
>
> g **Pronunciation**. A potentially sensitive area in Britain, involving education, social class and regional accent.

a Identify some of the features from the linguistic guidelines (a–g) in these sentences.
  1 This timetable is subject to alteration.
  2 We apologise for any inconvenience caused by this delay.
  3 We regret to inform you that the concert has been cancelled due to circumstances beyond our control.
  4 Would you mind waiting a moment?
  5 Thanks a lot.
  6 That bloke's a right pain in the neck.
  7 Following your recent application, we would like to invite you for interview.
  8 Got a light?
  9 This behaviour is totally unacceptable.
  10 I wonder if I could have a word?
  11 Walking towards the barn, he noticed something strange in the doorway.
  12 Taking into account the recession, the figures are far higher than could reasonably have been expected.
  13 Australia took another step towards retaining the Cup when they beat the Netherlands 3-2 yesterday.
  14 They don't stand a cat in hell's chance of getting into the World Cup.

b Decide where you would be likely to find each of the sentences above. Would it be spoken or written? Who would use it and why? Is it formal or informal?

3 Choose four of the sentences above and rewrite them in a different register, saying when you could use the rewritten versions.

Dictionary skills

4 Use a dictionary to find the difference in meaning and use between the words in each group. Consider register, connotation and collocation.

a language	dialect	jargon	lingo
b gesture	shrug	nudge	wink
c etiquette	politeness	behaviour	snobbery
d discourteous	rude	brusque	tactless
e culture	civilisation	custom	sophistication

L I S T E N I N G 2

1 Listen to the six short dialogues. Which one is the most formal? Why?

2 Listen to each one again and try to identify:

   a the relationship between the two speakers
   b where they are

3 Listen to the last two dialogues again and fill in the speech bubbles in these cartoons.
Check your version with the transcript on pages 167–168.

4 Which of the following made the above exercise more difficult? Discuss your choices with the rest of the class.
   • unknown vocabulary
   • speakers talking too fast
   • speakers not pronouncing the words clearly
   • use of idiom
   • use of ellipsis (i.e. missing words out)
   • two or more words being pushed together and pronounced as though they were one word

5 Read the transcripts of the other dialogues. Are they easier to understand when reading them than when listening to them? Why (not)?

1 Read the following text. As you read, think about the subject of each paragraph: in what ways is it different from the preceding and succeeding paragraphs?

2 Now work with a partner and suggest headings for each paragraph.

THE WAY WE DO THINGS ROUND HERE

1   Language is not just the words people speak. It is body language, dress, manners, etiquette, ideas, the things people do – their behaviour. And like language, <u>behaviour</u> has <u>a</u> <u>grammar</u>, <u>an</u> <u>internal</u> <u>logic</u> that is possible to understand and master.

Some of <u>the</u> <u>differences</u> may seem superficial – dress, etiquette, food, hours of work. Often it is simply 5 <u>a question</u> of getting used to them, like <u>the</u> <u>climate</u> or the plumbing, while one gets on with the business.

Some of the differences, it is grudgingly admitted, may be an improvement. <u>People</u> are more courteous, service is better, you ask for something to be done and it happens without having to follow it up. Others can be irritating, like the conventions of punctuality. If you invite people to a party at 7 o'clock your guests will consider it polite to turn up on the dot in Germany, five minutes early in the 10 American Midwest, an hour early in Japan, 15 minutes afterwards in the UK, up to an hour afterwards in Italy and some time in the evening in Greece. I deliberately avoided the more emotive word 'late' because there is nothing wrong in it. It is the accepted convention.

<u>The</u> <u>problems</u> begin when <u>differences</u> interfere with getting <u>the</u> <u>job</u> done. Delivery promises are not kept or suppliers are not flexible. There are no procedures or there are too many procedures. People never 15 get together and thrash things out or meetings drag on all day. Decisions are postponed or they are taken without proper study. And so on.

When asked how he played evil men so convincingly, the actor Vincent Price replied that he did not play evil men. They did what seemed right to them at the time. The way others do things is not different out of stupidity or carelessness or incompetence or malice, although it may appear so. Most 20 people do what seems the right thing to do at the time. The judgement of what is right is rooted in habit, tradition, beliefs, values, attitudes, accepted norms. In other words, the culture to which that person belongs.

An investigation into what lies at the heart of cultural differences leads into history, sociology, philosophy, theology, mythology, in fact every branch of the humanities. It is a 25 fascinating study but outside the scope and length of this book which deals with how those underlying differences manifest themselves in people's day-to-day behaviour at work.

Culture is a woolly, flakey, pretentious, unbusinesslike, mildly derisive word like 'intellectual' or 'bureaucratic'. There have been attempts to find alternatives, such as climate or organisational ideology, but they are equally unsatisfactory. Culture has been defined in many ways, including the following:

30   *A collective programming of the mind.*
    The sum total of all the beliefs, values and norms shared by a group of people.
    The methods a society evolves to solve problems.
    Everything we take for granted.
    Patterned ways of thinking, feeling and reacting, acquired and transmitted mainly by symbols, constituting the
35   *distinctive achievements of human groups including their embodiment in artefacts; the essential core of culture*
    consists of traditional ideas and especially their attached values. In many ways, culture could be described as the
    personality of society. The definition of culture as it is used from this point on in the book is:
    The way we do things round here.

3 Where do you think this extract was taken from? Choose from the following:

a an informal guide for international business people

b a piece of political propaganda

c a scholarly analysis of international ethics

4 Now answer the following questions on the meaning of specific passages from the extract.

a Why is it *grudgingly admitted* (line 6) that some of the differences are improvements?

b What do you understand by *thrash things out* (line 15)? Use clues in the sentence and paragraph to work out the meaning.

c What is the relevance of the story about Vincent Price?

d Explain in your own words what the author feels about the word *culture* (line 21).

e Look at the definitions of culture at the end of the passage. Which do you think is the best definition? Where do you think the definitions were taken from? Are they all meant to be serious?

GRAMMAR

Articles

The definite article.

The London Underground can be confusing.
The pub I was telling you about is in Broad Street.

The indefinite article.

A foreigner can easily get lost in Tokyo.
'Les Miserables' is a popular musical.

Zero article.

Society has become more violent.
Birds fly south in winter.

1 In the following pairs of sentences, the second uses the definite article while the first sentence uses the indefinite or zero article.
Explain the difference in the meaning of the noun caused by the change of article.

a History is boring.
The history I studied at school was boring.

b A man I saw yesterday phoned me this morning.
The man I saw yesterday phoned me this morning.

c I sold a car last week.
I sold the car last week.

d Too much excitement is bad for your heart.
The excitement died down.

e Work is rarely enjoyable and only sometimes profitable.
He's been there three weeks now and loves the work.

f Music is frozen architecture.
The music of Schoenberg and Webern shocked contemporary audiences.

g Bread is good for you.
Where's the bread?

h I lost my purse and some money. The police found a purse.
I lost my purse and some money. The police found the purse.

i I bought my daughter a computer for her birthday. She's always wanted a computer.
I bought my daughter the computer she's always wanted for her birthday.

2 Match each rule on the use of articles in the table below with the appropriate example sentence. There may be more than one example for each rule. Some examples may also be used more than once.

Then write the correct article (*a, the* or zero) next to each rule in the box provided. The first example has been done for you.

Example sentences:

a This is more than a piece of advice: it's <u>a rule</u>. <u>The rule</u> must be followed at all times.

b <u>The other drivers</u> seemed totally unaware that an accident had taken place.

c <u>The sun</u> rose above the low hills.

d She gave me <u>the information</u> I required.

e <u>Nature</u> abhors a vacuum.

f I went to see <u>a football match</u> last night.

g <u>The book</u> you lent me the other day is excellent.

h I see <u>a fox</u> in my garden sometimes.

i <u>Children</u> were playing on the sand by the sea.

Rules	Example Sentence	Article
can be used with plural countable nouns e.g. *dogs*	b/i	the/zero
can be used with singular countable nouns e.g. *dog*		
can be used with uncountable nouns e.g. *furniture*		
used to refer to something of which there is only one, e.g. *the earth*		
used to refer to an unspecified thing of which there are many examples		
referring to a specific thing known to both speaker and listener		
used with abstract uncountable nouns, e.g. *life*		
first reference to something the listener/reader doesn't know about		
second reference to something		

3 Look at the words that have been underlined in the text in READING 2. Explain the use or non-use of the articles in each case.

4 Abstract uncountable nouns normally take the zero article when referring generally, e.g. *Life can be hard.*

a Add to this list of abstract uncountable nouns.

work	society	life
nature	knowledge	history
misery	excitement	happiness
truth	imagination	health

However, abstract uncountable nouns can take the definite article when used to talk about one specific example. This can be done by:

- a relative clause: *The knowledge (which) he gained in business helped him organise other ventures.*
- a participle (*-ing*): *The information being gathered will be of considerable value.* This is really another kind of relative clause: *The information **which is being** gathered. . .*)
- a preposition following the noun (especially '*of*'): *We are involved in the development of new drugs; The space between the desks is too narrow.*

b Find an example of an abstract uncountable noun being used specifically in exercise **1**.

c From the list of abstract nouns in **a** above, take two or three examples and write sentences to show how they could be used generally and specifically.

L E X I S

Collocation

have and *take* + noun

In READING 1, the Japanese professor talks about *taking a bath*. He could also have said *having a bath* without changing the meaning.

Here are some more nouns which collocate with both *have* and *take*.

a bath	a holiday	a look
a break	a rest	a bite
a shower	a nap	

1 *take* + noun

These nouns collocate only with *take*. Put them into the appropriate sentences below. (Note also the prepositions used in some of these combinations.)

responsibility	offence
the lead	the blame
office	courage
the trouble	the/a decision
shape	the/a risk

a You must take .... for your own decisions.
b This project is finally beginning to take ....
c He was such a good example that everyone took their .... from him.
d Don't take .... , I wasn't trying to criticise.
e The President has been in poor health since he took ....
f He took .... although in fact he hadn't done anything wrong.
g Okay, you might fail. But it's worth taking ....
h Thank you for taking .... to come and see me. I know you're very busy.
i It sometimes takes .... to tell the truth.
j I eventually took .... to fire him.

2 *Give* is often used with nouns that refer to sounds made orally. For example you can *give*:

a shout	a sigh
a yell	a whistle
a groan	(or with facial actions):
a gasp	a smile, a grimace,
a cry	a yawn.

If you use one of these combinations rather than the more common verb (*to cry, to shout,* etc.) it suggests that the expression or noise is involuntary or that you haven't thought about it.

Which of the combinations with *give* could you use in these situations?

a somebody stands on your foot
b you are told a terrible joke
c you think of something amusing
d you are bored
e somebody gives you a nasty surprise
f you think somebody's suggestion is stupid
g you see somebody walk out in front of a car

3 Many other nouns can be used with *give*.
Examples
The Chancellor is trying to give the economy a kick start.
He was given a warm welcome by his hosts.
Give us a clue.

Add any other examples you can think of.

WRITING

1 As manager of a restaurant, you have received a letter of complaint and you ask your secretary to draft a reply. Read the following draft (ignore any mistakes) and decide what the original letter was complaining about.

Trout Café
Snowdon Place
Hampstead
London NW3 4NJ

☎ 071 431 4027

Dear Mrs. _____
Thank you for the letter and I'm sorry you have found cause to complain. This is the first complaint I have received since I have worked here and I only wished, you had complained, whilst you were hear. Actually I was very surprised you found the fish overcokked and rubbery since I have been told that if you cook fish too much it does not get rubbery. If you had told the waiter I'm sure he would have given you another one, although I feel that the cooking of fish is a personal prefrence and the fact that it was cold as well is puzzling as it must of come straight from the kitchen.

I have spoken to our cleaners regarding the dirty tablecloth and it appears there was some problems on that day with the laundry. This problem has now been resolved, which I thank you for drawing this matter to my attention.

Naturally we do inspect our toilets and I am well aware that there have been problems regarding the water for some time and I wish to apologise to you about your shoes. We do try to keep our restaurant in good running order and I hope you'll agree it's looking pretty good. Especially with the economic climate being what it is it is not easy to keep things up to the standerds people expect.

Once again, I apologies for any inconvenience this has caused you and i hope this letter is good enough.

Yours sincerely
Drad Richies

2 Unfortunately, your secretary is rather young and inexperienced and the draft reply handed to you for approval needs improvement. Read it again and, with a partner, decide:
   • which parts are unnecessary.
   • if anything needs to be added.

3 Now decide which parts need to be rephrased in order to achieve an appropriate register. (You will also need to correct your secretary's spelling and grammar mistakes!)

4 Now rewrite the whole letter in pairs. When you have finished, compare your final version with that of another pair.

LEXIS

Idioms and phrases using gesture

1 In what situations would you do the following?
   a shake hands with someone
   b grab someone by the hand
   c hold hands with someone
   d lay your hands on someone
   e clap your hands
   f wring your hands
   g put your hand up
   h put your hands up

2 What is meant by these idiomatic phrases?
   a Could you give me a hand carrying this?
   b Why don't you try your hand at golf?
   c He's a hired hand.
   d If you need advice on the job, talk to Bernard: he's an old hand at it.
   e This information must not fall into the wrong hands.
   f The situation is starting to get out of hand.
   g That boy needs taking in hand.

3 The following phrases use idioms or common collocations.
   In what situations would you do the following?
   a tip somebody the wink
   b make a conciliatory gesture
   c shrug something off
   d blow somebody a kiss
   e gesticulate frantically
   f raise your eyebrows

4 Register

In the word pairs below decide whether each word is formal, informal or not particularly either.
   1 bloke   man
   2 exhort   encourage
   3 horrible   abhorrent
   4 lethargic   sleepy
   5 agree   comply

5 Phrases with *give*

Put the most suitable phrases into the sentences below. Make any changes necessary.

give way to	give someone hell
give one's right arm	give as good as one gets
give someone a ring	give notice
give rise to	give the game away
give-and-take	give or take

   a She must be 40, ... a year or two.
   b The Prime Minister's comments .... speculation that he was about to call an election.
   c If he makes that mistake again I'm going to ....
   d I'd .... to be able to paint as well as she can.
   e Eventually, they were forced to .... his demands.
   f She never backs down: she always ....
   g Negotiations like these must involve some ....
   h .... if you want to go out this evening.
   i Sarah kept laughing and ....
   j They were .... 3 weeks ....

6 Choose one of the four words to fill the blanks in the sentences below.
   1 'Teacher Talk Time' and 'Intonation Patterns' are examples of English teachers' ....
   a) language b) dialect c) jargon d) lingo
   2 I gave him a .... to try and wake him up.
   a) gesture b) shrug c) nudge d) wink
   3 Priding oneself on disliking aristocrats could be a form of inverted ....
   a) etiquette b) politeness c) behaviour
   d) snobbery
   4 Inadvertently drawing attention to somebody's past failures could be described as ....
   a) discourteous b) rude c) brusque d) tactless
   5 The ability to converse with ease on a wide range of subjects is a mark of ....
   a) culture b) civilisation c) custom
   d) sophistication

GRAMMAR

The definite article

We use the definite article if we are sure that both the listener and the speaker (or reader/writer) share the same knowledge of what is being referred to.

Let me show you the picture.
Let me show you a picture.

In the first example, the listener knows which picture is being talked about. In the second, he/she doesn't.

1 Deciding whether to use a definite article is made easier if there is only one of something. Add to this list:

> *the Pope*
> *the government* (if we have already established which country we are talking about)
> *the earth*

2 Institutional reference

> *He bought the morning paper.*
> *I went to the cinema/theatre last night.*
> *She's on the phone.*
> *I'll take the train.*

In all of these examples, there are presumably several alternatives, i.e. several phones in the office, several different morning papers, a choice of trains, etc. . Since they are all common institutions, however, we treat them as a single class so the definite article is used.

Change the above four examples so that they take the indefinite article. One of them now sounds very odd, even impossible.

Which one?

How has the meaning of the other three examples changed?

3 Generic reference

The definite article is sometimes used as in the following examples. What do they have in common?

> *The dog can be a vicious animal.*
> *The car is a necessary evil.*
> *The mini-skirt was fashionable in the sixties.*

(These 3 examples are quite formal. It is more usual to say *Dogs can be vicious animals.* etc.)

This use of the definite article is most common in the following three categories. Add one or two more examples to each category.

1 Musical instruments
Example: *He's learning to play the clarinet.*
2 Dances
Example: *The waltz is in three time.*
3 With plural nouns, used to refer to national or family groups:
Examples: *The Americans invaded Grenada.*
The Smiths have bought a new car.

4 The zero article

The nouns on the right below change meaning slightly according to whether they take the zero article on the one hand, or '*a*' or '*the*' on the other. How?

be in/go (to) { church
bed
prison
school
hospital
home

5 Can we use articles with meals? If so, how?
Example
lunch, tea, supper, breakfast

6 Some illnesses are preceded by '*a*' while others take the zero article. Divide this list into two groups according to whether they normally take the indefinite or zero article.

cancer	diabetes	headache
fever	stomach ache	temperature
cold	flu	

7 In the following extract from the opening of a novel, decide for each of the following gaps what sort of article is required.

> It was only [1] ....*a*.... two-day crossing from [2] .... Piraeus to [3] .... Alexandria, but as soon as I saw [4] .... dingy little Greek steamer I felt I ought to have made other arrangements. Even from [5] .... quay it looked overcrowded, like [6] .... refugee ship; and when I went aboard I found there wasn't enough room for everybody.
> There was no deck to speak of. [7] .... bar, open on two sides to [8] .... January wind, was [9] .... size of [10] .... cupboard. Three made [11] .... crowd there, and behind his little counter [12] .... little Greek barman, serving [13] .... bad coffee, was in [14] .... bad mood. Many of [15] .... chairs in [16] .... small smoking-room, and [17] .... good deal of [18] .... floor space, had been seized by [19] .... overnight passengers from Italy, among them [20] .... party of overgrown American schoolchildren in their mid-teens, white and subdued but watchful. [21] .... only other public room was [22] .... dining-room, and that was being got ready for [23] .... first of [24] .... lunch sittings by [25] .... stewards who were as tired and bad-tempered as [26] .... barman.

UNIT 3 Jobs and Giraffes

FOCUS

1 Are you doing the job you most wanted to do when you were a teenager? If not, why not?

2 What factors do people have to consider when they look for a job?

3 What qualities do you think are needed for a person doing these jobs:

- speech therapist
- vet
- international banker
- dentist
- chicken farmer
- theatrical designer
- police pathologist
- translator

In your opinion why do people choose these jobs?

4 What is the difference between *a job*, *a vocation* and *a career*?

5 Is it normal, or even expected, in your country to do any of the following:
- start your own business?
- work for the same company all your working life?
- continue the family business?
- have more than one career during your working life?
- have two or more jobs simultaneously?
- help your family financially or to be independent?

READING 1

These three extracts are from an article about David Taylor. Read the first extract to find out who he is.

1 A BIG MAN, with a world traveller's tan, David Taylor is a veterinary surgeon with a case list that sounds like the sick parade aboard Noah's 5 Ark. In a week he can be treating dolphins for ulcers, prescribing a diet for an overweight orang-utan and injections for pandas. He has written more than a dozen popular books 10 including his best selling *Zoo Vet* series which went on to form the basis of the highly successful BBC TV series *One by One*.

Based in Surrey, with a partner in 15 Keighley, Yorkshire and another in Winchester, David Taylor runs the International Zoo Veterinary Group. His work involves anything to do with exotic animals and takes him all over 20 the world. Most of the time he is at zoos and safari parks but he is often called on during the making of TV commercials and films. As a result of his jet set vetting he tots up around 25 half a million miles a year.

Born in Rochdale, Lancashire, he recalls that from the age of six he wanted to be a vet and nothing else. It was the study of disease that he found 30 so intriguing as well as helping animals in trouble.

'It was the tadpole that had fungus on it that fascinated me and the sheep that I found dying in hollows on the moors 35 around Rochdale.'

David went on to study veterinary medicine at Glasgow University where he stayed on a further year to do a postgraduate course in comparative 40 pathology. Every morning he would go to the Western Infirmary and cut up human corpses. This paid off later when he did his Fellowship in primates in 1968. Primate disease, medi- 45 cine and surgery are virtually the same as human medicine. His was the first postgraduate qualification in exotic animals ever obtained by a vet.

From Glasgow he made the unusual 50 step from research to becoming a partner in a Rochdale mixed practice. This was the biggest agricultural practice in Great Britain. Being a Lancashire cotton town, there were

55 many farms with small numbers of cattle on the edge of the Pennines. There was also the zoo, cart horses from timber yards and breweries, children's ponies and small animal work. He learnt all the basic skills and 60 formed some basic opinions:

Now read the extract again in order to answer these questions.

1 a In how many ways can David Taylor's career be described as 'unusual'?

  b How many university courses did he follow?

  c Why did he need to *cut up human corpses*?

2 Find these phrasal verbs and explain their meaning in the context.

went on	called on
tot up	cut up
paid off	stayed on

3 How many examples of medical words and phrases can you find?

4 a What is similar about the construction of the first sentence in each of the first three paragraphs?

   Can you think why the writer uses this construction so much?

  b Look at the structure of the two sentences starting on lines 28 and 32. They are known as **cleft sentences**.
Rewrite them using a normal subject/verb/object word order. How does the emphasis change?

---

5 a Before you read the second extract, say which of these animals you think would be most difficult for a vet to deal with.

tigers	pandas	killer whales
horses	king cobras	gorillas

  b How do you think a vet manages to treat dangerous animals?

Extract 2

'Horses are stupid animals, they're very dangerous, they're delicate and they have classic problems. I've
65 had more trouble with horses than I've ever had with tigers, giant pandas, gorillas or killer whales. I've been more frightened by them than by king cobras or anything else.
70 'If you can handle, diagnose and treat the horse, which is big, powerful, dangerous and not all that bright but at the same time delicate and prone to wobblies, you can
75 handle anything. Until recently the horse was the classic teaching instrument.'
Fundamental things happened at the time that would revolutionise zoo
80 medicine. The cross-bow dart guns and blow pipes became available, enabling vets to lob drug laden syringes through the air. Then one of Britain's big drug companies
85 produced an injectable anaesthetic. Now the zoo vet had the tools to get at the animals. David Taylor was immediately involved in developing techniques. They had a massive
90 number of exotic animals at Belle Vue Zoo and he was still learning. There are over two million or more different animal species on this planet and theoretically the zoo vet
95 works with all of them.

6 Explain the meaning of these phrases:
not all that bright (line 73)
prone to wobblies (line 74)
to lob drug laden syringes (lines 83–84)

7 a How did animals use to be anaesthetised?

  b Why was the horse the classic teaching instrument?

33

8 Before reading this last extract, with a partner, think of as many ways as possible of transporting a giraffe from one country to another. What problems might be encountered?

Extract 3

Giraffes, he found, are very difficult to transport. There are two ways of doing it; either you transport them 100 when they're still small and they will fit into a big jet like a 747, or you shorten them by making them lie down, not on their side but on their breastbone.

105 'This is a tricky thing to do. They have a curious circulation to the brain and tend to faint very easily. Even mild doses of sedatives make them faint and that can be disastrous for an animal which comes 110 walloping down from such a great height.'

A three-day trip he made with two elephants and a giraffe from north of Madrid by road to south of 115 Barcelona remains particularly marked on his memory.

'I didn't realise how many cables, electricity and telephone wires run across the roads in Spain. There are 120 millions of them and every one had to be lifted up so that the giraffe's head could go under. We went through the villages lifting the wires with forked sticks.'

125 One night they stopped at a little hotel. They parked the huge wagon with the elephants and the giraffe under some trees and went to eat

and sleep. The trees were Medlars 130 laden with ripe fruit and the elephants gorged themselves. During the night everyone was woken by the riotous sound of drunken elephants.

135 'They were joyously out of their minds. We'd set off with a brand new low-loading truck and those drunken elephants completely destroyed it, they wrenched off 140 everything they could and pushed the sides out. They had a marvellous time. We arrived with a still-running but tattered open truck.'

World Magazine

9 From what you have read, decide whether these statements are true or false?

	True	False
a Young giraffes can be transported on large jets.	☐	☐
b Giraffes are anaesthetised on planes.	☐	☐
c They had to get the giraffe's head under the telephone wires.	☐	☐
d The elephants made themselves sick.	☐	☐
e The truck wouldn't go because the elephants destroyed it.	☐	☐
f The elephants pulled off parts of the truck.	☐	☐

10 Here are some standard collocations and common phrases. Find each one in the passage and check you know its meaning.

a tricky thing to do	mild doses
out of their minds	completely destroyed
had a marvellous time	brand new

Now think of other situations in which you could use each phrase.

11 Note down the language you have learned from studying these three extracts. Compare your notes with those of a partner.

LISTENING 1

1 If you turn on a radio in the middle of a programme it can take a moment to understand what it is about.
Listen to the first part of this recording. What are the two people talking about and where are they?

2 Now listen to the complete recording. As you listen, list the different aspects of the topic that they talk about.

3 What is meant by:

the unbroken ones	a roan
a healthy respect	they like fuss
a bovine animal	parrot fashion

4 Listen to this extract and fill in the gaps in the transcript.

> ***Pat:*** Er he erm he .... in self-defence because that's their natural erm attack...............
> .... because flight is their, is their ....
> .... you see. . .
>
> ***Richard:*** Yes.
>
> ***Pat:*** Whereas a .... animal with .... will turn around and attack, won't run away. . .
>
> ***Richard:*** Right.
>
> ***Pat:*** and isn't ....
> .... except their heels.
>
> ***Richard:*** Yes, yes.
>
> ***Pat:*** But these have ....
> ....
> .... except their heels.

LEXIS

Animal idioms

1 What characteristics do you associate with these animals?

dogs	cats	pigs	sheep	bulls

2 Say what is meant by the following idioms. Which idioms, if any, do they correspond to in your own language? In what situations could you use them?

a He's always being pushed around by his wife. He *leads a dog's life*.
b They were having a furious argument and their poor son was caught as *piggy-in-the-middle*.
c Stop being so *pig-headed*. Learn to compromise a little.
d What have you been doing? You *look like something the cat's dragged in*.
e The boss will be away all next week. *While the cat's away. . .*
f He *looked a bit sheepish* when I found out what he had been doing.
g Things aren't what they used to be, you know. This country's *going to the dogs*.

3 In these idioms, choose one of the animals from exercise 1 to fill in the gaps.

a He lives in a tiny flat. There's not enough room to swing a .....cat...... .
b You've got to be courageous and take the .... by the horns.
c 'I'm going to be Prime Minister.'
'................. s might fly.'
d He's in the .... house again. His wife refused to talk to him.
e You're very quiet. .... got your tongue?
f He was charging around the house like a .... in a china shop.
g After his spell in prison, Ian was regarded as the black .... of the family.
h I'm going to tell him everything. That'll set the .... among the pigeons.
i It was supposed to be a secret but somebody let the .... out of the bag.

READING 2

1 a Put these adjectives into two lists:
   a those that can be used to describe a job.
   b those that can be used to describe the qualitites required of job applicants.

responsible	challenging	high-calibre
well-qualified	demanding	experienced
innovative	committed	exciting
rewarding	ambitious	confident

   b Do these adjectives have positive or negative connotations?

2 Add the words below to the two lists you made in exercise 1a. Choose only those words which you feel have positive connotations in a work context.

talented	expanding	renowned
self-serving	aggressive	thrilling
judgemental	single-minded	reputable
mundane	time-consuming	

3 Look through the advertisements opposite to find out the following:
   a What does each company do?
   b What is the job?
   c Do the advertisements have any similarities in the way the jobs are presented? If so, what?
   d Which are the most vague about what the job involves? Do you think this vagueness is deliberate and if so, why?

4 a How many of the adjectives listed above in exercises 1 and 2 are used in the advertisements?
   b Only one of the advertisements mentions the word *salary*. How do the other three refer to money?
   c Two of the advertisements, (BBC, DG) require a candidate with certain *skills*. What skills are these and what do you think they involve?
   d Which words or phrases collocate with these nouns:

ACIS	BBC	DG
record	changes	opportunity
applicant	communication	reputation
		market
		trade

5 Style and register

   a How could you describe the style and register that these advertisements are written in? Choose from these adjectives:

friendly	downbeat
enthusiastic	boastful
impersonal	honest

   b Are there any differences in style? Could any be described as more formal or informal than the others?
   c What phrases are used instead of 'We want to employ. . .'?
   d Do any of them refer to *'You'* directly? How do they manage to be indirect?
   e When listing the qualifications and skills required, what phrases are used instead of 'You must have. . . '?

6 Tell your partner which of these jobs, if any, you would like to do and what you like/dislike about them.

WRITING 1

In small groups, write a similar advertisement, imitating the style of the examples.

Choose a job that you know something about. Here are some ideas:

translator	tourist guide
zoo manager	computer programmer
teacher	nurse
your own job	bus driver

Consider these points when writing your advertisements.
   • What does the company/employer do?
   • What exactly does the job involve?
   • What sort of person are you looking for?
   • What range of skills must they have?
   • What salary and bonuses are you offering?
   • What is the application procedure?
   • What is the most effective layout?

Assistant Editor, Presentation

Presentation is responsible for the transmission of the two BBC Television Networks. Working to one of four duty Presentation Editors, you will look after the detailed planning and transmission of BBC1 and BBC2 schedules. This involves the construction of programme junctions, placing of trails and making sure that the networks run to time and complement each other effectively; the job also requires an awareness of and co-ordination with World Service Television and the BBC National and English Regions. You deputise for the Editor and take full editorial and managerial responsibility, as needed, for both networks on air, in both planned situations and when last minute changes are required.

You must have proven co-ordination skills, editorial judgement, an eye for detail and the ability to communicate effectively and deal with staff at all levels. The selected candidate will be expected to work varied work patterns covering all transmission hours.

Salary £24,795-£34,208 p.a. (contract) plus an unpredictability allowance of £1,500 p.a. Based West London.

For further details contact **Janet Hoenig** on **081-576-1235.**

(Ref: 9024/EO/AG)

WHY PEOPLE WORK IN THE FINANCIAL SERVICES SECTOR

Since Milldon & Co Ltd was launched in 1972, we have been recruiting and training people in Financial Sales where they have proved to be very successful indeed. Many are high business producers who have become managers within a couple of years, opening up their own branches with five to ten sales people working for them. And women have been as successful as men.

Because of its 1991 expansion programme, Milldon & Co. Ltd, part of an £8.3 billion organisation, is recruiting more high calibre trainees for its London office.

If you relish the prospect of developing a business of your own with high earnings potential, together with working conventions to such places as the Seychelles, Rio and Thailand, then telephone:

AGO9
Sarah Savins
071 222 7495

Head of Marketing
Deutsche Grammophon

An exciting opportunity has arisen within the PolyGram group of companies – that of Head of Marketing for the renowned classical music recording label. Deutsche Grammophon, DG, or the yellow label as it is often known, enjoys an enviable reputation for the quality and diversity of its recordings and its roster of major international recording artists.

Reporting to the Divisional Director – Classics, PolyGram UK, the Head of Marketing has responsibility for all aspects of marketing DG's artists and their product in the UK. The job encompasses all the traditional marketing tasks – planning release schedules, budgeting, devising and effecting campaigns, briefing the sales division – as well as being able to take advantage of and develop the increasing popularity of classical music within the mass market.

We are seeking a talented and experienced marketing person with excellent musical knowledge. Candidates must be able to demonstrate an innovative approach to, and a successful background in, marketing whilst possessing the social and creative skills essential to achieving success in this role. Knowledge of the retail trade would be extremely useful as would a second European language. A very competitive package which will include car, medical insurance, bonus etc. will be offered to the successful candidate.

If you would like further information, please telephone Veronica Spicer on 081-846 8515 ext 5008. Written applications, including a detailed cv, should be sent to Veronica Spicer, Group Personnel Department, PolyGram UK Limited, 1 Sussex Place, London W6 9XS.

ACIS   *The Educational Travel Division of AIFS*

AMERICAN COUNCIL FOR INTERNATIONAL STUDIES
37 Queens Gate London SW7 5HR
ACIS is an American company specialising in tours of Europe for U.S. school groups. We are looking for individuals with a sound academic record and good communication skills to act as tour directors. Successful applicants will need to be fluent in a major European language, with a good knowledge of European history. The work is seasonal, but remuneration is competitive. Please contact Annie Dickson: 071-581 9498.
Ref AGO9

LEXIS

Adjective/noun collocation

I In pairs, match these nouns with the appropriate collocating adjectives and find out the meaning of each phrase. Some adjectives collocate with more than one noun.

   a work   c workmanship   e worker
   b task   d job(s)   f career

backbreaking	distinguished	odd
blue-collar	exquisite	part-time
brilliant	hard	promising
checkered	hopeless	shoddy
cushy	fine	steady
delicate	fruitless	unpleasant
dirty	monumental	unskilled

2 a What sort of person is a *high flier*?

   b What sort of person *never does a stroke of work*?

'*I was quite pleased to find a job which allows me to see more of my husband*'

LISTENING 2

Look at the ACIS advertisement on page 37. You will hear some extracts from a conversation with one of the people who interviews candidates for this job.

I Listen to the first extract. How much more do you learn about the job that is <u>not</u> in the advertisement?

2 Now answer these questions:

   a Why does she stress the word 'we' in *Well I can tell you what we do. . . ?*

   b What does she mean by *the logistics of the trip?*

   c What does she mean by *or whatever* near the end of the extract?

3 Listen to the second extract. Are the following sentences true or false according to what is said?

		True	*False*
a	They interview every applicant.	☐	☐
b	They wouldn't employ anyone who didn't meet all the requirements mentioned in the advertisement.	☐	☐
c	It is suggested that a person whose knowledge of countries is weak could learn about them before starting the job.	☐	☐
d	Extroverts are more likely to be employed than introverts.	☐	☐

4 Before you listen to the last extract, write down some phrases that you could use to tell people their interview had not been successful. Would you use different language on the telephone and in a letter?

5 a Now listen and note down the phrases that the interviewer mentions.

   b What can you say about the level of formality of these phrases and what does that tell you about the kind of organisation ACIS is?

   c If someone had failed the interview because their personality wasn't what was required, and they wanted to know why they hadn't got the job, what would you say?

SPEAKING

Job Interview

*Try to overcome your natural modesty.
You're here to talk about yourself.*

1 Working in groups of five, role play the interviews for ACIS. Two students should be interviewers and the rest candidates for the job. Remember that the interviews should be relaxed and informal.

Prepare for the interview using the following notes to help you.

Interviewers:

• Decide how the interview should start: how do you relax the candidate if he/she is nervous? What preliminary questions do you ask?

• You need to find out about the candidate's qualifications and experience. If these are limited, how do you allow the interviewee to present themselves in a positive way?

• Personality is very important in this job. How are you going to find out whether the candidate is confident and outgoing enough for the job?

• You may feel you want to think about the exact wording of some of your questions. Make notes on this now.

• Think about the tone and register of your questions: you want to be relaxed and informal, but on the other hand you have never met this person before.

Candidates:

• You need to present yourself in a positive light. If your qualifications and experience for this job are limited, how can you persuade the interviewers that you are still the person they are looking for?

• You realise that they are looking for a confident, outgoing sort of personality. How do you show them that you are this sort of person without appearing to be arrogant or smug?

• Think about the tone and register of your answers. You want to appear relaxed and friendly but not too familiar or casual: you haven't met the interviewers before and they are in a dominant position because they are interviewing you.

Agree with your teacher on a time limit for each interview.

Each candidate should be interviewed in turn (the other interviewees can observe).

The interviewers should then decide, giving reasons, who they will give the job to.

2 When you have finished all the interviews look at this list and decide which were a problem for you and which presented no problems during the interviews.

• trying to find the right word
• understanding what other people were saying
• speaking at a reasonable speed
• grammatical accuracy
• pronunciation
• using the appropriate tone and register

WRITING 2

APPROPRIACY

Following a recent series of interviews, your boss asks you to draft a standard rejection letter to be sent to all unsuccessful candidates.

These are the guidelines you were given. Pay careful attention to the register.

Be nice to them – they should not be made to feel that they were useless. Tell them there were many candidates and that standards were very high – a pleasure meeting you ... unfortunately ... we wish you every success ... etc.

LEXIS

Phrasal verbs

Phrasal verbs consist of a verb and a particle (*on, off, up*, etc.) used in combination.

There are four types of phrasal verb.
1. *We need to be careful and* **plan ahead**.
2. *Take these figures and* **add** *them* **up** *for me.*
3. *You can always* **call on** *me if you need help.*
4. *I'm not going to* **put up with** *this much longer.*

1 a Which of the four types of phrasal verb above are **transitive** and which are **intransitive**?

b In which can the verb and the particle be separated?

c Can you think of any more examples of the fourth type with two particles?

2 Here are some more common phrasal verbs. Decide which of the four categories listed above they belong to.

Be particularly careful with the second category: the verb and particle are normally only separated by a pronoun or short object.

Example
Can you **add** *all the expenses and wages* **up** *for me?*
is normally said:
Can you **add up** *all the expenses and wages for me?*

a I *look forward to* seeing you.
b I enjoy *working out* at weekends.
c I'm afraid I've *left out* the most important part.
d I'll *give* that book *back* to you next week.
e He *stayed on* at school for an extra term.
f I'll *look into* the problem as soon as I have time.
g You must *hand in* your application by the 15th April.
h A high degree of expertise is *called for* in this job.

Particles

3 Look at these phrasal verbs from the texts in READING 1 and 2. Give the meaning of each one. In which of the phrasal verbs is the meaning obvious, and in which is it less obvious?
a We'd *set off* with a brand new low loading truck. . .
b . . . they *wrenched off* everything they could. . .
c . . . every one had to be *lifted up*
d . . . *opening up* their own branches. . .

Can you pick out any other phrasal verbs in the texts?

Meanings of *on*

David **went on** *to study veterinary medicine in Glasgow University.*

What is the meaning of the particle '*on*' in this phrasal verb?

The three most common meanings of '*on*' as a particle are:

a the literal meaning of movement or place
- *I* **got on** *the bus.*
- *He* **poured** *milk* **on** *his cornflakes.*

or of attaching or adding something
- **Put** *your clothes* **on**.
- **Hang** *your coat* **on** *the peg.*

or metaphorically
- *I've been* **stuck on** *this exercise for half an hour.*
- *It took him a while to* **catch on**.
  (i.e. *understand*. As if physically catching hold of the idea)

b continuing or progressing
- **Carry on** *with whatever you are doing.*
- *They* **struggled on**, *regardless.*
- *If he doesn't answer,* **keep on** *ringing.*
- **Hang on**, *will you?* (i.e. *continue waiting*)

c the idea of starting something
- **Switch on** *the light.*
- **Turn on** *the engine.*

4 In these sentences, look at the phrasal verb and decide which meaning of the particle '*on*' is being used.

Are there any which don't fit into categories, a, b, or c above? If so, what do you think the function of '*on*' is?

a He was *spurred on* by his ambition.
b What was he *going on* about?
c *Turn* the radio *on* please.
d Her cold was *brought on* by getting caught in the rain.
e It was hard going but they *soldiered on* doggedly.
f Can you *sew* this button *on* for me?
g She's *signed on* for another two years with the company.
h Wearing jeans to work is generally *frowned on* in Britain.
i I don't like to *impose on* your time.

5 In pairs, list all the other phrasal verbs you know which use '*on*'. How many of them fit into the categories mentioned above?

GRAMMAR

Participle and verbless clauses

1 Circle the subject of each of these sentences. The first one has been done for you.

   a Driving home, Ⓘ suddenly had an idea.
   b Jumping and shouting, children ran into the playground.
   c Realising it was getting late, John got ready to leave.
   d Tired and miserable, they made their way home.
   e Reaching the gate, they turned to admire the view.
   f He stood for some time, silent and morose, before speaking.
   g Angered by what he saw as unnecessary bureaucracy, Dominic slammed the phone down.

In each of these sentences, the **subordinate clause** contains a **past participle** (-ed), a **present participle** (-ing) or is **verbless**. The subject of the **subordinate clause** is the same as that of the **main clause**.

2 Looking at the sentences above, answer these questions on the relationship between the two halves of each sentence (main clause and subordinate clause).

   a Which sentences have verbless clauses?

   b Which show two things happening at the same time?

   c Which show one thing happening immediately after another?

   d Which use a past form in the subordinate clause to emphasise that the action in the clause happens first?

   e Which subordinate clauses give the reason for the action in the main clause?

   f Which subordinate clause has a passive meaning?

3 Rewrite the sentences in exercise 1, if possible, using verbs with full tense forms.
   Example
   a *While I was driving home, I suddenly had an idea.*
   b Not possible

4 It is possible to use a different subject in the two clauses.
   Example
   The meeting finished, we got up and left.
   He moved towards her, tears streaming down his face.
   The subject having been raised, they turned their attention to it.

   Do you think the structures seen above are more common in spoken or written English?

5 Work in small groups. Look at the set of subordinate clauses, a–l, and the set of main clauses below. Match as many as you can.

   a Peering into her ear,
   b The sun having set,
   c The letter not having arrived,
   d Having married at an early age,
   e Born and brought up in Burnley,
   f Tanned and healthy,
   g Used to giving orders,
   h Expertly trained,
   i Convinced he was right,
   j Having worked out the combination,
   k Feeling very important,
   l Grumbling and dragging his feet,

   1 *they finally left Corfu.*
   2 *she found it difficult to adapt to the new job.*
   3 *he was a grandfather at 40.*
   4 *he viewed other towns with suspicion.*
   5 *Fred was the perfect dog.*
   6 *the mosquitoes became worse.*
   7 *the small boy was ordered to bed.*
   8 *the doctor noticed an infection.*
   9 *she phoned the company.*
   10 *Ian argued interminably.*
   11 *breaking into the safe he found easy.*
   12 *he climbed onto the rostrum.*

LEXIS

Phrasal verbs: *on*

'On' is used with a number of transitive verbs describing actions. The noun following 'on' in these combinations refers to the person or thing that is affected by the action.

Example
It slowly dawned on me that I was on the wrong train.
I want to improve on the services we offer.

1 Say what is meant by the following combinations with 'on'.

a Gradually, we *gained on* the car in front.
b He *doted on* his grandaughter.
c I didn't like the taste at first but it *grows on* you.
d He went to the police and *split on* his co-conspirators.
e Some companies pay people to *spy on* their competitors.
f The defence counsel *seized on* his words as proof that he was lying.
g Playing practical jokes like that may well *rebound on* you.
h They *lavished* hospitality *on* all their guests.
i Eating with your fingers is *frowned on* in most Western restaurants.
j She *forced* more and more food *on* me until I felt bloated.
k There is no need for me to further *impress on* you the necessity of caution.

2 One small group of verbs with 'on' is used to indicate attack. Explain the meaning of these verbs.

a Get out or I'll *set* my dog *on* you.
b The other members *rounded on* her and accused her of disloyalty.
c Most of the time she's fairly friendly but she can suddenly *turn on* you like a cornered animal.
d The cat crouched, then *pounced on* the unsuspecting bird.

3 a In the above two exercises, are the phrasal verbs transitive or intransitive?
b In how many of them can the verb and particle be separated?

4 Replace the words underlined in the sentences below with other phrasal verbs from UNIT 3 page 40. What differences in connotation, register, etc. are there between the two alternatives?

a He was <u>egged</u> <u>on</u> by an ambitious wife.
b What's he <u>rabbiting</u> <u>on</u> about?
c Wearing jeans to work is generally <u>looked</u> <u>down</u> <u>on</u>.
d She'll never <u>cotton</u> <u>on</u>. She's far too slow.
e I know it's difficult but you've got to <u>keep</u> <u>on</u>.
f My button's fallen off and I don't know how to <u>put</u> it <u>back</u> <u>on</u>.

Idioms with *on*

Use these idiomatic phrases to complete the sentences below. Make any changes that are necessary.

be on at somebody	be on about something
be on to a good thing	be on to somebody
be on the look-out for sb/sth	have a lot on
on and off	on the house

a These drinks are ....
b My mother is always .... me to get a proper job.
c What's he .... ? It doesn't make any sense to me.
d I'm afraid I can't make it on Friday: I ....
e She now gets twice the money for half the work. It strikes me she's ....
f He's been staying in my flat .... for the last year.
g I've been .... a cheap computer for ages.
h He needs to be careful or he'll have the police ....

Collocation

Add a suitable collocating adjective from those on page 38 to complete these sentences.

a This is *supposed* to be a hand-carved chair. All I can say is that it's pretty .... workmanship.
b He hasn't really got a full-time job. He does .... jobs for people who ask him.
c She had a very .... career as a diplomat before being given an honorary title and retiring to write her memoirs.
d She's got a really .... job. Loads of money and only three days a week.
e Cleaning out the garden shed is .... work.

f   A .... career in politics came to nothing as the result of the scandal.

g   We'll never finish this. It's a ....task.

Animal idioms

This exercise revises the idioms on page 35 and adds some new ones.

Choose the appropriate animal to complete these idioms.

1   He ate everything he could and made a real .... of himself.
    a) pig b) dog c) donkey

2   There's no point in dodging the issue. You've got to take the .... by the horns.
    a) goat b) bull c) cow

3   The competition is far too tough. We don't stand a .... in hell's chance of winning.
    a) dog b) cat c) fish

4   You've got to do it. You can't .... out now.
    a) mouse b) rat c) chicken

5   You're far too stubborn. Stop being so................. headed.
    a) donkey b) horse c) pig

6   It was great to see him again. We haven't met for .... 's years.
    a) tortoise b) donkey c) elephant

7   Don't worry about her. She wouldn't hurt a ....
    a) horse b) mouse c) fly

8   He's going to tell the boss. That will set the cat amongst the ....
    a) mice b) pigeons c) chickens

9   You can't do anything around here. We lead a ....'s life.
    a) pig b) dog c) horse

10 Things aren't what they used to be. This country's going to the ....
    a) pigs b) dogs c) sheep

GRAMMAR

Participle and verbless clauses

1   Rephrase these sentences using a participle or verbless clause. Does the change make any difference to the emphasis or tone of the sentence?

Example

I knew how he would react and chose not to tell him what had happened.

Knowing how he would react, I chose not to tell him what had happened.

a   The room was damp and dirty and smelt disgusting.

b   When I had finished the chapter, I put the light out and sat in the dark, thinking.

c   He was born in Maldon and grew up in Oxfordshire.

d   She felt embarrassed and offered an apology.

e   This book is disgusting and immoral and should be banned.

f   Since they were responsible for the damage, they should pay for the repairs.

g   The archaeologist used a fine brush to remove the remaining earth from the skeleton.

h   The management looks down on the blue-collar workers and so create tensions within the firm.

2   Complete this passage using participle clauses with *-ing* or *-ed,* or a verbless clause.

Dawn was breaking [1] *cold and grey,* as I walked slowly and disconsolately home. [2] *Thinking about it.,* it had been a fruitless night's work: nothing had gone according to plan. [3] ...., I turned into my road, [4] ...., and vowed never to make the same mistake again. If Jack had been more trustworthy things might have been better. But Jack, [5] ...., was a worthless good-for-nothing, as I would have seen sooner if I'd kept my eyes open. [6] ...., I put my key in the lock. And then froze. [7] .... the sound of running water was coming from somewhere inside. I turned the key and burst in, [8] .... Water, [9] ...., was everywhere and standing in the middle of the lake that used to be my living-room, [10] ...., was Jack.

3   Decide which of the sentences below are **cleft sentences**.

a   I danced all night with Angela.

b   He went to university in Leeds.

c   It's bananas that I'm allergic to.

d   He walked all the way to Glasgow.

e   I left school in 1978.

f   I find her pronunciation the biggest barrier to communication.

Look at the sentences above and transform those which have a *subject/verb/object* order to cleft sentences.

Example

I eventually found the book on Wednesday.

It was on Wednesday *that I eventually found the book.*

How is the emphasis changed? Do the different structures assume different things about the knowledge of the reader?

Creating an Atmosphere

FOCUS

1 Make a list of some situations in which it might be necessary to describe a place (e.g. *estate agents*, *holiday brochures*). In each case, how much detail would you give?

2 Look at your list and decide if the different contexts would require different types of language. If so, how would the language be different?

3 Look at these three descriptions. Where might they come from and how is the language different?

1 Summer died, after lingering on into a golden early October. The city became a place of sodium-lighted rainswept canyons, of blazing shop windows, of shopping crowds in crisp Saturday-afternoon air, a city that sprawled out on all sides of its tightly knit centre in a web of access roads and dark back streets glimpsed mostly from the interiors of swaying buses.

2 *The property is situated on a plot approx. 133' by 65' and the gardens are all at the rear.*
The front of the property is approached via a five bar gate leading to the driveway with space for two to three cars.
GARAGE 17' by 8' with fuel bunker attached.

3 In order to appreciate the variety of Oxford, one should visit Keble College in Parks Road. John Ruskin, who was the leading exponent of architecture in the 19th Century, considered the college so ugly that he diverted his morning walk to avoid it. But the college, designed by Butterfield, is a classic of its kind; if its frenzied brickwork and embellishments would seem happier on the set of a Hammer Horror movie, it is, at least, enormously striking.

4 What other ways of describing places are there apart from what they look like?

LISTENING 1

1 Listen to these short extracts of people describing places. Note down what sort of place you think each one is talking about.

1 ....

2 ....

3 ....

4 ....

5 ....

6 ....

In pairs, compare your answers.

2 Listen again to each extract. Which of the following ways of describing does each speaker use? Tick the most suitable boxes. Note any words or phrases which you think are useful for describing places.

	1	2	3	4	5	6
a						
b						
c						
d						

a comparing it to somewhere else

b giving a personal reaction to it

c trying to give a general impression

d focusing on details

3 a How can you best convey the atmosphere of a place? Give reasons.

b Which description is the least interesting? Why?

4 Which speaker do you find most difficult to understand? Why?

Does it become easier to understand with repeated listening?

SPEAKING

1 Work in pairs. Briefly describe to each other a place you know well.

2 a When you have finished, look back at the techniques in question 2 of the LISTENING section. How many of these did you use?

  b Think of ways in which you could make your descriptions more interesting and varied in structure. Consider the following:
   • relative clauses
   • conditionals
   • adjectives
   • phrases to introduce comparisons
    – *such as. . .*
    – *as though. . .*
    – *like. . .*

  c Think what vocabulary you could use to improve your description. Note it down.

3 Now describe the same place again using the techniques, structures and vocabulary you have just been working on. Your partner should ask questions if anything is unclear.

4 Did you find this task easier with or without preparation?
  Which of your partner's descriptions gave you the best idea of the place?

LEXIS

Adverbs describing place

The box below contains some words which are used as adverbs to describe position. If possible, use them in the sentences (a–h). Some sentences may have more than one answer.

abroad	aloft	ashore
downstream	downwind	halfway
inland	nearby	offshore
overhead	overseas	underfoot

  a The plane was flying directly ....
  b He held the trophy triumphantly .... for all to see.
  c It had been raining and the ground was wet .... as I walked through the forest.
  d The wreckage of the river boat was swept several miles ....

  e The port authorities radioed him while he was some distance ....
  f When the ferry docked at Calais they finally stepped .... after a long week at sea.
  g He paused .... down the stairs.
  h Many years ago most Corsicans lived .... since the coastal areas of the island were infected with malaria.

Now write similar sentences for the four remaining words.

READING 1

The text opposite is taken from a newspaper article in which a journalist compares various hotels around Gatwick airport near London.

1 Look at these words and phrases.

sumptuous	rather formal	traditional
dimly-lit	higher-minded	tiny
grubby	reasonable	unappetising
well-thought-out	cold	mean

What do you think each adjective could refer to when talking about international hotels?

2 a In pairs, read either **Text A** on page 47 or **Text B** on page 164.

  b Briefly note what the passage you read says about the following things.
   1 Room:
    • size
    • furniture
    • bathroom
   2 Room service
   3 Restaurant
   4 Service and facilities

  c Now compare your answers with those of a pair who read the other article.
  Which hotel would you rather stay in? Why?

Text A

TRAVEL
John Diamond
Gatwick Stopover

Effingham Park Hotel
£70 to £150

1 I stayed in a business-grade room – halfway between a standard room and a suite. The room itself was bigger than my
5 whole flat: had I been so minded I could have played badminton in it and never once run into the bed. As the bed was seven feet wide this is some claim indeed:
10 three sets of pillows were needed to fill its width. The furniture – easy chairs, dining chairs, arm chairs, a small dinner table, the wardrobe and
15 so on – were in purest mahogany. If anything, it was all a little too sumptuous, with its maroon hangings and the rather formal carpet and wall
20 coverings; given the choice I might have gone for one of the smaller oaken rooms. The bathroom was equally vast, loaded with unguents, thick
25 towels and a bathrobe hung behind the door.

Room service came in a trice from a well-thought-out menu and was silver served on a cloth
30 laid on my table. The hotel has two restaurants: the McLaren serves solid snack-to-supper food, and the jacket-and-tie Wellingtonia runs a rather
35 higher-minded menu.

There is a health club based in the hotel which is, for the most part, free to residents.

There is also a hair-dressing
40 and beauty salon, a nine-hole golf course, croquet lawn and putting green.

Generally the service was that of one of the more
45 traditional London hotels. The service directory covers everything from ticket booking to picnic hampers. And where else nowadays can a gentleman
50 leave his shoes outside his room at night in the knowledge that they will return, gleaming, the next morning.

The Sunday Times

3 The writer refers to some things which he assumes his British readers are familiar with. Students who read **Text A** should look at the article again and explain the following words. Students who read **Text B** should look back at page 164 and explain the words from their text.

Text A

a *badminton*
b *maroon hangings*
c *oaken rooms*
d *a bathrobe*
e *silver service*
f *a croquet lawn*
g *a putting green*
h *a picnic hamper*

4 a Which of the adjectives in exercise **1** are used in your text and what do they refer to?

b How many comparisons does the author use? What purpose do they serve?

5 Look back at the list of words and structures in the SPEAKING section. Which of these does the journalist use?

6 How would these descriptions change if they were:
a written in a novel?
b written in a tour guide?
c spoken to a friend?

GRAMMAR

Adjectives

1 Decide if these statements about adjectives are true or false.
  Look at the adjectives used in the hotel descriptions to help you.

		True	False
a	Adjectives describe nouns.	☐	☐
b	Some adjectives are used after verbs.	☐	☐
c	Some adjectives change their meaning depending on their position in the sentence.	☐	☐
d	It is sometimes difficult to decide if a word is a verb or an adjective.	☐	☐
e	Nouns can be used as adjectives.	☐	☐
f	Sometimes you can put an adverb before an adjective.	☐	☐
g	You can change the meaning of adjectives by adding prefixes or suffixes.	☐	☐
h	Compound adjectives are made up of two or more words.	☐	☐

Now look at the explanations on the right of the page to see if you were correct.

2 Most adjectives can be used both before nouns and after certain verbs.
  Look at this list of verbs which can be followed by adjectives. These verbs are sometimes known as **link verbs**.

be	become	get/grow(=become)
keep	make	taste
smell	sound	appear
look (= appear)	seem	turn (=become)
feel		

Example
I feel tired.
The weather's turned nasty.

Take care not to confuse adjectives and adverbs:
John looked angry. = adjective describing John's appearance
John looked angrily (at her). = adverb describing John's way of looking

Think of an adjective and a situation for each verb in the list above.

3 What is the difference in the meaning of the adjective in these pairs?

  a the *present* circumstances
    the people *present*
  b an *involved* explanation
    the people *involved*
  c the *proper* time
    the city *proper*
  d a *concerned* expression
    the people *concerned*
  e the *early/late* train
    the train was *early/late*
  f *criminal* law
    the law is *criminal*

Explanations: exercise 1

a True. Although sometimes they may modify other adjectives, for example a *great big horse.*
b True. Example: *The room itself was bigger than my whole flat.*
c True. Example: *a responsible person* (= *trustworthy*)
  the person responsible (= *answerable*)
d True. Example: *She is (very) calculating.* (= adjective: *She is a scheming, cunning sort of person.*)
  She is calculating. (= participle: *She is working something out.*)
e True. Example: *a ham sandwich*
f True. Example: *highly enjoyable*
g True. Example: *meaningless, disreputable*
h True. Example: *dimly-lit, dark-haired*

LEXIS

Adjectives of atmosphere

As well as describing the physical appearance of a place, you can also describe its atmosphere.
Example
oppressive, exhilarating

1 Look at this list of adjectives.

austere	godforsaken	remote
spartan	depressing	roomy
grandiose	comfy	spooky
anonymous	antiseptic	snug
desolate	cosy	grotesque

a Which do you feel best describe the photographs 1–4. Give reasons for your answers.

b Which of the words do you feel have the most negative connotations?

c Which of these adjectives describe the place itself and which describe its atmosphere?

d Add your own adjectives to the list.

2 How would you describe the atmosphere of:
- a crowded shopping centre?
- a deserted town?
- a residential street?
- a seaside resort out of season?
- the foyer of an international hotel?

READING 2

1 Read the following two extracts from different novels. Which do you prefer and why?

Text A

1 It was 7.45 a.m. by the clock on the south face of St Frideswide's as Morris walked up to Carfax and then through Queen Street and down to the bottom of St. Ebbe's, where he stopped in front of a rangy three-storeyed stuccoed building
5 set back from the street behind bright yellow railings. Nailed on to the high wooden gate which guarded the narrow path to the front door was a flaking notice-board announcing in faded capitals ST FRIDESWIDE'S CHURCH AND OXFORD PASTORATE. The gate itself was half-open; and
10 as Morris stood self-consciously and indecisively in the deserted street a whistling paper-boy rode up on his bicycle and inserted a copy of *The Times* through the front door. No inside hand withdrew the newspaper, and Morris walked slowly away from the house and just as slowly back. On the
15 top floor a pale yellow strip of neon lighting suggested the presence of someone on the premises, and he walked cautiously up to the front door where he rapped gently on the ugly black knocker. With no sound of movement from within, he tried again, a little louder. There must be
20 someone, surely, in the rambling old vicarage. Students up on the top floor, probably? A housekeeper, perhaps? But again as he held his ear close to the door he could hear no movement; and conscious that his heart was beating fast against his ribs he tried the door. It was locked.

Text B

1 She turned into a gateway. Untidy pink rhododendrons flanked the short drive. It had been raining earlier and the shrubbery was soaked and dripping in the dank air. She rang the bell beside a door with coloured glass in
5 its upper half. A thin slatternly woman with metal curlers in her hair answered and the girl looked past her with dismay at the peeling dark-brown paint and the grubby wallpaper in the hall. An unpleasant odour caught at her nostrils and revulsion made her step a
10 few paces back.

2 In your opinion which of the texts is the most successful in describing places? Consider the following:
- the number of things described (enough or too many?)
- the evocation of atmosphere
- how many senses (smell, sight, sound etc.) are involved?
- do the reactions of the characters help us imagine the place more vividly?
- does the description help us understand the plot or the characters?

3 a One of these extracts is from a detective novel. Which one is it? How do you know?

b Do you think the subject affects the description the author uses?

4 If you were the author of one of these extracts, is there anything you would want to change or revise?

LISTENING 2

In this recording you will hear an interview with Colin Dexter, the author of *'Service of All the Dead'*, the novel from which **Text A** in READING 2 is taken. He is talking about the use of description in his novels.

1 a What reasons do you think Colin Dexter will give for using description in his novels?

b Now listen and make notes on what he says about each of the following words and phrases from the recording.
- some *visual aspect*
- *spurious reality*
- *a particular shade of maroon carpeting*

2 a How many specific places does Colin Dexter mention?

b From what he says, what do you think 'The Randolph' is?

3 Do you think the author's technique of writing about real places is unusual? Can you think of any other examples of this technique in novels you have read?

LEXIS

Describing smell

1 a Divide these nouns into pleasant and unpleasant smells.

stink	whiff	odour	fragrance
aroma	bouquet	stench	reek	pong

b Which nouns could be used to describe the smell of:
- cooking
- flowers
- wine
- dirty socks
- rotting vegetables

2 Match the adjectives describing smells on the left to suitable nouns on the right. Sometimes more than one answer is possible. Collocation is often important as well as meaning.

Rancid – smelling or tasting like rank stale fat	rotting flesh
Acrid – bitterly pungent	smoke
Musty – mouldy, stale	bad water
Putrid – decomposed, rotten, foul, noxious; corrupt	an old house
Foul – containing noxious matter (foul air etc.)	old butter

WRITING

1 Write a short paragraph describing a place, for example, a house, town, street etc. . It can be real or imaginary.

Consider the following:

- what details to include and exclude
- how to convey the atmosphere of the place
- whether the time of year or weather affects your description
- the purpose of the description, for example to set the scene, reflect the mood of the characters
- how the atmosphere of a place can be evoked without using adjectives

2 When you have finished, show the paragraph you have written to a partner and decide which are its best features.

LITERARY EXTENSION

Read the first two verses of this poem by Philip Larkin which describes a train journey from the north east coast of England to London.

What sort of atmosphere does he try to convey?

How many things does he describe?

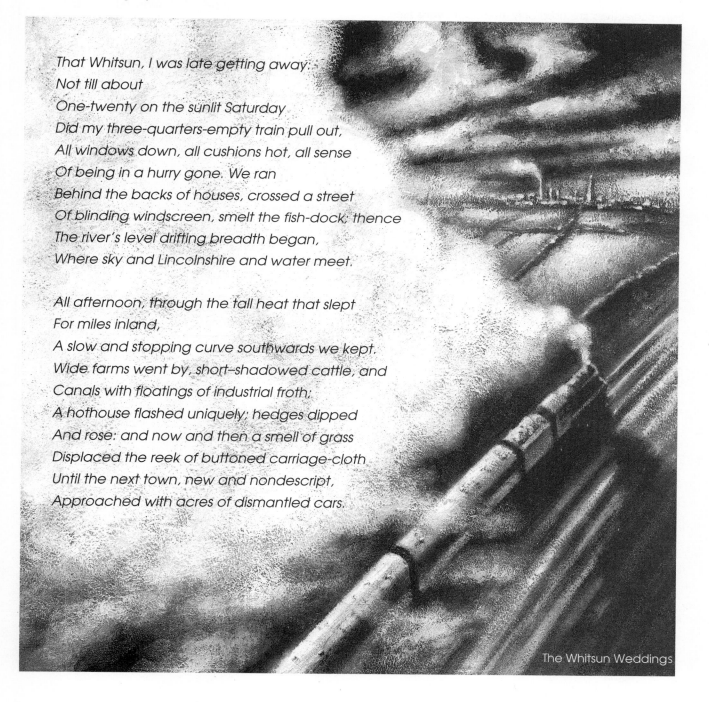

That Whitsun, I was late getting away:
Not till about
One-twenty on the sunlit Saturday
Did my three-quarters-empty train pull out,
All windows down, all cushions hot, all sense
Of being in a hurry gone. We ran
Behind the backs of houses, crossed a street
Of blinding windscreen, smelt the fish-dock; thence
The river's level drifting breadth began,
Where sky and Lincolnshire and water meet.

All afternoon, through the tall heat that slept
For miles inland,
A slow and stopping curve southwards we kept.
Wide farms went by, short-shadowed cattle, and
Canals with floatings of industrial froth;
A hothouse flashed uniquely; hedges dipped
And rose: and now and then a smell of grass
Displaced the reek of buttoned carriage-cloth
Until the next town, new and nondescript,
Approached with acres of dismantled cars.

The Whitsun Weddings

GRAMMAR

Position of adjectives

Some adjectives are used only after a **link verb** (see UNIT 4 page 48) and never before a noun. Others are almost always used before a noun and never, or rarely, after a link verb.

1 a Divide the following adjectives into two groups, those which go after link verbs and those which go before nouns.

eventual	content	asleep	ready
aware	occasional	adoring	fond
reminiscent	existing	alive	glad
cardiac	alone	ill	unable

Adjectives after link verb	Adjectives before noun

b Add any more adjectives you can think of to either list.

2 How many of these adjectives are used in collocation with other nouns, verbs or prepositions?
Example
cardiac arrest

3 Some adjectives that are used after verbs usually need to be followed by a clause beginning with '*to*' + infinitive.
Example
She **was able to complete** her thesis in time.
Complete these sentences in any suitable way using this structure.
a I'm afraid it's bound. . .
b I'd be willing. . .
c I am loath. . .
d The situation is liable. . .
e I am inclined. . .
f I think you should be prepared. . .

4 Here are some adjectives which are often followed by a *that* clause.

aware	certain	afraid	sorry
surprised	upset	worried	sad
anxious	sure	frightened	confident

Example
I **am pleased that** *you've found a good job.*

a What do these adjectives have in common?
b Apart from a *that* clause, what prepositions can follow these adjectives?

LEXIS

Adjectives

1 A small number of adjectives are used before nouns in a limited number of collocations.
Put these adjectives into the appropriate gaps in the sentences that follow.

| scant flagrant commanding chequered paltry |
| belated searing thankless knotty fleeting |

a He showed .... regard for the safety of his fellow passengers.
b It was a .... problem that took a while to solve.
c The report was a .... indictment of government malpractice.
d They indulged in .... violations of human rights.
e She eventually sent a .... apology.
f Organising meetings is a .... task.
g It was only a .... visit but she promised to stay longer next time.
h They paid him a .... sum for his services.
i She's had a rather .... career.
j Oxford swiftly built up a .... lead over Cambridge.

2 Match the compound adjectives on the left with the collocating nouns on the right. Think of a context for each collocation.

a labour-saving   1 citizen
b far-reaching   2 change of plan
c low-cut   3 device
d long-standing   4 tactics
e second-class   5 dress
f last-minute   6 credit
g one-sided   7 favourite
h all-out   8 formula
i deep-seated   9 argument
j interest-free   10 resentment
k face-saving   11 consequences
l odds-on   12 attack
m strong-arm   13 agreement

3 These four adjectives can only be used immediately after a noun. What do they mean and what sort of nouns can they be used with?

| designate | elect | incarnate | galore |

4 a From memory, write as many words as you can that you learned for the first time in UNIT 4.

b Look back at UNIT 4. Approximately what percentage of the total number of words that you learned in UNIT 4 have you remembered?

c Is this test fair? Do you feel you would remember more if you were given more time to think about it?

d What do you think is the difference between 'active' and 'passive' knowledge of vocabulary?

e If you were asked to perform the same task next week, do you think you would remember more or fewer words? What about next month?

GRAMMAR

As

1 How many functions of 'as' can you identify in the following sentences?

a He fell as he was walking down the steps.

b He could never run as fast as me.

c As you have to leave early, perhaps we'd better start with you, Kate.

d Tired as he was, he still insisted on working until midnight to get it finished.

e Leave it as you found it.

f The film stars Robert De Niro as a rather unlikely priest.

g I think he's a complete idiot, as are the rest of his family.

2 'As' is also used in a number of standard phrases. Put a suitable phrase from the following list into the sentences below.

as if/as though	as opposed to
as for	such as
so as to	as good as
as long as	as such

a I have never been in favour of corporal punishment .... , but I think some element of physical hardship is involved in most forms of institutional punishment.

b He stared at me .... he wished I would vanish.

c There are innumerable arguments against the plan, ... that it destroys the environment and is ugly to look at.

d Nuclear fusion, ... nuclear fission, is apparently almost impossible to achieve.

e Okay. I'll go with you .... you promise it won't take long.

f She was .... her word and delivered her report on precisely the day she had promised.

g They arrived early .... secure the best seats.

h Karen achieved everything she had set out to achieve. .... her brother, his success surprised everybody.

UNIT 5 *In a Jam*

FOCUS

1 a Calculate roughly how many hours you spend in a car in an average working week. Compare your total with others in the class.

b How much time do you spend in other forms of transport?

c How much of this time is essential travelling? Check with other people in the class that your definition of *essential* is the same as theirs.

2 A serious increase in traffic in recent years has caused a major problem in many of the world's cities. In small groups, list:

a the reasons why this traffic problem has become serious.

b the problems that heavy traffic causes.

3 In the not-too-distant future, the increase in traffic might well have reached a point where drastic measures have to be taken to limit the use of private cars.

What practical steps could be taken to achieve this? List as many suggestions as you can.

READING 1

1 Look at the headline and the picture below. Was this one of the solutions you listed in question **3** of the FOCUS section?

2 Scan the article in order to find reference to these amounts of money. What are they for?
Example
£5.5 billion – the cost of building the tunnels.
   a £2   c £500   e £1 million
   b £1.4 billion d £2 billion

3 What do the following figures refer to?
Example
70 – the number of miles of tunnels
   a 80   c 8   e 35
   b 111   d 100   f 5,000

Move to 'bury' London's traffic crisis

Subterranean traffic: a tunnel network, left, could link up London's main arteries, leaving the capital's streets clean, quiet and uncongested; right, how the proposed system of tunnels might look

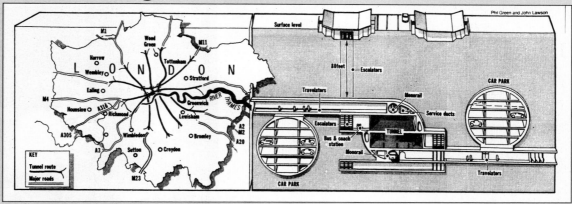

Phil Green and John Lawson

by Nick Rufford

1 Department of Transport engineers are examining a proposal to divert half the capital's traffic below the surface in a 70-mile network of underground tunnels.

2 The £5.5 billion plan has been given more urgency after two weeks of the worst pre-Christmas traffic jams the city has seen. It is backed by an anonymous consortium which includes a leading firm of architects and one of the top construction companies.

3 Its promoters claim it would cure crippling traffic congestion, as well as reduce noise and fumes. The scheme would be financed by private investors and repaid from a £2 toll paid by drivers.

4 The proposals are among a number submitted by private developers to the Department of Transport for coping with the rapid growth of traffic on Britain's roads.

5 Transport officials are privately worried that without drastic improvements in London, the traffic crisis will worsen. Already there are more than 1.5m vehicle movements in the capital each day – a total which is expected to increase.

6 The scheme, described as no more costly or ambitious than the Channel tunnel, would consist of six 80ft-deep 'underways', three running north to south and three east to west. Each would link up with a national motorway. At 'interchange points', where the motorways cross British Rail or London Underground lines, underground parking would be provided to allow drivers to continue their journey by train.

7 Jerry Matthews, chairman of Covell Matthews International, one of the backers, claims that tunnels are the only answer to traffic congestion. 'None of the proposals put forward in the last five years is capable of easing London's traffic problems,' he said. 'Flyovers and road improvement schemes only provide temporary stop-gaps. This scheme is viable; it can pay its own keep and needs only the government's sanction.'

8 The proposals have been welcomed by road and environment lobbies, including the British Road Federation and the Noise Abatement Society, which want urgent action on traffic congestion, public transport hold-ups, pollution, road safety, parking and 'rat running' – taking shortcuts.

9 A typical London driver spends 111 hours a year sitting in stationary or slow traffic. The total cost in wasted time and fuel is estimated at £1.4 billion, an annual bill of £500 each. The roads have become so clogged that in the heart of the city vehicles travel at only 8 mph. – as slowly as a horse and cart did 100 years ago.

10 A hold-up on a key road can set off a chain reaction, causing the capital to seize up. Last week traffic was locked solid throughout most of central London after a gas leak in Wandsworth, south London, caused homes to be evacuated and roads closed.

11 The previous week, thousands of vehicles ground to a halt after students staged a protest on Westminster bridge. The jam, which stretched from the City to Marble Arch and from King's Cross to the Oval, was described by the Automobile Association as the worst on record.

12 Some experts are sceptical about the scheme and believe it would encourage more drivers into the capital. Martin Mogridge, of University College's transport studies group, said: 'Building more roads will mean more cars and more congestion.'

13 A scheme to build a £2 billion network under Paris to relieve traffic congestion is already being planned. Known as Laser, an acronym for underground regional automobile express, the scheme involves 35 miles of toll roads and 5,000 parking places. A £1m study, supported by Jacques Chirac, the mayor and former prime minister, is nearly complete. Brussels already has a network of roads under the city.

The Sunday Times

4 Now read the text again and make notes under the following headings:

  a What the scheme is
  b Means of financing the scheme
  c Reasons for urgency
  d Advantages of this scheme over others
  e People who support the scheme
  f People against the scheme
  g Reasons for not supporting it
  h 2 examples of London's traffic crisis
  i 2 examples of similar schemes

5 What is your reaction to the scheme? Would such a scheme be practical in your own town?

LEXIS

1 a Look again at the article on page 55 and find words which mean:

  1 to make traffic take a different route (paragraph 1)
  2 money paid by drivers who used a road (paragraph 3)
  3 a quicker route than the ordinary one (paragraph 8)
  4 a delay (paragraph 10)

  b Look at the phrase *causing the capital to seize up* in paragraph 10. Find another adjective or adjectival phrase in paragraph 9 which is similar in meaning to *seized up*.
  In what other situations could you use it?

2 Find the following words or phrases in the article on page 55:

  a two nouns used instead of *plan* (paragraphs 1 and 6)
  b a word meaning *supported financially* (paragraph 2)
  c a word which means *a group of companies working together* (paragraph 2)
  d two words used to describe *people who support a plan* (paragraph 3 and 7)
  e the word for *a person who puts money into something in order to make a profit* (paragraph 3)

Collocation

3 *Traffic*, as an adjective, is used in the text in collocation with four nouns, for example *traffic jams* (paragraph 2). Find the other three.

4 Find four verbs which collocate with *proposals*.

5 Find the adjectives which commonly collocate with these nouns:

  a growth (paragraph 4)
  b improvements (paragraph 5)
  c action (paragraph 8)

6 Use the context to help you explain these phrases:

  a *pay its own keep* (paragraph 7)
  b *set off a chain reaction* (paragraph 10)
  c *grind to a halt* (paragraph 11)
  d *stage a protest* (paragraph 11)

LISTENING 1

In this recording you will hear a conversation with someone from Oxford City Planning Department about some of the traffic problems in Oxford. Listen and answer the questions.

1 Which of the following disadvantages of building a tram network are mentioned?

  ☐ the city is too small
  ☐ not enough people use public transport
  ☐ it's too expensive
  ☐ trams are too fast and therefore dangerous
  ☐ buses provide a better service
  ☐ it might involve knocking buildings down
  ☐ trams are ugly

2 What advantages and disadvantages of conventional buses are mentioned?

3 What disadvantages does he mention of building more roads?

4 The planning officer in this conversation uses some official-sounding language that contains jargon. Listen again and say what is meant by the following words and phrases:

a *density of passenger flows*

b *commercially viable*

c *dense heavy flows on particular corridors*

d *a large articulated vehicle*

e *create conditions whereby you can provide dedicated routes*

f *rapid transit system*

g *very heavily constrained*

h *not tenable as a solution*

i *catenary*

5 What do you think is the most pollution-free form of public transport?

S P E A K I N G   1

APPROPRIACY

1 Decide which of these phrases would not normally be used in a formal business meeting.

a While I am in broad agreement with you, I nevertheless feel. . .

b If I could intervene at this point. . .

c With respect, that is simply not the case. . .

d That's a load of rubbish and you know it!

e May I suggest. . .

f May I interrupt you just for a moment?

g One possibility which we have not considered yet. . .

h Could I just ask you to clarify that point?

i I feel that the case is being overstated.

j Wait a minute. What are you on about?

k What we would like to propose is. . .

2 Put the phrases above into the chart below according to what they are used for.

polite disagreement	interrupting	making proposals

3 Add similar phrases to each group making sure that they are suitably formal.

4 Role playing a formal business meeting

A large historic city has severe traffic problems. Work in groups, as if you were members of the city council. Your task is to propose and agree on a relatively uncontroversial, effective and cheap way of easing this traffic problem. You will also have to find ways of raising the capital to finance your plans.

One person should act as the chairman and another as secretary in a formal meeting called to discuss the problem. The chairman must control the discussion. Disagreements should be voiced politely and formally.

The situation

You should take the following points into consideration:

• The city gets a large part of its income from tourists.

• Pollution is destroying the historic buildings.

• There is a shortage of parking spaces in the city's medieval streets, many of which are too narrow for buses.

• Businesses complain that the lack of mobility loses them millions each year.

• Tourist organisations want to turn the city centre into a pedestrians only area; local residents say they have a right to drive to their own houses, and complain that it is the tourists who cause the problem.

• Taxi drivers threaten to strike if anything affects their business.

Political considerations

• The city council is short of money.

• Local elections are not far away and if you upset too many people you will not be re-elected.

• You won't get re-elected unless you do something about the traffic problem.

57

WRITING

Reports

1 Why are reports on business meetings necessary? Who are they for?

2 What sort of information would be included in such a report?

   Choose from the following:

   a names of people present
   b date and time
   c itinerary of meeting
   d length of time each point took to discuss
   e detailed analysis of all the points raised
   f summary of all the points raised
   g summary of main points agreed on
   h summary of suggestions that were rejected
   i anything else

3 What is the appropriate format for such a report?

4 What register would it be written in?

5 Write a report of the council meeting from the SPEAKING section on page 57. It should be as clear and concise as possible.

LEXIS

1 Verbs of movement

These verbs can all be used in connection with driving. Complete each of the sentences below by using an appropriate verb from those in the box. Change the tense where necessary.

swerve	cruise
skid	pull in(to)
cut in	crawl
draw up	weave in and out
accelerate	pull out

a He .... along the motorway at a steady 70 mph.
b Inevitably, there were some cars .... along in the slow lane.
c One idiot in a hurry was .... of the lanes, trying to dodge the traffic.
d He .... into the fast lane in order to overtake.
e He had to .... in order to get past as the other car speeded up.
f The previous week, a car had .... on a patch of oil.
g He had had to .... in order to avoid it.
h The traffic was heavy in the inside lane and in order to get to the exit he had to ....
i Once off the motorway he .... the side of the road to get his breath back.
j He eventually .... outside his house half an hour later than usual.

2 Adjectives followed by prepositions

Some adjectives are followed by prepositions when used **predicatively** (i.e. after the verb *be*)

Example
*It **is characteristic of** this government to make promises and do nothing.*

Complete these sentences using an appropriate preposition.

a Her behaviour is devoid .... common sense.
b I am well aware .... the problems involved.
c He became resigned .... failure.
d This idea is hardly compatible .... our existing plans.
e He was filled .... remorse.
f This service is subject .... further delay.
g They are totally incapable .... doing the job properly.
h That man is completely bereft .... any understanding.
i She has always been prone .... illness.
j As a leader, he seems impervious .... criticism.

READING 2

1   Read the following article and explain the meaning of the headline, which includes a pun on the idiomatic phrase *'Life in the fast lane.'*

Strife in the fast lane takes its toll

by Tim Walker

M25: Hell on wheels.

1   It was 8 a.m. on the south-west stretch of the M25 and the traffic was, as the man on the radio put it, 'building up. . .'

2   It was not so much building up as solidifying. It looked as if thousands would be rather late for work on Friday.

3   Most people now despair for the M25 — the diseased heart of Britain's motorway network. Last week the Controller and Auditor General said he wanted it upgraded to a four-lane highway. The AA suggested an outer ring-road. Mr Peter Bottomley, the Transport Minister, is considering the situation. And meanwhile the motorists are waiting ... and waiting.

4   It is inevitably taking its toll on the unhappy band who use the motorway, and yesterday Inspector Terry Hawker of the Hertfordshire Constabulary said, by letting the M25 get to them, drivers were being their own worst enemies.

5   'If you have got enough highly-strung, bad-tempered people on the M25, it will be unpleasant driving along it, no matter what the physical conditions are like,' he said.

6   Mr Cary Cooper, a professor of organisational psychology at Manchester University, divided drivers into two types: A and B. Type A drivers, he said, are 'assertive, ambitious, impatient and extra-ordinarily hyper- active. . .'

7   On Friday they were there for all to see. On the few open stretches they jockeyed frantically for position in the fast lane and, as they approached the slip roads they wanted, played the 'last one in is the winner' game.

8   Braking along the M25 is frequently necessary but these drivers, predominantly male, wearing a shirt and tie and travelling alone, always left it to the very last moment and each time registered looks of profound shock and anguish at being delayed.

9   They peered with bitterness at a sign, towards the Chertsey turn-off, that announced a 'Police speed check area'. Chain-smoking, incessant fidgeting and a menacing tapping of steering wheels were *de rigueur* in queues for the fast lane set.

10   The type B drivers, Professor Cooper's theory goes on, are 'unassertive, unambitious, patient and extraordinarily inactive. . .' They were the ones meandering contentedly in the middle and inside lanes. Common traits were humming along to their car radios and giving way to women motorists at every opportunity.

11   On the rare occasions they strayed into the fast lane, they tended, quite obliviously, to cause long convoys of angry type A drivers to build up tightly behind them. They would return to the central lane long after the act of overtaking, bemused rather than angered by the flashing headlamps and abusive hand gestures from the overtaking vehicles.

12   Mrs Mary Evans, a 67-year-old widow from Slough who had broken down on the hard shoulder near the Leatherhead turn-off, seemed to support the Cooper theory.

13   'It's not that the road is too crowded, it's the aggressiveness of some of the people that use it that makes driving along it such an unpleasant experience. It must have been obvious my car was playing up, but when I began to decelerate all people did was start flashing and hooting me.'

The Observer

2   The article contains a number of expressions and idiomatic phrases. Working with a partner, use a dictionary to understand the following phrases:

It was not so much building up as solidifying
taking its toll on that unhappy band
by letting the M25 get to them
physical conditions
jockeyed frantically for position
de rigueur
the fast lane set
my car was playing up

3   a   Make two lists, one containing the words and phrases which characterise type A drivers and the other those which relate to type B drivers and their behaviour.

   b   Add other words and phrases to the two lists that could also be used.

Which category would you put yourself in?

SPEAKING 2

Role-play

A type A driver has been speeding on the motorway. He braked too late when coming up to a jam and very lightly touched the back of the car of a type B driver. There is some minor damage to both cars. Nobody is hurt. Two policemen sitting in a patrol car nearby witnessed the accident and are now interviewing the two drivers beside the road.

Before you start, list some of the phrases you could use.

Drivers: accusation and denial

Example

'What do you think you're doing?'

Police: calming and official

Example

'If you would just let the other gentleman give his version of events, Sir.'

Now work in small groups to role-play the situation. The type A driver starts by getting out of his/her car and accusing the other driver immediately after the accident. The police arrive on the scene shortly after.

> **Type A driver.**
> You are convinced it was the other driver's fault for going too slowly and causing an obstruction. You are late for an appointment. You are very angry and capable of making some rather irrational accusations.

> **Type B driver.**
> You are normally a mild mannered sort of person but the other driver is starting to get on your nerves with his/her accusations. You think people like that shouldn't be allowed to drive.

> **Two policemen.**
> You are going to book the type A driver for speeding and also warn him/her that he/she may be charged with dangerous driving. You witnessed the whole accident and know he/she was to blame. Speak formally, authoritatively, but calmly. Try to stop an argument developing. Take the names and addresses of those involved.

GRAMMAR

Relative clauses

I Look at these extracts from the READING sections and from LISTENING 1 and underline the examples of relative clauses.

1 It is backed by an anonymous consortium which includes a leading firm of architects and one of the top construction companies.

2 Already there are more than 1.5m vehicle movements in the capital each day – a total which is expected to increase.

3 The proposals have been welcomed by road and environmental lobbies, including the British Road Federation and the Noise Abatement Society, which want urgent action on traffic congestion, public transport hold-ups, pollution, road safety, parking and 'rat running'.

4 The jam, which stretched from the City to Marble Arch and from King's Cross to the Oval, was described by the Automobile Association as the worst on record.

5 It is inevitably taking its toll on that unhappy band who use the motorway every day.

6 Mrs Mary Evans, a 67-year-old widow from Slough who had broken down on the hard shoulder near the Leatherhead turn-off, seemed to support the Cooper theory.

7 'I think we haven't got the size of a city and the density of passenger flows that will make it commercially viable.'

8 . . . the conventional bus, which has the flexibility of being able to move off the route at any point and into the residential areas, in Oxford has the potential to provide a much better service.'

Defining relative clauses describe the preceding noun in order to distinguish it from other nouns of the same class.

Example

*The drivers **who stayed in the slow lane** tended to be more relaxed.*

(Not the drivers in other lanes.)

The rest of the sentence tends not to have much meaning if the relative clause is omitted:

Example

The drivers tended to be more relaxed.

(Which drivers?)

Non-defining relative clauses give extra, non-essential information about the preceding noun.

Example

Myles, who had enjoyed the summer, was now thinking about doing some serious work.

Here, the relative clause can be omitted and the rest of the sentence will still make sense.

2 Decide for each of the relative clauses you underlined in the extracts on page 60 whether it is defining or non-defining.

3 Here are some rules on the use of relative clauses. Decide for each whether it refers to defining or non-defining clauses.

	Defining	Non-defining
a 'that' is often used instead of 'which', 'who' and 'whom'* in spoken English Example *What was the name of the guy that won the World Championship?*	☐	☐
b 'that' is never used Example *Madame Bovary, that was written by Flaubert in 1857, was recently made into a film starring Isabelle Hupert.* (This sentence is incorrect: 'which' should be used rather than 'that')	☐	☐
c The subordinate clause is usually separated from the main clause by commas Example *The wind, which had blown up before breakfast, slowly died down.*	☐	☐
d Commas are never used Example *The new road that they're building by the leisure centre still hasn't been finished.*	☐	☐

	Defining	Non-defining
e This structure is used mainly in written rather than spoken English Example *The report, which has already been criticised, will be published next week.*	☐	☐
f If the relative pronoun is not the subject of the relative clause, it can be left out altogether. Example *The cheque you said you had posted still hasn't arrived.*	☐	☐

*Note: 'Whom' is very formal and is rarely used these days, except in a written form.

4 Look at these examples and answer the questions.

a *My mother who is in India phoned me yesterday.*
Why is this sentence strange?

b *George, that stood by the door, was an old friend.*
Is this sentence correct?

c *We agreed to meet in a place I suggested.*
Why does this sentence have no relative pronoun?

d *I recently met someone who had been to Borneo.*
Can the relative pronoun be omitted in this sentence?

e *The driver that I was shouting at the other morning turned out to be my boss.*
Is this sentence correct?

f *He saw the waiter who served him.*
He saw the waiter, who served him.
What is the difference between these two sentences?

'Which' is often used as a relative pronoun referring back to a whole clause or sentence or series of sentences. The clause with 'which' is commonly preceded by a comma.

Examples

The rain poured down and the match had to be abandoned, which was a great pity.

Their marriage is a great success, which I find surprising.

All of which may explain his behaviour.
(used at the end of a paragraph listing reasons.)

I think it's going to rain, in which case there's no point going out.

5 Explain the difference between these two sentences:

a She saw the little boy who made her smile.

b She saw the little boy, which made her smile.

Participle clauses.

Participle clauses (see UNIT 3) can be used in a similar way to **defining relative clauses**.

Examples

The girl walking down the road is Hilda Godfrey.
(The girl who you can see walking. . .)

Any vehicles parked in this space without authorisation are liable to be removed.
(Any vehicles which are parked. . .)

A document containing some serious allegations was handed in to the investigating department.
(A document which contains/contained. . .)

6 Rewrite the following sentences using a participle clause instead of a relative clause.

　a　The cleaner who was tidying the room when you came in is retiring soon.

　b　A stone which was hurled by one of the rioters whistled past his ear.

　c　The proposal which deals with the motorway extension will be considered this afternoon.

　d　Your contact is the man who will be carrying a rolled umbrella.

1 **a** Would you ever consider cycling to work? Why (not)?

　b Do you think anybody enjoys spending an hour driving to work? Why (not)?

2 Listen to the first part of this conversation between Sharon and Dominic about commuting to work and answer these questions.

　a How far does Dominic travel every morning?

　b How long does it take him?

　c How does he feel about it?

　d What is Sharon's reaction to what he does?

3 Now listen to the second part and tick the correct box to say whether these statements are true or false.

		True	False
a	Sharon always cycles.	☐	☐
b	She lives fourteen miles from work.	☐	☐
c	On hot days the ride is very pleasant.	☐	☐
d	She's tired when she gets home.	☐	☐
e	She used to come along the A40.	☐	☐
f	Her new route is two miles longer.	☐	☐

4 Now listen to the whole recording again and answer these questions.

　a Why does Dominic say, *'I'm not saying it's always been my ambition to be a commuter'* ?

　b What does he say about *'getting in gear'* ?

　c What does Sharon do as she's riding?

　d What does she mean when she says, *'I'm whacked'* and *'I sort of clicked'* ?

5 Listen to the questions that are asked in the conversation. Do the speakers' voices go up or down at the end of the questions? Can you work out any rules about intonation when asking questions?

LEXIS

Phrasal Verbs: *Up*

'Up' is one of the most common particles to be used in phrasal verbs and is therefore often highly idiomatic. However, although there are many exceptions, there are two main groups of meaning. Sometimes it is necessary to think metaphorically with phrasal verbs:

A *In an upwards direction; increasing, growing, improving*
Example
Her father blew the balloon up for her. (= inflate)
She was brought up in Bedford. (= raise, educate)
We must step up production. (= increase)

B *Stopping; completion of act; finality*
Example
Where will we end up? (= finish our journey)
I give up! (= abandon the attempt)
We pulled up suddenly. (= braked)

I Fit these phrasal verbs from the READING and LISTENING texts into the above categories.

Are there any which are too idiomatic to fit?

	Type A	Type B
*Each would **link up** with a national motorway.*	☐	☐
*. . .causing the capital **to seize up**.*	☐	☐
*. . . all the buses **piled up** in the centre of the city. . .*	☐	☐
*. . . traffic was. . . **building up**.*	☐	☐
*It must have been obvious my car **was playing up**.*	☐	☐

2 Categorise these examples.

*We've **done** the house **up**.* (=re-decorate)
*This doesn't **add up**.* (= reach a coherent conclusion)
Shut up! (= stop talking)
*Trade is **picking up**.* (= getting better)
*I can't **keep up** with the pace.* (= stay at the same level)
*We were **held up** in the fog.* (= delayed)
*Shall we **settle up** and go?* (= pay the bill)
*He **hung up** on me.** (= put the phone down)
*Did you **stay up** all night?* (= not go to bed)
*You've **made** yourself **up**.* (= use cosmetics)
Cheer up! (= be cheerful)
*They **blew up** the bridge.* (= destroy by explosion)
*We're **selling up** and leaving.* (= selling everything)

* This expression dates back to old-fashioned telephones.

3 Explain what difference the phrasal verb makes in the following pairs of sentences:

a He was beaten.
 He was beaten up.
b They drank their beer.
 They drank up.
c He shut the door.
 He shut up shop.
d She cleaned the table.
 She cleaned up the mess.
e He used the sugar to make a cake.
 He used up the sugar to make a cake.
f There was ice on the lock.
 The lock had iced up.

4 In pairs, list as many other phrasal verbs using *'up'* as you can. Decide which category, **A** or **B**, each belongs to.

GRAMMAR

Relative clauses

1 Add the following information to the story using relative clauses. The first one has been done for you.

> 1 *We hadn't seen her for five years.*
> 2 *She had been a teacher all her life.*
> 3 *My sister and I were only about seven or eight at the time.*
> 4 *She intended to ignore her 90th birthday totally.*
> 5 *We normally had our evening meal at eight o'clock.*
> 6 *The lane went past the back of the house.*
> 7 *The trees lined either side of the lane.*
> 8 *Great aunt Edith showed no signs of tiredness.*

> It was on Sunday that my great aunt Edith, *who we hadn't seen for five years*, came to stay. She was a formidable lady and terrified both my sister and me. Despite the fact that she was approaching her 90th birthday she showed no sign of infirmity, either mental or physical. At eight o'clock in the evening she announced that she was going for a walk down the lane. My sister and I followed her, hiding behind the trees. Three quarters of an hour later, great aunt Edith finally returned and announced that she was hungry now.

2 In the following sentences, provide commas and a relative pronoun if they are necessary.

a Sarah, ...*whose*... birthday is in July, is my niece.

b Her friends .... remembered it bought her a present.

c The boy .... you saw her with is her brother, Barry.

d The only car .... I've ever had is a Rover.

e Trams .... used to be in most English cities are now found in very few.

f I had a student .... was a bus driver in Rome .... he lived.

3 Look at these sentences with relative clauses and decide which are more formal and why.

a There's a job being advertised that I think I'll try for.

b He is a man for whom I have immense respect.

c The house in which I was born has long since been demolished.

d The flat I'm living in at the moment is a bit small.

e The person to whom this is addressed is no longer with us.

f The person I gave it to looked nothing like that.

* Note: 'Whom' is preferred to 'who' if preceded by a preposition.

4 Rewrite each of the following sentences so that the meaning remains unchanged.

Example

The village I lived in for eighteen years is called Wingerworth.

The village in which I lived for eighteen years is called Wingerworth.

a The road the man ran along was long and straight.

The road along ....

b I was born in a small town which has grown enormously.

The small town ....

c The man whose book I borrowed has asked for it back.

The man I borrowed ....

d There is no way to prevent this disease from spreading.

There is no way in ....

e This language is spoken by different cultures, each of which use it differently.

This language is spoken by different cultures which ....

LEXIS

Phrasal verbs: *Up*

1 What are the connections between the phrasal verbs in these groups? Do any of them fit the categories on page 63?

1 She *crept up on* me and caught me unawares.
A young man *came up* and asked me a question.
They *came up against* all sorts of problems.
He *went up to* the man on the door and gave him his ticket.

2 I've *come up with* a great idea.
How did you *dream* that one *up*?
That's a great story but I bet you're *making* it *up*.
I think we should *draw up* plans for the attack.

3 In the late nineteenth century, Africa was *carved up* among the colonial powers.
Cut the cake *up* into sixteen pieces.
The band eventually *split up* in 1987.
Chop up a large onion and add it to the mixture.

4 The subject *came up* in discussion.
Don't *bring* that *up* again: I've heard enough about it.
Look who's *turned up*!
He finally *showed up* half an hour late.

Adjectives and prepositions

2 Use a dictionary to find the prepositions which commonly follow these adjectives:

resistant	heedless	mindful
conversant	fraught	lacking
riddled	reminiscent	similar
averse	devoted	susceptible

3 Collocation

Which of the above adjectives are frequently used in connection with:

a danger
b illness
c bullet holes, errors
d one's family, or work
e personal qualities like common sense
f responsibilities

Collocation: *Drive*

4 Explain what is meant by these idiomatic collocations:

a He is the *driving force* behind the project.
b They went out into the *driving rain*.
c This job is enough to *drive one to drink*.
d That girl *drives me up the wall*.
e You *drive a hard bargain*.
f She *drove the point home* by quoting several examples.
g He was *driven into a corner* by the force of her arguments.
h What are you *driving at*?

Verbs of movement

5 Look at this list of verbs of movement. Which can be used to describe the movement of a car? In what contexts can the other verbs be used?

soar	swerve	plunge	overtake
skid	brake	cut in	pull out
crawl	flow	hurtle	drift
freewheel	draw up	rush	glide
gallop	take off	stroll	spin

FOCUS

1 What are the main news stories at the moment?

2 Do you know of any major events which are not being given much media coverage?
For what reasons do you think they are being ignored?

3 Discuss these statements with a partner.
Which do you agree with or disagree with? Why?

a TV news is as good as the papers, if not better.

b Most news is boring and irrelevant.

c Buying a newspaper is a waste of money because nobody ever reads all of it.

d Home news is, on average, more relevant to most people than foreign news.

e The news is always about things that have gone wrong: good news is hardly ever reported.

4 What do you know about British newspapers?
Find out as much as you can about their names and political orientation.

Which are considered to be quality and which are popular papers?

READING 1

1 Work in small groups.

a What sort of problems do you think television journalists have when reporting on violence in other countries? List as many as you can, then compare and discuss the items on your list with another group.

b Do you think there are any disadvantages in television news companies competing with each other to be first in reporting a news story?

2 Read the text opposite by Kate Adie, who was Chief Correspondent in Beijing for the BBC during the 1989 student demonstrations in Tiananmen Square.

Does it mention any problems other than those you have just discussed?

Kate Adie

Just after midnight, on the Saturday in Beijing, I was in the NBC bedroom that was their headquarters. They had two-way radios and five crews deployed. We had three crews out at the time and two were back. I then heard on the two-way radio, at 7 minutes past 12, one of their crews ferrying a message: 'Firing has begun. There is gunfire. There is gunfire in the area of a hospital.' He named it. I knew the hospital. I could hear the sound of heavy firing over the two-way radio.

I went with a crew, virtually hijacking a car. Within seven minutes we were near that hospital, but there was so much gunfire between us and the hospital I never got there. In front of us was a horrendous scene, one of great confusion that, only days later, I worked out. In fact, what was happening was that the vehicles of the 38th Army, which had come in 24 hours earlier, were sitting, abandoned, on a large street intersection. They had been set on fire by some local people, and were now being crashed into by the 27th Army coming into town. None of that information was available when I saw what was going on; it was just a scene of confusion, a great deal of shooting, quite a number of corpses, people being shot in front of us. There was panic and a lot of people running around, unaware of the seriousness of the situation.

Question: Do you go back to the hotel and file that, or do you stay to try to find out a bit more? When is your deadline? Is there someone else from another news company going back to be the first with the news? It is getting to be a more difficult decision, especially as there are claims made now in the competitive news media, particularly in the newer ones, that being first at breaking the news is a great prize we should win.

We stayed 45 minutes in that area, until it became too difficult for us to remain. I then decided that I had to get some idea of the damage being done; so I tried to get to another hospital. I had a real stroke of luck in that we came across a group of people with a woman very severely injured. We took her in the car - one of the few vehicles on the road that night - to hospital, and there I got some idea of the scale of things, seeing something like 120 people come past me, severely injured, with some dead. At which point, again you think, do I get across town to go on air? Or do I film more? Do I pull the crew out of this?

This is not a whinge, it's not a complaint, it's just a worry, an awareness of the pressures. Do they want us first or do they want us fullest?

But there is a big problem about letting the cameras tell the story: the pictures don't tell the whole story. Since I've come back, so many people have said, 'We saw the pictures of the massacre.' Oh, no, you didn't! You saw hardly anyone actually killed on camera and very few corpses. You saw some injuries. Because of the 'considered evidential nature' of what we covered, people say, 'But where were all the bodies?' Well, the fact is that it happened so quickly and so violently, and the confusion was so great, even the best cameraman in the world could not behave like a feature film cameraman and have the time, the angles and the luxury to record death.

It's not like in the movies. I've tested this to a certain extent with people: 'You've just been shot - how do you die?' Most people would turn in a terrific performance. They would stagger, a few steps to the left, look for a wall, slide down, have a few last words. It doesn't happen like that. Down - one eighth of a second. People die of shock from a high velocity bullet at under 750 yards. The cameraman turns - they're gone, down on the floor. You don't see it on the television cameras.

The other thing is that people actually run to help and drag people away: they don't leave them, as they would on a battlefield. They're gone. People don't realise they are dead.

The Listener

3 Look at the text again.
  a What is the main theme of each paragraph?
  b What cohesive devices are used to connect the paragraphs with each other?
  c At what point does there seem to be a break in coherence?

4 What adjectives could you use to describe the style of this extract? Justify your choices by considering:
  • the length and complexity of the sentences
  • the use of questions
  • the use (or non-use) of adjectives
  • the sophistication (or lack of it) of the vocabulary
  • whether the points are made effectively

Choose from this list:

| direct | simple | colloquial |
| rhetorical | discursive | convoluted |

5 Is the style suitable for the purpose of the article? Justify your opinions.

6 Do newspaper journalists and those working for TV companies face similar problems? Justify your opinions.

LISTENING 1

1 Would you prefer to work as a journalist for a TV company or for a newspaper? Why?

2 Listen to this interview with a newspaper journalist. He is talking about his experiences as a reporter during the war in Yugoslavia between Croatia and Serbia. Make a list of the difficulties he encountered as a reporter. Then compare your list with a partner.

3 Listen again, if necessary, and say what the journalist means by the following:

a *It's very much the basics of who, what, why, when.*

b *. . . and that was a question of going into and through another physical, if not mental, jurisdiction.*

c *. . . there were small autonomous groups. . .*

d *. . . there's a technical problem attached to straying too far away from a telephone.*

e *. . . communication is fragmented. . .*

4 How different are this journalist's experiences to those of Kate Adie?

LEXIS

Newspaper vocabulary

The following extracts are from an article on 'journalese' by Keith Waterhouse, a well-known writer and journalist.

1 Match the words in italics with the definitions below.

> Except in urgent telegrams, no one else writes like this:
> The Prime Minister is *backing* Prince Charles in his *bid* to *curb* sex and violence on television, it was *revealed* last night.
> The *go-ahead* has been given for a *battery* of new *controls* to ensure programmes are fit for family viewing when a broadcasting *free-for-all* is *unveiled* next month.
> The *curbs* will be far more stringent than TV *chiefs* expected, and the government is *braced* for protests that they are being *shackled* and censored.

a attempt
b prepared
c directors
d range
e limit/control (verb)
f limits/controls (noun)
g guidelines or laws
h announced (twice)
i tightly controlled
j deregulation
k supporting
l permission

2 In the second example Keith Waterhouse looks at how some collocations have become clichéd. Rephrase the clichés in italics. The first sentence has been done for you.
Example
Official reports with surprising conclusions ask the government to take action. The government is about to make some major alterations.

> In journalese *shock reports* forever *call* on the government, which in turn is *set* to make *sweeping changes*. Plans are *under attack* or *facing broadsides*, commitments are *spelled out*, remarks are *certain to spark off a new political storm*, steps are *urged* to *curb growing menaces*, ministers *sound clear warnings*, new crises *loom*, new crazes *reach epidemic proportion*s There are so many *drama*s in the dramatic world of journalese that when one reads a headline in 'The Independent', CHANNEL 4 EXPANDS DRAMA, one reads on in growing expectation of a drama involving Channel 4's territorial ambitions rather than an account of how Channel 4 proposes to expand its drama output.

Headlines

3 The language of 'journalese' is particularly in evidence in headlines. What can you say about the style of headlines?

4 Using the glossary below, explain as fully as you can what these headlines mean.

Example

Quake death toll tops 40,000

The number of people who are reported to have been killed in the earthquake now exceeds 40,000.

ban	–	*forbid, exclude*	libel	–	*false injurous statement*
blast	–	*explosion*	oust	–	*expel*
brew	–	*grow, gather strength*	poll	–	*election*
curb	–	*limit, check*	row	–	*controversy*
flee	–	*escape*	shun	–	*avoid*
foil	–	*prevent*	split	–	*division*
key	–	*most important*	top	–	*exceed*

a Row brews over jobs threat

b Interest rate to fall

c 300 die in Greek Heatwave

d Border talks

e 'War crimes' enquiry call

f Alert as police foil car bomb plot

g Decision time for poll-weary Portugal

h Nasser son flees Cairo press attack

i Austrian President to sue for libel

j Rooftop drama

k Cabinet split over alcohol ban

l Key players ousted

m Blast injures 4

n Americans shun Europe

o Divers face work curb

5 Look again at the headlines above.
   a What can you say about the role of adjectives and nouns in headlines?
   b How many headlines have no verb?
   c Which tense is used to report all present and past events? Why?
   d What form is used to indicate the future?

6 Choose four headlines from an English newspaper and rewrite them as full sentences. Avoid using 'journalese'.

GRAMMAR

Infinitive future

Be to + infinitive is a formal way of referring to future plans and arrangements. It is also used to give orders. The structure is often seen in notices and instructions as well as news reports.

Examples
*The Prime Minister **is to meet** industrial leaders today.*
*You **are to make sure** that the door remains closed at all times.*
*The factory **is to be closed** down.*

1 Make statements for the following situations using the *be to + infinitive* structure.
a A wedding.
b A parent giving instructions to a child.
c A government policy announcement.

2 In newspaper headlines, the verb *be* is very often omitted.

Examples
Railways to go private.
President to offer arms deal.

Write headlines for the following situations.
a A trade union is planning to persuade its members to go on strike.
b A film star is planning to take a newspaper to court for libel.
c Nuclear arms reduction negotiations are scheduled to take place in January.

3 The form can be varied by using *about* or *due*. Explain what is meant in these phrases.
a I'm about to go out to meet someone.
b The train is due to arrive at 6.32 a.m.
c What time are you due to arrive in Paris?
d I'm not about to complain so you needn't worry.

Is there any difference in register between *be about to* and *be due to*?

LISTENING 2

1 Listen to these three extracts from a radio news broadcast.

Make notes about the following.

a Australian prisoner
   Murray Stewart
   Buckinghamshire
   Springhill Open Prison
   Geoffrey Dicken

b South London off-licence
   Mavid Sadiq
   Saturday night
   27

c Derek Bentley
   Iris Bentley
   The Home Secretary
   1953

2 Work in groups of three.
a Look at the transcript of the item about Derek Bentley on page 171. In each sentence, mark the stressed words.
   Then listen to the recording again and check.
b Look at each sentence again and think about the intonation. Look especially at the ends of the sentences. Should your voice go up or down?
c Practise saying a few sentences until you think they sound right, then listen to the tape and compare your version with that of the person speaking.
d Taking one part each (newscaster, reporter and Iris Bentley) read the item using the same speed as the people on the tape. If possible, record yourself and listen again to check your stress and intonation.

READING 2

The following two newspaper articles are about one of the items you have just heard on the radio news.

1 Work in pairs. One person should read **Text A** and the other **Text B** on page 165. Make notes on the following:
a Although the main events took place in 1952-3, this story is in the news again. Why?
b What exactly took place at the scene of the crime?
c Why was Bentley hanged?
d What evidence is there now that he was innocent?

2 Now compare notes with your partner. Do both articles contain the same information? Do they give any different information? If so, tell your partner what other information you have found.

3 Iris Bentley comments that the hanging of her brother was a grave miscarriage of justice.
From the evidence you have gathered, do you agree with her?

Text A

Sister's hopes rise for Bentley pardon

As the campaign to pardon Derek Bentley grows, Christopher Lockwood meets the woman behind it

Derek Bentley's sister marked the 39th anniversary of his execution yesterday by laying carnations at the gates of Wandsworth prison where he was
5 hanged for his part in the murder of a policeman.

On a note tied to the wreath she wrote: 'To my dear brother. I hope it won't be long now until your
10 pardon, and the truth will be told. Your loving sister Iris.'

At 9a.m. - the time of the execution on Jan 28, 1953 - Miss Iris Bentley, 59, and her daughter
15 Maria, joined the prison chaplain in prayer. She said afterwards: 'I felt Derek at my side, and I told him it would not be long.'

Miss Bentley, who is suffering
20 from cancer, then delivered a letter to the Home Office, renewing her call for a posthumous pardon.

Bentley was 19 when he went to the gallows for his part in the
25 murder of Pc Sidney Miles, shot dead by 16-year-old Christopher Craig, in 1952 on a warehouse roof in Croydon.

Craig was too young to hang, but
30 Bentley, an epileptic with a mental age of 11, was sentenced to death. Three policemen claimed Bentley had shouted to Craig: 'Let him have it, Chris.'
35 In her letter to Mr Baker, Home Secretary, Miss Bentley wrote: 'Thirty-nine years ago this morning my brother Derek Bentley was hanged for a murder he did not
40 commit.

'Many people believe this to have been one of the gravest miscarriages of justice ever witnessed.

'Over the last year a great deal of
45 new evidence has come to light which conclusively proves Derek's innocence. That report is now on your desk.'

A Metropolitan Police report
50 submitted to the Home Office last week contains evidence from five witnesses who were not called at the time of Bentley's trial. One, Pc Claude Pain, also on the roof at the
55 time of the shooting, denies Bentley ever said: 'Let him have it.'

Craig, released from prison in 1963, gave a television interview last year in which he protested
60 Bentley's innocence, while admitting his own guilt. A lie-detector test appeared to confirm his claim that Bentley never made the remark.
65 A decision on whether to grant a pardon to Bentley is still being considered by the Home Office.

A Commons question to Mr Baker asking for a statement on the
70 Bentley case was tabled yesterday by Mr Simon Hughes, Liberal Democrat MP for Bermondsey.

Iris Bentley

The Daily Telegraph

71

GRAMMAR

The passive

1 The passive is much more common in informative than in imaginative writing. Give reasons why.

2 Look at these examples of the passive and the reasons for using it below. Match the examples with the reasons. (You may find there is more than one reason for each example.)

1 *The meeting has been postponed.*

2 *I've been robbed.*

3 *She was sentenced to three months' imprisonment.*

4 *The company accepted the comments and said that steps would be taken to prevent any repetition of the events.*

5 *His success can be attributed to hard work.*

6 *The finance minister arrived in Brussels and was met by his French counterpart.*

Reasons for using the passive

a The agent has already been mentioned and you want to avoid repetition.

b The action is more important than the agent.

c The agent is 'people in general'.

d You do not know who the agent is.

e It avoids an awkward change of grammatical subject in the middle of a sentence.

f It is obvious from the context who the agent is, so it is not necessary to mention it.

3 a Find all the examples of the passive in **Text B** on page 165. There are twelve of them.
Look at each example and decide why the passive is used.

b Now look at some of the active verbs and decide why the passive is not used.

LEXIS

Reporting verbs

If you are unsure whether what you are reporting is true, you can use one of the following verbs in a passive form followed by *to be* or *to have*.

| allege | report | consider | fear |
| expect | say | believe | rumour |

Examples

*It **is rumoured to be** a considerable fortune.*

*The President **is expected to have** talks with the French Prime Minister next month.*

*The accused **is alleged to have** hurled insults at the actor.*

1 Find an example of this structure in the fourth paragraph of **Text B** on page 165.

2 Report some current events using other verbs from the list above.

3 When reporting what people have said, variety and extra meaning can be gained from using a number of verbs other than *say*.

acknowledge	concede	remark
add	declare	report
admit	deny	request
allege	hint	reveal
assert	imply	state
assure	insist	stipulate
believe	maintain	suggest
claim	object	threaten
comment	reassure	urge

All these verbs can be followed by a *that* clause.

Examples

The defendant admitted that he had been drinking.

He hinted that an announcement would be made soon.

The policeman reassured him that this would be taken into account.

What examples of reporting verbs are used in paragraphs six and ten of **Text A** on page 71?

4 Look at the list of verbs again.

a Decide which ones might be used to make a strong assertion about something.

b Which might be used if someone is having to deal with accusations made against them?

5 Use one of the verbs above to report the following quotations.

a 'OK, I did phone her. But I didn't shoot her.'

b 'The Government really must take action as soon as possible.'

c 'It's an interesting idea.'

d 'I'm innocent.'

e 'How many more times do I have to say it? I have never seen this man before in my life.'

f 'I will do it only on condition there is no publicity.'

g 'You stole my wallet!'

h 'I don't think you should try to go any faster.'

i 'That's an unfair comment.'

j 'There's a small boat on the port bow, sir.'

WRITING

News report

You are a journalist on a tabloid paper. Read the following information:

*There is a presidential election in two months' time. The current president is very unpopular and may be defeated if the opposition can find a good candidate. The leading opposition candidate, Will Clapton, is beginning to look as if he could win the election when suddenly a nightclub singer, Jenny Orchid, announces on television that she has had a twelve-year affair with the married Clapton. Clapton denies it.
His wife stands by him. Who is lying?*

Jenny Orchid holds a news conference to repeat her allegations. You go to the conference and take the notes on the right.

Write your report on the news conference. Your readers already know about the election, of course, but you can speculate on the consequences of the scandal for the result. Your readers have also heard of Jenny Orchid; she has been on every TV news programme for the past two days, as have Will Clapton and his wife.

Orchid: pretty, blonde. Obviously rehearsed her part.

On Clapton: 'His denials make me sick. . . I loved him. . . can't be trusted. . . abandoned me for his ambition. . . deceived his wife. . . promised to leave wife and marry me. He's a worm.'

Visited her regularly. Gave her a Porsche for her 30th birthday. Produces tapes of their telephone conversations. Poor quality, sounds like Clapton but can't be sure. Not much intimate stuff, mainly about arranging meetings. Claims he'll never forget their 'magical time in Florida together'

Rumour: Orchid being paid $100,000 by a rival tabloid newspaper for her story! Refuses to answer questions. Leaves with tabloid journalist.

GRAMMAR

The passive

Look at each of these sentences and decide whether it would be better expressed in the passive. They are all written reports or notices. Rewrite it in a more suitable form.

Example

The staff in this shop speak English.

English is spoken here.

a We do not accept traveller's cheques here.

b The law does not allow children under sixteen in this bar.

c The judge sentenced her to three years' detention.

d People have suggested that the Governor may be considering withdrawing from the Presidential race.

e Various journalists have been claiming that Miss America is the victim of blackmail.

f If the current economic decline continues, it will not be long before several other countries overtake Great Britain in terms of industrial output.

g Doctors were treating a teenage joyrider in hospital last night, after he crashed into four cars and injured four people.

LEXIS

Newspaper phrases

Rewrite these newspaper phrases avoiding journalese.

Example

Minister's TV remarks spark off political storm

The remarks made on television by a government minister have started a controversy.

a The City Council is backing moves to change parliamentary boundaries in the city.

b New plea for lights after death crash.

c Tax bills slashed to hit target.

d Kidlington residents face 100% tax jump to help stave off a cash crisis.

e A Labour councillor has called for more resources for the police in the wake of recent attacks on the elderly.

f Companies are being urged to review standards as part of the European Year of Health and Safety.

g Couple demand curb on cars parked outside home.

h Boat owners living at controversial moorings on the River Thames could face eviction in a row over insurance.

i The Prime Minister vowed yesterday to transform public services in the 1990s.

j Lord Moynihan, the fugitive peer, slipped secretly back to Britain months before his death, it was revealed last night.

Reporting with nouns

Use an appropriate form of the word in brackets to complete these sentences.

a The negotiating team had to make a number of .... before agreement could be reached. (*concede*)

b Her only .... was that she should not be asked questions about her recent marriage. (*stipulate*)

c We have received .... of military manoeuvres in this area. (*notify*)

d He made several disgraceful .... against his former employer. (*allege*)

e He issued a complete .... of any involvement in the affair. (*deny*)

f The long-term .... of the break up of the Soviet Union are still far from clear. (*imply*)

g He was trailing in the polls following a series of damaging .... about his private life. (*reveal*)

h He raised no .... to spending further amounts on the project. (*object*)

News broadcast

Complete these news broadcasts with the words and phrases listed below.

The Home Office is being ....¹ to ....² into how an Australian drug smuggler escaped from an open prison in Buckinghamshire. ....³ that Murray Stewart, who was ....⁴ a five-year sentence for a £40 million computer swindle, just walked out of Springhill Open Prison in Aylesbury seven weeks ago. Conservative MP and law and order campaigner Geoffrey Dicken says Stewart should have been more ....⁵.

A 15-year-old boy who ....⁶ a gunman during a raid on a south London off-licence has died. Saddiq was shot in the chest as he ....⁷ with the raider on Saturday night. A 27-year-old man has been ....⁸ the raid.

The sister of Derek Bentley will today lay a wreath at the gates of the prison where he was hanged 39 years ago. Iris Bentley will also ....⁹ a letter to the Home Secretary calling for an ....¹⁰ on a long awaited posthumous pardon. James Bays reports.

'Derek Bentley was nineteen when he was ....¹¹ in 1953 at Wandsworth prison for his part in shooting dead a policeman. A ....¹² enquiry has ....¹³ that Bentley shouted "Let him have it!" just before the officer was shot. His sister Iris is praying a decision on a pardon will come today.'

"Even though it is 39 years, when I go there each year I always feel that I'm going in to see Derek. And if it comes in, I shall feel that I want to go in to get him, bring him home. And I know I can't." 'But, she says, even if the decision ....¹⁴ her brother, she's ....¹⁵.'

vowing to fight on	tackled
charged in connection with	struggled
heavily guarded	serving
cast doubts on claims	pressed
sent to the gallows	goes against
it's been revealed	fresh
launch an urgent enquiry	hand in
immediate decision	

Collocation

1 Look at these reporting verbs and decide which of them commonly collocate with the words below.

acknowledge	concede	report
add	declare	request
admit	deny	reveal
allege	hint	state
assert	imply	stipulate
assure	insist	suggest
believe	maintain	threaten
claim	object	urge
comment	remark	

- gratefully
- defeat
- firmly
- categorically
- stubbornly
- violently
- in passing
- clearly
- war
- strongly

2 Many of the reporting verbs above can also function as nouns without changing their form.
Example
to submit a report
Decide which of them would commonly collocate with these words when used as nouns.

to submit a	to file a	a casual
a scathing	an urgent	
to drop a	an uncontrollable	

3 How many of these nouns can be followed by the preposition 'on'?

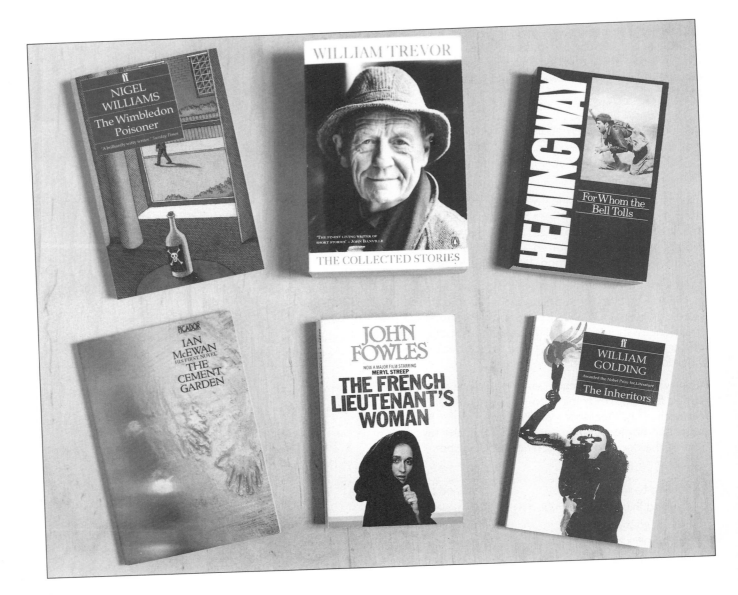

FOCUS

1 Why do people in all cultures need to read or listen to stories?

2 What stories did you hear as a child? How universal are they?

3 What common forms of story telling are there in modern society?

4 What makes a story interesting?

5 What sort of novels do you like to read and why? If you don't read novels, say why not.

6 Read this short account of a strange event. Do you
think the story, so far, is interesting? Does it describe
the scene well? Say why or why not. How could it
be improved?

> One day, when I was a child, a truck came into the courtyard of our
> apartment house and some men carried a large and heavy machine into our
> smoking room. This machine, my father explained, was the working model of an
> invention with tremendous possibilities, which he had decided to finance.
> 'What does it do?' asked my mother. 'You will see,' he said. 'The inventor,
> Professor Nathan, will demonstrate it himself.' The Professor arrived and
> for a couple of hours he worked on the machine, which was operated by
> electricity. In the end there was a big flash and all the lights in the flat
> went out. The Professor said he would come back the next day to fix it.

R E A D I N G   1

Now read the original version of the story above which is taken from Arthur Koestler's
autobiography, *Arrow in the Blue,* set in Budapest before the First World War.

Is it better than the version above?

1 One day – I must have been seven or eight at the
time – a truck drawn by six horses rumbled into the
courtyard of our apartment house, and half a dozen
men, sweating and groaning, carried a monstrous
5 machine up the stairs into our smoking-room. This
machine, my father explained with his usual
enthusiasm, was the working model of an invention
with tremendous possibilities, which he had
decided to finance. 'But what does it do?' asked my
10 mother. 'You will see,' he said, beaming. 'The
inventor will demonstrate it to us himself. He is a
genius, called Professor Nathan.' A few minutes
later, the inventor arrived, an astonishingly dirty
little man, hunchbacked and bearded, who looked
15 like one of Snow White's seven dwarfs. For a
couple of hours he fiddled with the wires, wheels,
and levers in the belly of the machine, causing it to
emit an occasional frightening spark, for the
contraption was operated by electricity. In the end
20 there came a big flash, darkness descended over the
flat, accompanied by the smell of burnt rubber and
the shrieks of the cook and maid who had joined
the family to watch the proceedings. Professor
Nathan, unperturbed, declared that there had been
25 a short-circuit, and that he would be back the next
day with some wire and other essential ingredients.

Koestler uses a number of techniques to make the story more vivid and to help the reader imagine the scene.

- He uses precise and vivid vocabulary, rather than the more obvious words, for example *rumbled* (line 2) not *rolled*.

- He selects a few descriptive details which help the reader to imagine the scene more exactly, but which are not necessary for the purpose of the story, for example *sweating and groaning*.

- He uses metaphors and comparisons.

I   Would anything have been lost or gained from the story if Koestler had used *complaining, large* and *smiling* rather than *groaning, monstrous* and *beaming*?

2   Find other examples of descriptive details. What do they add to your understanding of the scene?

3   a   What image is conveyed by the phrase *in the belly of the machine*?

   b   How is the image changed by the phrase *essential ingredients*?

   c   What comparison is used to describe the professor?

Now read the next section of the text to find out what the machine is for.

I was given my supper by romantic candle light and spent most of the night sleepless with excitement, trying to guess what the
30 machine was for. The next morning, after breakfast, Professor Nathan arrived and went to work again. I was only permitted to watch the proceedings through the doorway because, my mother insisted, the machine was
35 dangerous and might explode. After an hour or so the thing really started to work. It rumbled and clattered like an old-fashioned printing press, and its huge body, which occupied half the length of a wall, trembled so violently that
40 all the ash-trays, bronze nymphs, and cuspidors in the smoking-room danced on their bases. My father shook Professor Nathan solemnly by the hand, and now at last proceeded to demonstrate the purpose of the machine to the
45 assembled household. While we watched with bulging eyes, the Professor handed him a briefcase which contained a bundle of tattered envelopes of various sizes. My father took the bundle and pushed the sealed envelopes, one
50 by one, into a slot in the machine while Professor Nathan, standing on tip-toe at the other end, extracted from a second slot the same envelopes after they had passed through the machine – waving each over his head with
55 earnest pride, like a conjurer displaying a rabbit. The envelopes which had entered the machine sealed were now cut open.

4   Find examples from the text above of the three techniques Koestler uses to help the reader imagine a situation and list them under the following headings.

Precise, vivid vocabulary	Descriptive details	Metaphors or comparisons

5   Do you think there is too much detail or not enough?

6   From the description, make a rough diagram of the scene as you imagine it. Working with a partner, compare ideas. If your diagrams are very different, try to justify your version by finding evidence in the text.

7   The main purpose of storytelling is to illustrate the actions and feelings of people. Do you agree?

8   What do you know about the father, mother and author from the text? How do you expect each of them to react to the demonstration of the machine?

Read this last extract to find out what the father, mother and author's reactions are. Are they different to what you expected?

'Isn't it a stupendous invention?' cried my father, happy as a child. 'Stupendous,'
60 'grandiose,' 'fabulous,' and 'colossal,' were his favourite expressions. If business was 'colossal', it meant, on his scale of semantics, that it was moderately good. If it was merely wonderful, we
65 were on the verge of bankruptcy.

'But what is it for?' asked my mother, displaying the nervous tic which made its appearance whenever she was worried or agitated. The tic consisted of a twitching of her
70 eyebrows and a slight tremor of her chin, accompanied by a faint clucking noise in her throat which was only audible when you knew about it. But my father did know about it; that faint sound was enough to prick the bubble of
75 his happiness instantaneously.

'But can't you see that it is tremendous?' he cried. 'Imagine the millions of working hours it will save those American firms with their colossal number of incoming letters!' He went on talking
80 with an enthusiasm which by now had become artificial; the maid and the cook had slunk back to the kitchen; my mother, without a word but with an audible cluck-cluck, went to her room, and still he continued talking, now only to me,
85 sole disciple of a lonely prophet, ready to betray him before the cock crowed thrice, until I burst into tears.

Soon afterwards the envelope-cutting wonder machine disappeared from the flat, never to be
90 mentioned again, leaving as its only memory a large patch of scorched wallpaper in the smoking-room. The next fabulous adventure that I remember came a few years later, when my father opened the first factory in Europe for
95 the manufacture of radio-active toilet soap.

9 a Why does his mother ask *'But what is it for?'* when it has already been demonstrated?

b What is meant by *that faint sound was enough to prick the bubble of his happiness?*

c Explain the word *slunk* (line 81) and the image it conveys.

d Why had his father's enthusiasm *become artificial?*

e What is being referred to in the phrase *ready to betray him before the cock crowed thrice?* What does the reference reveal about how the author feels about his father?

f Why do you think the machine was *never mentioned again?*

g What image of his mother is conveyed by her *audible cluck-cluck?*

h What is the author's attitude towards his parents? Choose from the following:

cynical	sympathetic
humorous	sentimental
tolerant	ironic
detached	unfeeling

LEXIS

Onomatopoeia

Onomatopoeia means that a word sounds like the noise or thing it is describing, for example *rumble* or *splash*.

There are a large number of words like this in English. Here is a selection. They can all be used as both verbs and nouns.

blare	crack	hum	sizzle
boom	crackle	jingle	slam
bubble	crash	plop	snuffle
buzz	drone	rattle	squelch
clang	drum	rumble	thud
clatter	groan	rustle	whine
click	hiss	sigh	whirr

a Which of these sounds can be made by the human voice?

b Which might be associated with cooking?

c How many can describe gunfire?

d Which are long sounds and which are short?

e Find words from the list on page 79 which describe the following sounds:

1 walking in mud
2 a distant plane
3 insects
4 a fire
5 a small animal in the bushes
6 the sound of bells
7 car horns
8 thunder

SPEAKING

1 a When discussing something with a friend, what words or phrases can you use to elicit the other person's opinions?
Add to this list:
What about. . . ?
What do you think about. . . ?

b List words or phrases you can use to agree with someone's opinions.

2 🔲 Listen to this sentence on the tape said in two different ways.
'That's rather odd, isn't it?'

a How is the intonation different?

b Which of the two versions is a genuine question and which is just asking for agreement or confirmation?

3 Practise saying these sentences with both intonation patterns.

a He goes there quite often, doesn't he?
b This agreement won't last very long, will it?
c We can't stay much longer, can we?
d They haven't told the others yet, have they?

4 Work in pairs. Write down four statements that you think your partner will agree with. Then use the above structure (statement + question tag) with suitable intonation to get your partner to agree with you.

5 Look at these opening sentences. Four are from novels and one is from a short story.

1 *Lok was running as fast as he could.*
2 *I did not kill my father, but I sometimes felt I had helped him on his way.*
3 *He had, romantically, a bad reputation.*
4 *Henry Farr did not, precisely, decide to murder his wife.*
5 *He lay flat on the brown, pine-needle floor of the forest, his chin on his folded arms, and high overhead the wind blew in the tops of the pine trees.*

Work with a partner and answer these questions about the five opening sentences. Use the language you have just practised to elicit your partner's opinions.

a Which gives the most information about the plot of the story?

b Do we learn anything about any of the characters?

c How does the author make us want to read on?

d Why do two of them use the pronoun *'he'* when we don't know who it refers to?

e Why does the first one use a continuous tense?

f Why does the last one say **the** forest and not **a** forest?

g Which one are you most tempted to continue reading? Why?

h Are there any that you would definitely not read? Why not?

LISTENING 1

You will hear extracts from a recording of two people discussing the opening sentences in exercise **5** of the SPEAKING section.

1 Look at these adjectives used in the recording to describe some of the sentences. Which sentence do you think each refers to?

ironic	conventional
miserable	macabre
wry	immature
fun	maudlin
arresting	unpretentious

2 Now listen to the extracts to see if you were right. Do you agree or disagree with any of their opinions?

3 Listen again to each extract. Note the ways in which the two speakers elicit agreement and agree. Compare these notes with those you made in exercise **1** of the SPEAKING section.

WRITING 1

Continue one of the sentences from exercise **5** of the SPEAKING section to complete the first paragraph of a novel.

Compare results with a partner. Say what you think is good about your partner's work. Have you got any suggestions on how it could be improved?

READING 2

1 a Working with a partner, choose two of the opening sentences from page 80 that you want to continue reading. Read the continuations.

1 Lok was running as fast as he could. His head was down and he carried his thorn bush horizontally for balance and smacked the drifts of vivid buds aside with his free hand. Liku rode him laughing, one hand clutched in the chestnut curls that lay on his neck and down his spine, the other holding the little Oa tucked under his chin. Lok's feet were clever. They saw. They threw him round the displayed roots of the beeches, leapt when a puddle of water lay across the trail. Liku beat his belly with her feet.

'Faster! Faster!'

His feet stabbed, he swerved and slowed. Now they could hear the river that lay parallel but hidden to their left. The beeches opened, the bush went away and they were in the little patch of flat mud where the log was.

'There, Liku.'

The onyx marsh water was spread before them, widening into the river. The trail along by the river began again on the other side on ground that rose until it was lost in the trees. Lok, grinning happily, took two paces towards the water and stopped. The grin faded and his mouth opened till the lower lip hung down. Liku slid to his knee then dropped to the ground. She put the little Oa's head to her mouth and looked over her.

Lok laughed uncertainly.

2 I did not kill my father, but I sometimes felt I had helped him on his way. And but for the fact that it coincided with a landmark in my own physical growth, his death seemed insignificant compared with what followed. My sisters and I talked about him the week after he died, and Sue certainly cried when the ambulance men tucked him up in a bright-red blanket and carried him away. He was a frail, irascible, obsessive man with yellowish hands and face. I am only including the little story of his death to explain how my sisters and I came to have such a large quantity of cement at our disposal.

In the early summer of my fourteenth year a lorry pulled up outside our house. I was sitting on the front step rereading a comic. The driver and another man came towards me. They were covered in a fine, pale dust which gave their faces a ghostly look. They were both whistling shrilly completely different tunes. I stood up and held the comic out of sight. I wished I had been reading the racing page of my father's paper, or the football results.

'Cement?' one of them said. I hooked my thumbs into my pockets, moved my weight on to one foot and narrowed my eyes a little. I wanted to say something terse and appropriate, but I was not sure I had heard them right. I left it too long, for the one who had spoken rolled his eyes towards the sky and with his hands on his hips stared past me at the front door. It opened and my father stepped out biting his pipe and holding a clipboard against his hip.

3 He had, romantically, a bad reputation. He had a wife and several children. His carry-on with Sarah Spence was a legend among a generation of girls, and the story was that none of it had stopped with Sarah Spence. His old red Ford Escort had been reported drawn up in quiet lay-bys; often he spent weekends away from home; Annie Green had come across him going somewhere on a train once, alone and morose in the buffet car. Nobody's parents were aware of the facts about him, nor were the other staff, nor even the boys at the school. His carry-on with Sarah Spence, and coming across him or his car, were a little tapestry of secrets that suddenly was yours when you became fifteen and a senior, a member of 2A. For the rest of your time at Foxton Comprehensive — for the rest of your life, preferably — you didn't breathe a word to people whose business it wasn't.

It was understandable when you looked at him that parents and staff didn't guess. It was also understandable that his activities were protected by the senior girls. He was forty years old. He had dark hair with a little grey in it, and a face that was boyish — like a French boy's, someone had once said, and the description had stuck, often to be repeated. There was a kind of ragamuffin innocence about his eyes. The cast of his lips suggested a melancholy nature and his smile, when it came, had sadness in it too. His name was Mr Tennyson. His subject was English.

Jenny, arriving one September in 2A, learnt all about him. She remembered Sarah Spence, a girl at the top of the school when she had been at the bottom, tall and beautiful.

4 Henry Farr did not, precisely, decide to murder his wife. It was simply that he could think of no other way of prolonging her absence from him indefinitely.

He had quite often, in the past, when she was being more than usually irritating, had fantasies about her death. She hurtled over cliffs in flaming cars or was brutally murdered on her way to the dry cleaners. But Henry was never actually responsible for the event. He was at the graveside looking mournful and interesting. Or he was coping with his daughter as she roamed the now deserted house, trying not to look as if he was glad to have the extra space. But he was never actually the instigator.

Once he had got the idea of killing her (and at first this fantasy did not seem very different from the reveries in which he wept by her open gave, comforted by young, fashionably dressed women) it took some time to appreciate that this scenario was of quite a different type from the others. It was a dream that could, if he so wished, become reality.

One Friday afternoon in September, he thought about strangling her. The Wimbledon Strangler. He liked that idea. He could see Edgar Lustgarten narrowing his eyes threateningly at the camera, as he paced out the length of Maple Drive. 'But Henry Farr,' Lustgarten was saying, 'with the folly of the criminal, the supreme arrogance of the murderer, had forgotten one vital thing. The shred of fibre that was to send Henry Farr to the gallows was –'

5 He lay flat on the brown, pine-needle floor of the forest, his chin on his folded arms, and high overhead the wind blew in the tops of the pine trees. The mountainside sloped gently where he lay; but below it was steep and he could see the dark of the oiled road winding through the pass. There was a stream alongside the road and far down the pass he saw a mill beside the stream and the falling water of the dam, white in the summer sunlight.

'Is that the mill?' he asked.

'Yes.'

'I do not remember it.'

'It was built since you were here. The old mill is farther down; much below the pass.'

He spread the photostated military map out on the forest floor and looked at it carefully. The old man looked over his shoulder. He was a short and solid old man in a black peasant's smock and grey iron-stiff trousers and he wore rope-soled shoes. He was breathing heavily from the climb and his hand rested on one of the two heavy packs they had been carrying.

'Then you cannot see the bridge from here?'

'No,' the old man said. 'This is the easy country of the pass where the stream flows gently. Below, where the road turns out of sight in the trees, it drops suddenly and there is a steep gorge –'

'I remember.'

'Across the gorge is the bridge.'

'And where are their posts?'

'There is a post at the mill that you see there.'

The young man, who was studying the country, took his glasses from the pocket of his faded, khaki flannel shirt, wiped the lenses with a handkerchief, screwed the eyepieces around until the boards of the mill showed suddenly clearly and he saw the wooden bench beside the door; the huge pile of sawdust that rose behind the open shed where the circular saw was, and a stretch of the flume that brought the logs down from the mountainside on the other bank of the stream. The stream showed clear and smooth-looking.

b Now answer the questions on page 83, comparing the two texts. Do not answer all the questions, just those that seem the most relevant to your choice of texts.

	Text 1	Text 2
Situation.		
Is what is happening perfectly clear? If not, why not? Is the situation unusual? Does it go directly into the action or does it spend time setting out the background to the story?		
Characters.		
1st or 3rd person narrative? How much do we learn about the characters? Which character do you most identify with?		
Style.		
Are the sentences complex or simple? Does the author seem interested simply in telling the story or in building character and atmosphere?		
Paragraphs.		
Are there significant differences between the subject matter of each paragraph? Is there a logical progression or contrast?		
Narrative/Description.		
How much is narrative and how much is descriptive writing? Does the description help us to understand the narrative? How? Are there any metaphors or similes? Any interesting (precise, surprising) vocabulary?		
Interest.		
Briefly list the techniques the author uses to attract and to hold the reader's attention.		
Personal reaction.		
Which text do you prefer? Why? Write down the phrase or sentence you like best. Why does it appeal to you?		

L I S T E N I N G   2

In this recording, you will hear the crime writer Colin Dexter, whom you heard in **Unit 4**, talking about how he writes.

1 Before you listen, discuss these questions with a partner.

If you were a writer of novels or stories:

a would you prefer to write the whole story, then revise it, or would you plan carefully and revise as you go?

b would you use a word processor or write in long-hand?

c when revising, do you think you would be more likely to cut a lot out or to add things?

d which would you find more difficult – the plot or the language?

e would you write for your own enjoyment or be very conscious of what your readers expect?

2 Now listen to the recording. What answers does Colin Dexter give to the above questions?

3 In what context does he mention the following?

   a   *. . . a very rough and ready way. . .*
   b   *. . . the fine pieces of writing. . .*
   c   *. . . a bit of a filter. . .*
   d   *Tart it up a bit. . .*
   e   *. . . you've almost had your chips.*

4 a What attitude do you think Dexter has towards his prose style? Give reasons for your answer.

   b Do you think his attitude is typical of professional writers?

GRAMMAR

Continuous aspect

We can give a verb a **continuous aspect** (sometimes called continuous or progressive tenses) by adding *be* and *-ing*.
Examples
We will be going there tomorrow.
They were talking about it as they made their way home.
What is he doing?

When a verb is used in its continuous aspect, the emphasis is on some or all of the following aspects of time:

1 Duration – it happens over a period of time
2 Limitation of duration – it is temporary
3 Possible incompleteness of action – we may not know when the action started or when it will finish

I Look at these pairs of sentences and say how the use of a simple or continuous form affects the meaning.

Activity verbs

   a He drank a pint of milk.
      What are you drinking?
   b It was raining when he went out.
      It rained for 40 days and 40 nights.
   c What have you been working on?
      I worked on the book until 10 o'clock.
   d What were you doing between 10 and 11 o'clock last night?
      I read from 10 o'clock till bedtime.
   e I've been writing a letter.
      I've written a letter.

Momentary verbs
(i.e. verbs which describe a very short action)

   a They banged on the door.
      They could hear someone banging on the door.
   b He nodded, wisely.
      He was nodding wisely.
   c Mark winked at me.
      Mark was winking at me.
   d Bernard jumped athletically over the fence.
      He was jumping up and down with excitement.

Transitional verbs are verbs which describe the change from one state to another.

   a The car is now drawing up by the door.
      The car drew up by the door.
   b It seemed as if he was falling for a long time.
      He fell on the slippery surface.
   c The economic stability of the country has been deteriorating for some time.
      His condition had deteriorated markedly.
   d The plane was landing as we arrived.
      The plane landed as we arrived.
   e I've lost my bag.
      I was obviously losing my mind.

State verbs normally describe a state rather than an action and are therefore not normally given a continuous aspect.
They include the following types:

- verbs to do with the senses: *see, hear, smell,* etc.
- verbs to do with understanding and knowing: *believe, hope, know, forget, imagine, think,* etc.
- verbs of having and being: *be, belong to, own, cost, have,* etc.

However, some of them can be used in the continuous to indicate an active sense. Compare these two sentences:
He is stupid. (**state**)

This is a comment on a person's character or intelligence, something that is unlikely to change.

He is being stupid. (**action**)

This is a comment on a person's current behaviour. He is not necessarily a stupid person but is acting in a stupid way at the moment.

2 Compare the following pairs of sentences. Why are the ones marked * not possible?

   a I know what you think, so I won't ask for your opinion.
      I know what you are thinking, but it's not true.
   b I have an elder sister.
      She's having a baby.
   c This box contains a number of documents.
      *This box is containing a number of documents.
   d I really don't like that new teacher.
      *I'm really not liking that new teacher.

3 Look back at the openings of the novels you read on page 80. How many examples of the continuous can you find, and why are they used?

LEXIS

Adverbs of manner

Adverbs can be used to describe actions more accurately. They are particularly useful in stories to emphasise the characteristics of people through their actions.

Example

*My father shook Professor Nathan **solemnly** by the hand.*

*. . . its huge body. . . trembled so **violently**. . .*

*. . . that faint sound was enough to prick the faint bubble of his happiness **instantaneously**.*

1 Choose four or five of these adverbs which describe the way people do things and think of a suitable verb and situation for each.

awkwardly	freely	ruthlessly
briskly	hastily	stiffly
casually	meticulously	systematically
discreetly	patiently	vigorously
fiercely	rigidly	warmly

2 Which of the adverbs above collocate with each of the verbs below.

Can any of these verbs collocate with any other adverbs?

welcome	deny	recall	retreat
eliminate	admit	reply	explain
defend	destroy	walk	examine

3 Make a list of other similar adverbs which you could use to describe the actions of people.

WRITING 2

Choose one of the following extracts from novels and short stories and continue them in any direction, for example lead up to the extract, use it as a starting point or use it in the middle of your piece.

The story does not have to be complete. Concentrate on character and making the situation interesting rather than inventing a complicated plot.

1 'You came, then?'

'Keep your voice down!'

'There's nobody here.'

The newcomer walked down the central aisle and the two men met halfway. They spoke in hushed voices, but the few snatches of conversation that carried to Ruth's ears were readily and frighteningly comprehensible.

2 When he drove up to the big building, he recognised it, but did not connect the girl he had driven home that night with the girl of the cinema. Even when she came to the door, and stood in the hall looking to see who he was, he did not recognise her.

3 The woman said nothing. Her look lasted two or three seconds at most; then she resumed her stare to the south. Ernestina plucked at Charles' sleeve, and he turned away, with a shrug and a smile at her.

4 It was Sunday afternoon in Port Benjamin. The sun was beginning to break through the heavy rain clouds that had hung over the town for so long, and for the first time in many months people had ventured out into the country in such numbers that the streets were nearly deserted.

GRAMMAR

Continuous aspect

State verbs

1 Decide which of the following sentences are possible. Put a line through those that are not.
   a She was feeling for the light switch in the dark.
   b ~~That is sounding like John's car outside.~~
   c We're having breakfast.
   d I'm thinking about your offer.
   e I am knowing this already.
   f She's being very helpful.
   g There's nothing there. You were imagining it.
   h It's a special price in our sale: it's only costing £35.99.
   i He's having dark hair and blue eyes.
   j She's being rather short and fat.
   k This product is containing no artificial preservatives.

2 In the following paragraphs, underline the most likely tense from the choice given.

   a I *opened/was opening* the door and immediately I *was seeing/saw* her: she *stood/was standing* on the other side of the road, the baby in her arms. The baby *was crying/cried* almost hysterically but she *didn't seem/wasn't seeming* to notice and, her apparent indifference *was starting/started* to attract the attention of passers-by.

   b I *have* often *wondered/was* often *wondering* whether other people find me boring. A couple of years ago I *found/was finding* myself sitting next to a fairly well-known politician at a dinner party. I *had been going on/had gone on* about some political matter or other for a few minutes when I *noticed/was noticing* that he *had been falling/had fallen* fast asleep and *started/was starting* to snore.

   c 'What on earth *are* you *doing/do* you *do*?' she *cried/was crying*, running into the room. I *looked/was looking* round innocently. 'Nothing. Why?' At the same time I *was* continually *trying/continually tried*, without much success, to put the incriminating evidence back under the bed. 'You *have been making/have made* one hell of a noise,' she said accusingly. 'I *was* just *trying/just tried* to clear up a bit,' I lied. 'It was a mess in here.'

3 In colloquial speech, the continuous has a special polite use with some of the verbs of understanding and knowing. It has the effect of making the statement more tentative and is therefore less direct or potentially confrontational.
   Example
   '*I was wondering if I could ask you a favour*,' gives the impression that you know the person you are speaking to is very busy and you will therefore quite understand if the person can't manage it.
   '*I'm hoping you'll come and help us*,' gives the listener a chance to say '*no*'. '*I hope you'll come and help us*,' could sound uncomfortably like a polite order.

   In what context could you say the following?
   a What were you wanting?
   b I think you are forgetting a number of factors.
   c I wonder if you could give us your opinions?
   d I hope you didn't mean what you said earlier.

4 A further colloquial use of the continuous is to describe a persistent or progressive activity, usually with words like *always, continually, constantly*, and *forever*.
   The tone of this structure is usually one of irritation or criticism.
   Example
   He's always going on at me about how I dress.
   They are constantly telling me what to do.
   I know this bloke who's always forgetting his phone number.
   Using this structure, write a couple of sentences about people or things that irritate you.

L E X I S

1 Facial expressions

These verbs all describe facial expressions. What emotions do they indicate?

smirk	glare	grimace
frown	beam	scowl
grin	pout	sneer

2 Adjectives describing character

a Divide the following list of adjectives describing character into those with positive or negative connotations.

exasperating	irrepressible	smug
embittered	frivolous	conceited
genial	gloomy	jovial
chirpy	sulky	considerate

b Think of some famous people to whom some of these words could apply.

c Add other adjectives of your own to the list.

3 Collocation

Choose the most appropriate verb from those in the box to fill each of the gaps in the sentences below. Make any changes necessary – some of them may need to be changed to nouns.

welcome	deny	recall	retreat
eliminate	admit	reply	explain
defend	destroy	walk	examine

a I vividly .... meeting her for the first time.

b I was warmly .... by the president of the association.

c He freely .... that he had killed the girl but vigorously .... that it had been on purpose.

d They set about systematically .... the evidence.

e Seeing there was no way forward, they beat a hasty ....

f They .... the surrounding area meticulously for fingerprints.

g Al Capone was known to ruthlessly .... anybody who stood against him.

h Once again, she patiently .... the rules to him.

4 Wish, Hope and Want

Fill the gaps in the following sentences with an appropriate form of *wish*, *hope*, or *want*, either as verb or noun.

a And your children are well also, I .... ?

b He hasn't got a .... in hell of passing. (Idiom)

c I .... I were ten years younger.

d The genie granted Sinbad three ....

e I wouldn't .... that illness on my worst enemy.

f Do you .... a cup of coffee?

g I .... and pray she gets better soon. (Idiomatic collocation)

h 'Bring him here immediately!' 'As you .... , sir.'

i In this luxury liner you will .... for nothing.

j Where there's life, there's .... (Idiom)

k Waste not, ... not. (Idiom)

5 Sounds

a What sorts of things would you associate with the following sounds?

rattle	hiss	rustle	peal

b Find other adjectives to add to this list which describe sound.

deafening	ear-splitting	shrill	audible

Equality of Opportunity

FOCUS

Discuss these points in small groups.

1 What justification is there for educating boys and girls separately?

2 In school, boys and girls learn how people of their sex should behave. They also learn a certain degree of contempt for the opposite sex. Do you agree?

3 The head teacher of a school decides that all pupils of both sexes should study sewing, cooking, carpentry, electronics, music and the history of sport as compulsory subjects up to the age of sixteen.

   What sort of reaction would this scheme have from:
   a pupils?
   b teachers?
   c parents?

4 In small groups, do the following tasks:
   a Name three famous female composers.
   b Name three famous female scientists.
   c Think of one female chess champion.
   d Say roughly what the balance is between male and female politicians in your country.
   e Say what the approximate balance in numbers is between male and female teachers that you have had.

Is there any imbalance in the numbers of men and women involved in the occupations above? If so, why?

LISTENING 1

1 Listen to these short extracts of children talking about school. As you listen, guess the age of each child and write it in the chart below.

Name	Age?	Opinions/Characteristics
1 Robbie		
2 Henry		
3 Edmund		
4 Neil		
5 Brent		
6 and 7 Sophie/Naomi		

2 Match the following opinions and characteristics with the correct child by writing the letter in the chart on the left. You can use any letter more than once.

  a is a bit vague about school activities
  b is too young for primary school
  c is good at Mathematics
  d thinks girls can be bossy
  e annoys the teachers
  f usually works with other people
  g thinks boys are badly behaved
  h is well behaved towards the teachers

3 Do you find any of the children hard to understand? Why? Listen to any difficult ones a few times to see if you can understand them better.

READING 1

1 Read the first three paragraphs of an article which appeared in *The Sunday Times* in order to find out why it was written.

1   The boys and girls in Mary Watson's French class at St Joan of Arc comprehensive in Rickmansworth, Hertfordshire, work co-operatively every day. And they were outraged at opinions expressed by Averil
5   Burgess in last week's New Society.
     Burgess, the headmistress of an independent London girls' school, who becomes president of the Girls' Schools Association this week, said she thought single-sex schools were better for girls. She
10 had observed that boys in co-educational schools dominate the classroom, ignoring girls' views and wrecking their confidence by treating them as second-class citizens.
     'It's not like that in our class,' says Howard
15 Milton, who was adamant that his teacher should contact *The Sunday Times* and put the record straight. 'We do all our French dialogues together in pairs – a girl and a boy.'

THE GREAT THING ABOUT GIRLS' SCHOOLS IS THAT THEY CAN CONCENTRATE ON THEIR WORK WITHOUT THINKING ABOUT BOYS

2 What do you think the rest of the article will be about? Choose from the following:

  a an analysis of Averil Burgess' views
  b a rebuttal of her views
  c a balanced discussion of the pros and cons of co-education
  d a humorous look at the relationships between teenagers

3 Now skim through the rest of the article on page 90 to see whether your predictions were right.

4 Suggest a suitable headline for the article.

5 The following extracts are taken from the article on page 90. Put them into the appropriate gaps in the text.

  a Back in the French class, Daniel and Jackie are practising a dialogue between a tourist and a French official.
  b But this fifth-year class works together in a new way,
  c The boys are more forward than the girls,
  d I wasn't too keen on the new arrangement at first,
  e The course is aimed at the world of work,
  f Jason Montgomery, a local pool champion, admits that such harmony does not reign everywhere.
  g No teacher should allow boys to get away with ignoring girls' contributions,
  h But apart from the French, one of the most important things is that TVEI is committed to avoiding sex stereotyping.

'We help each other out,' says
20 Melissa Larkin, his current partner.
Howard adds: 'The boys can't put the
girls down because if one needs help,
then you both do.'

¹ .... and then students agree it is
25 unusual. 'When we first started in the
fourth year, we all came in and
straightaway sat down next to our
friends: boys with boys and girls with
girls,' says Howard. 'But then Mrs
30 Watson said we were going to have this
new system of girls and boys sitting
together, and we said "why?", and she
explained. We have a new pair every
term, so we get to know more people,
35 and it's worked out really well.'

Watson is deputy head of the school,
which used to be a Catholic girls'
grammar school but went co-ed and
comprehensive in 1975. The vocational
40 French course that she teaches is part of
the school's technical and vocational
education initiative (TVEI), funded by
the government's Training Agency.

² .... and is designed for children
45 who are unlikely to go on to A-levels.
It concentrates on everyday practical
French. 'There is no grammar and lots
of conversation,' says Watson. 'They
learn some quite difficult skills, such as
50 taking a French answerphone message.

'And there are some tasks which even
French people might find difficult, like
filling in health insurance forms, or a
vehicle accident report. I know I find
55 that sort of thing hard in English.

³ '............ I have explained that to
them all, and pointed out that sitting in
separate groups is no good when you
will have to work together in the
60 outside world.'

Jackie Robinson and Daniel Clifford,
another pair, agree that boys and girls
behave differently in school. ⁴ '............'
says Jackie, who is quite shy. 'The
65 boys jump into things and the girls
hang back a bit. They don't like to be
sort of. . . well. . . aggressive.'

'But nowadays, when the boys start
showing off, the girls just take the
70 mick,' says Daniel. 'Like if I stand up
and make a fool of myself, no one
thinks that's so clever any more.'

⁵ '............' says Jackie. 'I didn't like it
at all. But now it's really good. You
75 learn things from each other. With
another girl, you see the same things,
but with boys you get a different point
of view.'

⁶ .... 'In some other classes, the
80 boys muck about, so the teacher gives
them special attention to get them on
the right track. If all classes were like
this one, that wouldn't be necessary.
I'm glad I'm taking this class. It's a
85 miles better course than what we were
doing before.'

Watson sees co-operative behaviour
between the sexes as a question of
good classroom management.
90 ⁷ '............' she says. 'Apart from
anything else, it's just plain rude.'

Her ideas are now being taken up by
other teachers in the school, and have
spread to the religious education
95 department, where discussions of
sensitive topics are made easier
because the two sexes know each other
better.

'I think they are relieved when we
100 make them sit together, and take the
choice away from them,' says Clare
Hallows, the head of RE. 'Because if a
boy and a girl choose to sit together and
get to know each other, they attract
105 attention and embarrassing remarks.'

⁸ .... 'Me and Jackie can get pretty
far in our French conversation now,'
says Daniel. 'No we can't,' giggles
Jackie. 'At least, I can't.' 'Yes you
110 can,' responds Daniel. 'You're pretty
good.'

The Sunday Times

L E X I S

1 Adjectives

a Which adjective in paragraph 1 on page 89 describes the feelings of the students?

b Which adjective in paragraph 3 describes the feelings of Howard Milton?

c What is the difference between the grammatical structures used before and after these two adjectives? Can they be used in any other way?

2 Phrases and idioms

a Find these phrases in the text and work out their meanings:

put the record straight (line 16)
take the mick (line 69)
get them on the right track (line 81)
miles better (line 85)

b Which of these phrases are the most informal?

3 Phrasal verbs

a Underline these phrasal verbs in the text:

help each other out (line 19)
put the girls down (line 21)
worked out (line 35)
pointed out (line 57)
hang back (line 66)
showing off (line 69)
muck about (line 80)
get away with (line 90)
taken up (line 92)

b Using your dictionary, try to find an exact one-word equivalent for each of these phrasal verbs. Check to see if there are any differences in register, connotation or collocation. Put your word in context by placing it at the appropriate place in the text. Does it have the same effect as the original phrasal verb?

WRITING

Writing a summary

As part of a follow-up article in a later edition of *The Sunday Times* newspaper, you are asked to summarise the arguments given in favour of compulsory boy/girl pairwork in the above article.

a Find the places where these opinions are given and underline them.

b Summarise each point in your own words.
Example
Boys can't dominate or show off. (lines 19-23 and 79-86).

c Put the arguments together into a coherent and cohesive paragraph, linking the ideas together where possible. (See UNIT 1 on cohesion for a reminder of the principles involved.)

d Is the register of your summary appropriate for a newspaper article in a 'quality newspaper' like *The Sunday Times?*

SPEAKING

Analysing your own mistakes

1 Look at this list of common difficulties which foreign learners encounter in English conversation.

  a Which do you think are the most serious?

- a strong accent which is difficult to understand
- not listening to, or responding to, other people's points
- risking causing offence by using the wrong register
- not answering or saying very much
- not using a plural 's' or a third person singular 's'
- using the wrong preposition
- using the wrong tense
- making long pauses in the middle of a sentence
- using incorrect intonation

  b Are there any other common errors that you or other people in the class make?

2 Working in small groups, choose three of the points, a–h, for discussion.
Spend about two minutes discussing each item. Justify your opinions and try to persuade the other members of the group who disagree with them.
One or two people in each group should act as observers, listening to the discussion and noting down any of the above errors made by the group. If possible, record the conversation and then analyse the recording afterwards.

a "Schools should teach vocational subjects such as accountancy, secretarial skills and engineering, rather than the traditional academic subjects like geography, history and science."

b **"Most of what you learn in school is useless in later life."**

c "Education should be compulsory for all people up to the age of 18."

d "The government should pay 100% of the fees of anyone who wants to go to University."

e *"Classes should be divided according to age, regardless of ability."*

f **"Pupils should be tested regularly, with those who fail being obliged to retake the year."**

g "Pupils should be able to choose the subjects they study and not have them imposed by teachers or education authorities."

h *"Personal and moral development is as much the job of the school as academic education."*

LISTENING 2

In this recording you will hear a teacher of 9–10 year olds in a state school.

1 The teacher talks about *learned helplessness on the part of the girls*. Before you listen, say what you think this means.

2 In pairs or small groups, discuss briefly what you think the teacher will say about each of the following subjects:

a the different approaches boys and girls have to Technology

b the teacher's job during Science lessons

c the difference between boys' and girls' behaviour in Science lessons

d the justification for single-sex groups

e the pupils' reaction to being forced to work with members of the opposite sex

f the justification for mixed-sex groups

3 Now listen to the recording. Are any of her views different from those you predicted?

4 What does she find *irritating* about pupils' behaviour during science experiments? Who does she appear to blame more: boys or girls?

5 a Look at the transcript on page 173. Are there any parts which don't appear to make sense?

b Listen to the recording while reading the transcript. Is the sense clearer when listening? Why?

c Rewrite and punctuate the last paragraph so that it becomes coherent and cohesive written English. (You may need to add or change words and sentence structure.)

LEXIS

Phrasal Verbs: *out*

'Out' as a particle has two main areas of meaning:

a Into the open, away from, not in or at a place, removal, (often contrasted with '*in*'):
Example
*The prisoners **broke out**.*
*They've **let** the secret **out**.*

Some examples are more metaphorical:
Example
*They've **fallen out**.* (= had an argument)
***Speak out**.* (= make views public)
*His work **stands out**.* (= is above average)

b Thoroughly/to completion (often indicating exhaustion or extinction):
Example
*The fire **burnt out**.*
*We've **run out** of sugar.*
*They **argued** it **out**.* (= They reached a conclusion.)

I Here are some more examples, including those from the text. Which category does each example belong to? (Some may belong to both categories.)

a We *help* each other *out*. (line 19)
b I. . . *pointed out* that. . . you will have to work together in the outside world. (line 57)
c I can just *make* it *out*. (= see with difficulty, distinguish)
d Let's *work* this problem *out*.
e He *passed out* in the heat. (= fainted)
f They are *bringing* the book *out* in March. (= publish)
g I'll *spell* it *out*. (= make it plain)
h I must *tidy out* this cupboard.
i It's time we *had* this *out*. (= discuss our disagreements)
j A shot *rang out*.

2 Some combinations with '*out*' deal with ideas or secrets, which people have in their minds, being communicated and coming out into the open.
Example

speak out	*'spit it out'*
act out	*blurt out*
read out	

In what situations could you use each of these phrasal verbs?

GRAMMAR

Conditional clauses

I Find the three examples of conditional sentences in READING 1 on page 90. (Starting on lines 22, 70 and 102.)
What tenses are used:
a in the *if* - clause?
b in the main clause?

What time is referred to in each: past, present or future?

2 The type of conditional sentence you have just looked at is by far the most common. However, many other tense/time combinations are possible.

In the exercise below, work in three groups to decide which of the phrases (a–e) can be used to complete each sentence naturally. Group 1 should work on numbers 1 and 2, group 2 on numbers 3 and 4 and group 3 on numbers 5 and 6.

There is more than one possibility for each example, depending on the context and the intention of the speaker.

Think of a context for each one. When you have completed the two examples in your group, discuss the possible answers as a class.

1 If you went to Scotland, ...
   a) you would have a great time.
   b) you might see Edith.
   c) why didn't you phone me?
   d) you're mad.
   e) you'll regret it.

2 If we are leaving, ...
   a) we're leaving immediately.
   b) you should have told someone.
   c) I must bring a jacket.
   d) we'd better tell someone.
   e) we'll be on time.

3 If they have told you, ...
  a) they would have told me.
  b) why don't you get angry?
  c) they'll tell me.
  d) they're stupid.
  e) then they've behaved irresponsibly.

4 If I had known about it, ...
  a) I could have done something.
  b) I can do something.
  c) I could do something.
  d) I told you.
  e) I wouldn't mind.

5 If he tells you the truth, ...
  a) what will you do?
  b) what did you do?
  c) what could you do?
  d) what are you going to do?
  e) what would you have done?

6 If Kennedy hadn't been assassinated in 1963, ...
  a) the Cold War might have ended sooner.
  b) how old would he be today?
  c) Ronald Reagan wouldn't have become President.
  d) America will be a different sort of country.
  e) the 1960s would be different.

In conditional sentences, the main clause (or result clause) follows the normal rules for tense and time. It is the *If* - clause that can be surprising.

If - clauses can be divided into two main types:
  • **REAL**: these deal with real possibilities.
  • **UNREAL**: these deal with hypothetical speculations, improbabilities or impossibilities.

3 Look at the real and unreal conditions in the table below.
  a Fill in the time column in the middle with 'Past', 'Present' and 'Future' in the appropriate places.

b Fill in the appropriate columns with the name of the tenses used.

c What pattern of difference is there between tenses used in real and unreal *If* - clauses?

d Write one of the following meanings in the table for each *if* - clause.
  1 *I don't know if they went there yesterday.*
  2 *I think it's very unlikely that they will go there.*
  3 *I'm not sure if they are going there tomorrow.*
  4 *They definitely didn't go there yesterday.*
  5 *I don't know if they have already set off.*
  6 *I think it is highly unlikely that they will be going there now.*
  7 *I don't know if they are going there.*

4 Look at these statements about *If* - clauses. Which are true and which are false?

		True	False
a	When referring to the future, we usually use *will* or *would* in the *If* - clause.	☐	☐
b	The verb form in unreal *If* - clauses is further in the past than the time reference.	☐	☐
c	In real *If* - clauses, tense and time correspond.	☐	☐
d	There is no difference in form between present and future *If* - clauses – only context can tell us which time period is being referred to.	☐	☐

REAL	Meaning	Tense	Time	UNREAL	Meaning	Tense
A If they went there yesterday, . . .	1	Past simple	Past	E If they had gone there yesterday, . . .		
B If they have gone there already, . . .				F If they went / were going there now, . . .		
C If they go there / are going now . . .						
D If they go / are going there tomorrow, . . .				G If they went / were going there tomorrow, . . .		

5 Look at the following examples of conditional sentences, a–k. Decide in each case:

- does it refer to past, present or future time?
- is the conditional clause real or unreal?

Note: Notice that real conditionals referring to the past, and unreal conditionals referring to the present or future have the same form.

Example

If I finished work early, we could go to the pub.
(unreal, future)

If I finished work early, I used to go for a walk.
(real, past)

The context will usually tell you which one it is.

a If you'd told me earlier, I could have helped.

b Why don't you simply ask her what she thinks? If you asked her, she'd tell you.

c If I tried harder, I'd get better results, but I'm afraid I just can't be bothered half the time.

d I probably wouldn't have got involved with this business if I'd known more about it at the beginning.

e 'I wonder if George called earlier this morning.'
'If he left a message while we were out my secretary will let us know.'

f Give us a call if you want to discuss it more.

g Why didn't you spit it out if you didn't like the taste?

h I'd still be there now if you hadn't come and rescued me.

i I'll give you a hand if you like.

j If you hadn't volunteered to work tomorrow, we would all have had to stay on until it was finished this evening.

k If she's damaged my car, there'll be trouble when she gets home.

6 In small groups, discuss the following:
How would things be/have been if …

a men got pregnant and had babies?

b Boris Yeltsin hadn't resisted the Soviet military coup in 1991?

c Beethoven had discovered the electric guitar?

d you had/hadn't taken your parents' advice?

e you hadn't started to learn English?

f you had gone to a better school?

g the atomic bomb had not been invented?

LEXIS

Sexism in language

1 There are a number of idioms that refer to the stereotypical portrayal of men and women in society. Say what is meant by the following. In your opinion, is it sexist to use these idioms?

a He's his own man.

b Let's talk man to man about this.

c He's a good family man.

d Act like a man!

e This'll make a man of you.

f He's a man of the world.

g He's a bit of a Jack the lad.

h Boys will be boys.

i Hell hath no fury like a woman scorned.

j It's time he made an honest woman out of you.

k She's a scarlet woman.

2 Now decide whether each of these words refers to women or men or both. How insulting are they?

wimp	bimbo	old woman	shrew
cow	old maid	bachelor	dragon
fishwife	whiz-kid	mate	

3 Words ending in *-man*, such as *chairman* or *fireman*, have annoyed some feminists who see them as sexist. Which of these suggested alternatives to the word *chairman*, either as a female or a sexless version, seem to you the best?

chairperson	Madam Chairman
chairwoman	the Chair

4 a What pronoun could you put in the gaps in these sentences?

'Anybody under 16 who wishes to join the trip should obtain written permission from .... parents.'

'Whether or not a student decides to continue in higher education often depends on the financial pressures .... is/are under.'

b English does not have a third person singular pronoun that is sexless. The following may be used, but every alternative has its supporters and its critics. What are the problems with each?

he, his – claiming that this is grammatically sexless
he/she, his/her
he or she, his or her
s/he
they, their

READING 2

1 The following extract is entitled *Stereotypic man*. What do you think this means?

2 These words are used in the extract. Bearing in mind the title, what do you think each of these words might refer to?

trivialising	emulate	breadwinner
expectations	glamorous	irresistible
predictable	brainwashed	

3 Now read the following extract to see if your predictions were correct.

4 How many stereotypes are described here? How many of them do you recognise easily and how many seem obscure?

5 a Do you think the author is male or female? Give reasons for your choice.

  b Do you think s/he is fair to men? Why (not)?

6 How difficult do you find this text to understand?
  a No problems.
  b Generally fine but there were difficult parts.
  c Very confusing.

If there are bits of the text that you don't understand, is this because of:
  a vocabulary, or strange phrases?
  b grammar or sentence structure?
  c difficulty in seeing the author's point?
  d something else (explain what)?

7 Find and underline those bits you find puzzling. Compare this with a partner: are there any parts you both don't understand?

Decide together the best strategy for dealing with problematic vocabulary in texts. Consider the following:
• it doesn't look very important: we can safely ignore it
• try and work it out slowly
• use a bilingual dictionary
• use an English/English dictionary
• ask somebody else
• ask the teacher
• give up and forget about it: it's simply too difficult

Stereotypic man

1 While feminists have pointed out how trivialising and restricting stereotypic images, especially media images, are on the lives of women, it seems to have escaped most men's notice that they are trivialised and
5 restricted too.

'Man and machine in perfect harmony,' goes a car commercial on television, implying more than its originators realise. Do men really want to be as smooth-running and predictable as machines? Surely not in real
10 life. But how do they resist when they are sold glamorous irresistible packages? The cool guy who never shows emotions but smokes a cigar instead. . . the superman, fast-living, risk-taking, getting admiring gasps from lesser mortals. . . the James Bond smoothie who's quick
15 on the draw. . . the beer-swilling hero who knows how to live rough, no frills, no fuss. Heroes all, and all guaranteed to get the girl (even though in real life terms they display potentially reckless or violent behaviour, considerable repression and give every indication of
20 becoming unrewarding lovers and companions).

And in contrast, there are the failure symbols, the warning signals to laugh at. . . the swot with glasses, the clumsy thickhead, the henpecked, the weedy, ineffective, accident-prone wimp. Some stereotypes can
25 become manipulative tools: to get out of the housework, there's the lost little boy, can't do a thing for himself, but who is still so lovable and a wow with women. And another type is the 'perfect husband', who gets on with being the breadwinner and taking the
30 dog for a walk, neither sissy nor sexy, the sober, production-line man – using his perfection in lieu of passion and involvement.

These images affect men's behaviour and women's expectations. There is the father image, stern and
35 uncommunicative or insensitive and uncommunicative, or violent and uncommunicative. And the divorced father, indifferent to his family, busy making it with younger women. There is the manager, ruthless whiz-kid, the irresistible
40 'bastard'. The good pal, beer-swilling, telling dirty jokes. And the doctor, remote and kindly – we're back to the uncommunicative man again.

These are not easy images to emulate and they have rather a bad effect, both on those who can
45 actually live up to them, and those who can't.

Women as well as men have been brainwashed into accepting the standards created by these characters. Unfortunately, those traits billed as most desirable are the kind most women would be better
50 off without – aloofness, tantalisingly hard to get, controlling, never admitting weaknesses. Versions of this sadistic figure turn up in movies, on television, in romantic fiction. What kind of promise do TV coppers or James Bond offer in the
55 way of meaningful relationships? Yet they are the unsmiling, inhuman hero figures that men have been taught to emulate and women have been taught to regard as desirable.

LEXIS

1 Phrasal verbs: *Down*

Look at the following examples:

put the girls down (READING 1 line 21)

look down on someone (=consider them inferior)

the scandal brought down the government

a What is the function of *down* in each?

b Can you think of other phrasal verbs with *down* which have a similar meaning?

2 Phrasal verbs: *Back*

Look at the following examples:

hang back

keep something back

hold something or someone back

a What is the function of *back* in each?

b Think of as many phrasal verbs with *back* as you can.

c Does *back* have any other functions in phrasal verbs?

Dictionary work

3 Which word is the odd one out?

adamant	unyielding	irresolute
obstinate	determined	

4 What are the differences in meaning between these verbs?

dominate	influence	conquer
dictate	domineer	

5 Put these words in order from the strongest to the mildest.

indignant	outraged	reproachful

6 Which is the strongest of these words and which can be followed by a preposition?

keen	enthusiastic	zealous	dedicated

GRAMMAR

Conditional clauses

1 Look at these examples of different conditional sentences. Using the real/unreal distinction, decide:

1 in what situation each example might be used.

2 what meaning the speaker conveys by the choice of tense.

(Concentrate on the *If* - clause. The result clauses are given to help with the context. Follow the examples a–c.)

a If you are telling the truth, we'd better tell the police.
   Situation: *Father talking to imaginative son who is telling him about a crime he has witnessed.*
   Meaning: *I don't know for certain if you are telling the truth.* (real - present)

b If John went to London last night, why didn't he tell us?
   Situation: *John has been promising to take us to London for ages.*
   Meaning: *I can't believe he went to London without telling us.* (real – past)

c If Pierre went to London, he could see all the theatre he wanted.
   Situation: *Pierre, who is lazy, is always complaining that there are no theatres in this town.*
   Meaning: *I don't think he'll go. I'm speaking hypothetically.* (unreal - future)

d If I were you, I'd have a rest.*

e If they've finished, they'll let us know.

f If you'd told me, I could have done something about it.

g If they were older, they'd behave better.

h If you're leaving, I'll get your coat.

i If they hadn't talked all the time, I'd have enjoyed it.

j If you were a bit more considerate, you'd offer me your seat.

k If you were leaving, I'd get your coat.

l If they talked all the time, we used to fall asleep.

m If you see Sue, tell her I'll be late home.

* Note: For reasons related to changes in the language over the years, '*If I was. . . .*' is informal and '*If I were . . .*' is formal. There is no difference in meaning.

2 In each group of sentences below, say whether
a) or b) or both can go before the italicised sentence
on the right.

1 a) I was often busy and had little time for socialising.
   b) I'm sorry but I'm going to be rushed off my feet.
   } *I would visit my aunt if I could.*

2 a) Jim thought about it. Was it true? Had he won the Pools?
   b) He can't be very well off, can he?
   } *If he was rich, he wouldn't spend all his time in a dump like this.*

3 a) I really like Sophie.
   b I'll try to pass the message to her today.
   } *If I don't, I'll let you know.*

4 a) When I was little, we used to play football in the park.
   b) The forecast is good. There's practically no chance of the weather turning bad.
   } *But if it rained, we'd have to stay at home.*

5 a) Do you want something else to eat?
   b) Have you finished what you wanted to do?
   } *If you don't, we could go.*

6 a) The Forth Bridge needs constant maintenance.
   b) Do you remember my old bike?
   } *If you didn't keep painting it, it would go rusty.*

7 a) You shouldn't have told lies.
   b) You shouldn't tell lies.
   } *If you had told the truth, this wouldn't have happened.*

8 a) Richard said the accident wasn't his fault, but I disagreed.
   b) Richard says the accident wasn't his fault, but I disagree.
   } *If he hadn't braked so suddenly, he wouldn't have fallen off his bike.*

9 a) You shouldn't have told him.
   b) You mustn't tell him.
   } *If he finds out, he'll kill me.*

10 a) You knew all about it. But you didn't tell her?
   b) It was supposed to be a secret. That's why I didn't tell you before.
   } *Would you have told her if you had known?*

Too smart to be taken in

FOCUS

1 What products do you think these British advertising slogans were used for? Choose from this list:

cars	cream cakes	toilet paper
diamond engagement rings		washing powder
camping holidays	carpets	tea

|c| **Persil washes whiter**

|a| *Naughty but nice*

|d| **Vorsprung durch Technik**

|b| **Longer and softer than ever before**

|e| **The best sights and the best sites**

|f| **Lifts the spirit.** *Comforts the soul.*

|g| **Works of art you can walk on.**

|h| **How else could a month's salary last a lifetime?**

2 Do any of these slogans strike you as:
a clever?
b ridiculous?
c meaningless?

3 Are there any particular advertisements, on radio, television or in newspapers or magazines, which you particularly dislike? Are there any which you particularly like? Why?

4 In small groups, discuss the following two statements. Which do you agree with?

> **'I have nothing to do with any aspects of advertising. . . But I trust the public to tell the difference between real life and the ads, which is more than many better-educated worthies seem willing to do.'**
> *Edwina Currie, MP, The Listener*

> **'The concepts of sexual love, manliness, femininity, maternal feeling are steadily devalued for us by their mercenary association with a brand-name – as though the real human values they represent can be purchased by rushing out and buying a new shaving lotion, a new deodorant, even a new washing-machine.'**
> *Frank Whitehead, Discrimination and Popular Culture*

LEXIS

Advertising vocabulary

Using a dictionary, discuss the following questions in small groups.

a What is the difference between *persuasion*, *indoctrination* and *manipulation*?

b How does *subliminal advertising* work?

c Where would you see a *hoarding* or a *billboard*?

d What is a *copywriter*?

e Is there a difference between *marketing* and *selling*?

f What exactly is an *advertising campaign*?

g What are *wholesalers*, *retailers* and *consumers*?

h What is the difference between a *headline*, a *slogan* and a *catchphrase*?

i How do you respond to *sales talk*?

j What is the difference between *hard sell* and *soft sell*?

LISTENING 1

In this recording, you will hear a conversation with Mark Roberts, a marketing consultant.

1 Listen to the first question. Rephrase it in a more concise way.

2 Now listen to the answer and fill in the chart.

Decisions to be made:
1
2
For example, *Head and Shoulders*, *Fairy Liquid*
3
Techniques:
example
a
b

3 Answer these questions. Listen again if you need to.
a What exactly is meant by *market niche*?
b How can people *fritter their money away*?
c What do you think *Head and Shoulders* and *Fairy Liquid* are?
d What is a *Torture Test*?

4 Can you think of any other advertisements you have seen which illustrate the strategies and techniques mentioned in the conversation?

1 Skim quickly through these advertisements. What do they have in common?

2 What techniques do they use to attract the reader's attention?

SKINNY LEGS

Try this new amazing scientific home method to ADD SHAPELY CURVES to ankles, calves, thighs and hips!

Skinny legs rob the rest of your figure of attractiveness. You too can try to help yourself improve underdeveloped legs, due to normal causes, and fill out any part of your legs you wish, or your legs all over as many women have by following this new scientific method. This tested and proven course was prepared by a well-known authority on legs. Requires only 15 minutes at home. Contains step-by-step instructions and illustrations of the easy scientific leg technique, with simple instructions for gaining shapely, stronger legs, plus leg measurement chart for each section of leg according to height and weight.

30 DAY TRIAL for the 'Shapely Legs Home Method' (in plain wrapper), send $7.95 plus 95 cents for shipping. Money back guarantee if not satisfied.

Modern Methods, Dept. 85 to 839
Box 2012 New Rochelle, NY 20002

Wrinkle Stick

Vikki LaMotta, Playboy Model at 53 Introduces Her New, Ultra-Rich, Purse-Size …
wrinkle stick
virtually FREE!
$8.00 RETAIL VALUE!

The new VH, formula LYL OIL WRINKLE STICK - for wrinkle protection day or night. In its sleek 'pop-up' case it glides on effortlessly and melts into skin instantly to plump up cells and fade fine line wrinkles that shout 'age' to the world! Perfect for eyes or all dry, flaky, ageing facial and neck areas. Enriched with vitamin E and Aloe.
Vikki wants YOU to share her personal anti-ageing secrets. Send just $2 for postage, handling and promo and Vikki will send you her fabulous new $8 value WRINKLE STICK plus her full Beauty Secrets Catalogue absolutely FREE!

To order: Mail this ad plus $2.00 to:
Vikki LaMotta Cosmetics Ltd.
Dept. WS-302404 Park Avenue S., New York, NY

inches of muscle power

Amazing New Body-Building System Packs SOLID INCHES OF MUSCLE and POWER A Super System for beginners! Where You Want It – FAST! Add 3" to your arms, 4" to your chest – so QUICK and EASY you'll hardly believe your eyes! The revolutionary NEW 'Instant-Action' POSITRAIN System does it for you in just 30 MINUTES A DAY! Used by 'Mr America' Champs! Simple instructions. Packed with easy-to-follow photos (by Mr America Champs – no cheap drawings!). GUARANTEED to make you a Muscular Powerhouse – whether you're skinny or fat, young or old – or money back! Send only $10.95 for Big Complete Course. Nothing more to pay. No annoying time payments. Better than course costing $40 or $50. FREE: 10 Extra Bonus Courses on how to be popular and successful, make women like you, etc. Also Adult Fitness Course.
MAIL COUPON TODAY!
DAN LURIE BARBELL CO., INC.219-10 South Conduit Avenue, Springfield Gardens, N.Y. 11413 Rush me complete 'Instant-Action' POSITRAIN course and FREE Bonus courses. Enclosed is $10.95 plus $1 for postage and handling.
NAME _____ADDRESS _____CITY _____STATE & ZIP _____For immediate service call 718-978-4200 and charge your order on master or visa card. Money-back guarantee.

ASHAMED OF PRUNE LIPS?

Are you self-conscious about those old-looking lines that surround your lips?

You don't have to be!

JTL WRINKLE CREAM is a unique lotion made up of collagen, jojoba, aloe, herbs and Vitamin E especially designed to fade away those ugly little wrinkles, yet will not alter skin structure. The amazing thing about *JTL WRINKLE CREAM* is that results occur after the first treatment, leaving your lips smooth and youthful again. Stop looking old because of aged prune lips. Look and feel younger with a more youthful and attractive appearance. Full money-back guarantee if you are not totally satisfied with the results. For a 90-day supply of JTL WRINKLE CREAM, send $12.95 plus $2 for postage and handling to:

JTL PRODUCTS, 5313-Y, Bakman Avenue, N. Hollywood. CA91601

3 With a partner, choose two of the advertisements to read more closely. Answer these questions on style.

a Which of these words would best describe the style? (More than one is possible). Why have the adverts used this particular style?

serious	enthusiastic	formal	scientific
literary	informal	impersonal	
personal	colloquial	rhetorical	

b How many exclamation marks are there? Why are they used?

c Find two or three examples of ellipsis. Why is this feature so common?

d Are the sentences long or short or a mixture? Which do you think are the most effective in advertisements?

4 Read through all four advertisements. Note the key phrases in the chart below that illustrate the features listed on the left.

	Prune Lips	Skinny Legs	Wrinkle Stick	Muscles
Claim to be the only one of its type or much better than anything else on the market	unique lotion			
Claim to scientific respectability				
Claim to be new				
Quick results				
Claim to make you feel, as well as look, better				
Suggestion that the product has been specially developed with the reader personally in mind				
Financial incentives/guarantees				

5 Work individually. For each statement, put a tick in the column which most accurately reflects your opinion.

	Agree	Disagree	It depends	Don't understand
a The basic assumption behind these advertisements is that there is an ideal physical appearance and that those who don't conform to it are ugly and failures.	☐	☐	☐	☐
b Advertisements such as these honestly try to help people who have real physical problems.	☐	☐	☐	☐
c If you buy these products, the advertisements imply, you will be irresistible to the opposite sex.	☐	☐	☐	☐
d If we can improve people's appearance, the world will be a happier place.	☐	☐	☐	☐
e These advertisements encourage people to come to terms with their physical appearance, including their less attractive features, and are therefore a good thing.	☐	☐	☐	☐
f They all imply that you would look fine if it weren't for that one little imperfection.	☐	☐	☐	☐
g These are ordinary advertisements aimed at ordinary people.	☐	☐	☐	☐
h Advertisements such as these have no motive other than to make money for the manufacturers.	☐	☐	☐	☐
i The subtle effect of this type of advertising is to increase people's feelings of inadequacy.	☐	☐	☐	☐
j You would have to be naive to buy one of these products.	☐	☐	☐	☐

Now compare your answers with a partner. Justify your opinions on any points about which you disagree. If you ticked **It depends**, say what it depends on.

WRITING 1

APPROPRIACY

1 Look at the list of copywriter's guidelines for writing an advertisement in the column on the right Briefly note what you think the reason for each particular guideline is. The first one has been done for you.

2 Look back at the advertisements on pages 100–101. How far do they conform to these guidlines?

3 Look at the advertisement on the opposite page. Is it better or worse than those on pages 100–101? Justify your opinions.

---

a Don't exaggerate or get hysterical. Be truthful and reasonable.
Reason
You must be credible. If people suspect you are lying, they won't buy.

b Avoid long words. Stick to short Anglo-Saxon words where possible, rather than Greek or Latin words.

c Be colloquial. Use the word *you*.

d Be wary of adjectives like '*exciting*', '*amazing*', '*incredible*'.

e Be positive. Avoid negative statements or questions such as '*Why not try one*'?

f Keep to the present tense. '*Look how it will brighten your home*' becomes '*Look how it brightens your home*'.

g Make sure there is a contrast in pace by varying the lengths of the sentences.

h Each sentence or paragraph should flow naturally into the next.

4 Look at this list of common link phrases. Check you know their meaning.

And of course …	That's only part of it …	Did you realise …	Just as … so …
More interesting still …	Not to mention …	Not only …	It's as if …
At the same time …	This includes …	You see …	Moreover …
Just as important …	As we said at the start …	When all's said and done …	We couldn't end without. . .
For example …	Naturally …	After all …	

a How many of these phrases would you certainly *not* use in a piece of formal academic writing?

b Which of these link phrases, a – e would you use for:
   a introducing additional information?
   b concluding?
   c introducing examples to illustrate your point?
   d persuading?
   e comparisons?

5 Working in groups, choose one of the following objects or products:
- mineral water
- dog food
- fashionable glasses
- a computer game
- a hair care product
- a tennis racket

As a group of copywriters, write an advertisement for the product, to be published in a magazine.

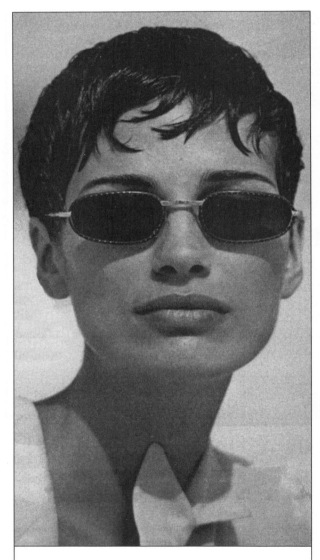

GIORGIO ARMANI
OCCHIALI

READING 2

I Before reading the next passage, in pairs quickly list all the reasons you can think of:
a for banning advertising
b to justify its existence

2 Compare your lists with another pair.

3 Now read the following extract. As you read, refer back to your lists. Tick those points on your lists which are included in the text and add any extra points that you find.

1   It is by no means difficult to find voices hostile to advertising. They range from the rabid far left, who however are as adept as anyone at the manipulative falsehoods of which they accuse the advertising business,
5 to conservative intellectuals who refuse to acknowledge that they, too, make choices about products and services, and that advertising is one of the sources of information on which those choices are based. In between these poles are the rest of us: those who consider themselves too
10 smart to be 'taken in' and feel secure enough to regard advertising with amused contempt; those who think that TV commercials are an insult to the intelligence (but what about most of the programmes?); those who see ads as a corrupting influence; those who charge advertisers
15 with trivialising the emotions; those who see in advertising an added production cost which is passed on to the consumer; and so on and on. As Roderick White notes in *Advertising: What it is and how to do it*, 'everyone knows all about advertising'.
20   In defence of itself, the advertising business can point to the jobs created by the stimulation of consumption; to (in Britain) the two television networks and hundreds of newspapers and magazines whose existence is made possible by advertising revenue; to the benefit of
25 advertising to the consumer in indicating what choices are available within a given product range; to the controls, both statutory and voluntary, which protect consumers from advertising excesses; and, *in extremis*, it can be pointed out that advertising people themselves
30 are decent men and women, loving husbands, wives, fathers and mothers, with the same variety of political attitudes and social beliefs and the same sense of responsibility as the rest of us.
   There is no resolving the argument, just as there is no
35 chance of changing the vote in a debate about God and Mammon (which some extremists take the argument about advertising to be), Marxism versus capitalism, or today's moral values against yesterday's. However, it is worth looking at the cases for the prosecution and the
40 defence in some detail, if only because it is good to shed light where there is prejudice.

Advertising

4 What do you think the author's own opinion of advertising is? Give reasons for your answer.

5 What is revealed about the author's attitude in these two statements?
but what about most of the programmes?
(line 12–13)
everyone knows all about advertising (lines 18–19)

6 Now answer these questions on cohesion.
  a What do these words refer to?
  which (line 4)
  they (line 4)
  they (line 6)
  these poles (line 8)
  those (line 9)
  which (line 27)
  b What is the relationship between *the rabid far left* (line 2) and *conservative intellectuals* (line 5)?

7 a What do these adjectives mean?
  hostile (line 1)
  adept   (line 3)
  statutory (line 27)
  voluntary (line 27)
  b What is the meaning of these verbs?
  taken in (line 10)
  trivialising (line 15)
  c What is the meaning of these noun phrases?
  rabid far left (line 2)
  manipulative falsehoods (line 3–4)
  the stimulation of consumption (line 21)
  a given product range (line 26)
  d What verbs collocate with these nouns?
  argument (line 34)
  light (line 41)

What can you do to help you remember how to use these words?
What else do you need to know about them apart from meaning?

LISTENING 2

1 Listen to these three radio advertisements.
  a Write down exactly what is being advertised in each.
  b Which do you think is the best advertisement? Why?

2 Listen again and answer the following questions.
  a What does the first advertisement tell you to look out for?
  b How many incentives are being offered to do business with the company in the second advertisement?
  c What exactly is new about the product in the third advertisement?

3 The next three advertisements are for the following:
  • a sale at a bicycle shop
  • a sale at a building and home improvement centre
  • a furniture shop

In pairs, choose one of these and write one or two phrases which you would expect to hear in the advertisement.

4 Listen to the three advertisements. Do they include the phrases you thought of?

5 Suggest ways in which you think any of these three advertisements could be improved.

WRITING 2

Presenting an argument

1 Look at the phrases below and decide if they are more characteristic of formal or informal argument.
What criteria help you to make your decision?

> Bearing this in mind, . . .
>
> While conceding/admitting that . . .
>
> It is also the case that . . .
>
> It is nevertheless true that . . .
>
> It should not be forgotten that . . .
>
> In defence of this/itself . . .
>
> It can/could be pointed out that . . .
>
> It can/could be argued that . . .
>
> However, it is worth looking at . . . , if only because . . .
>
> It is/would be by no means difficult to . . .
>
> There is no question of . . .
>
> In between two poles . . .
>
> There is no resolving the argument . . . that . . .
>
> It is clear that . . .
>
> It follows that . . .
>
> It will be seen from this that . . .
>
> Thus . . .

2 Which of these phrases are used in the text in READING 2?

3 In those examples where there is a choice of modal or auxiliary verb (for example *can, could, is, would, be*) what difference is there in meaning between the two alternatives?

4 Which of these phrases can be used for:
a drawing conclusions?
b refuting other arguments?
c defending arguments?

5 *'Advertising has changed the way we look at the world and it has changed it for the worse.'*

Write a short argument in favour of or against this statement. Write in a fairly formal style, similar to that used in the text in READING 2. Refer to some of the arguments of the opposing view, in order to discount them.

GRAMMAR

Pronouns

When reading a long passage, it is useful to be aware of the words which we use to refer back to something which has already been mentioned. We often use words such as *'this'*, *'that'*, *'these'*, *'those'*, *'so'* and *'such'* for this purpose.

1 In the following sentences, choose the best pronoun from the two given. If you think both are possible, decide how the meaning changes depending on which is used.
a It's been snowing for hours. *That/This* is why the traffic's so bad.
b Many Oxford colleges only admitted women for the first time in 1979. *This/That* decision had little impact on the academic standards of the University as a whole.
c My house is surrounded by trees. *These/Those* are mainly pines.
d The economy boomed in the years immediately following the war. Roads were built, railway lines laid and big businesses moved into the capital. All of *these/this* inevitably had an impact on the social structure of the country.
e As Minister for Health, I will continue to ensure that the Health Service is adequately funded and that *this/that* money will remain forthcoming for the foreseeable future.
f There are only two surviving examples of his sculpture and one of *these/those* is of questionable validity.
g *That/This* is a good idea. Why didn't you think of it before?

2 Working in small groups, try to work out some guidelines for the use of *'this'*, *'that'*, *'these'* and *'those'* from the above examples.
Compare your guidelines with another group.

3 a Find one word which can be used to fill all the gaps in the sentences below.
   1 Are you coming this evening? If ...., let me know.
   2 Nationalism has been on the increase in recent years and nowhere more .... than in the former Soviet Union.
   3 This machine is out of order and is likely to remain .... for some time.
   4 The place was packed out. I never expected it to be ....popular.
   5 Please bring this invitation with you. Those who fail to do .... will not be admitted.

b How many gaps can be filled by other words?

4 What one word can be used to fill all the gaps in the sentences below?

a The events of the last weekend were unacceptable and .... violence is to be deplored.

b Your daughter is rude, ill-disciplined and disruptive. .... behaviour will not be tolerated in my school!

c Schools like this sprang up all over the country. One .... school is owned by an immigrant family.

d He denied causing a disturbance, saying he had never before been involved in any .... thing.

e Car-related crime is on the increase according to figures released by the government. But .... statistics are frequently used to give a false impression of the dangers of living in cities.

5 The following sentences have exactly the same meaning:

It took nine hours. I haven't been on so long a trip for ages.

It took nine hours. I haven't been on such a long trip for ages.

a Which of these sentences is more common?

b What are the grammatical rules governing the transformation?

Reflexive pronouns are often used to emphasise or clarify who or what you are talking about.

Example

*The surrounding countryside was pleasant enough but the town **itself** looked run-down.*

6 Provide clauses or sentences preceding the sentences below that would justify the use of the reflexive pronouns.

Example

It is the things which are done in the name of religion which I abhor. I have no objection to religion itself.

a John himself rarely went out.

b I myself don't disapprove quite so strongly.

c The car itself was far from new.

d You just wait till you're a parent yourself!

LEXIS

Nouns referring back to spoken or written texts

List **A** contains a group of nouns which can be used to refer back in a general way to written or spoken comment.

A

allegation	assertion	boast
claim	declaration	contention
digression	remark	retort
plea	revelation	pronouncement
explanation	excuse	observation

Example

*Ian's **observations** on the meaning of life baffled me.*

These nouns are useful, for example, when discussing other people's arguments for or against a subject. Many of them are related to REPORTING VERBS, (see page 72).

I Many of these nouns also reveal your feelings and opinions about the value of what has been said. What does the choice of noun in these sentences reveal about the writer's opinions?

a The minister's *declaration* that the recession was over surprised many people.

b *Allegations* of misconduct by the judge were made in some of the tabloid newspapers.

Decide what feelings the other nouns in list **A** convey. Find a word with a similar meaning to each one, but which has different connotations.

Example

*If you talk about somebody's **plea** for help, you think they are in distress. If you talk about their **request** for help, it suggests something less desperate.*

The nouns in list **B** below refer to people's ideas or opinions.

B

conjecture	assumption	viewpoint
delusion	finding	view
insight	notion	position
vision	theory	idea

2 Add other similar nouns that you can think of to list B above.

3 If you use one of these nouns, what does it show about your attitude to those ideas?

Example

*If you talk about somebody's **assumption** it implies that you disagree with their arguments.*

4 Use the words in lists **A** and **B** to complete these sentences. Pay careful attention to the collocations.

a The .... that this product would stop the affects of ageing was discounted by the Consumer Protection Association.

b She was under the .... that she would become famous.

c There was no formal .... of war.

d The Party had a .... of how the country should be run.

e His years among the Indians enabled him to gain a deep .... into the workings of their culture.

f They had only a vague .... of where they were supposed to be going.

g The news of her past history was seen as an astounding ....

h This .... is still held by a number of people, though it has been widely discredited.

i The .... of this court is that no crime has been committed.

LEXIS

1 Advertising vocabulary

Fill in the blanks with the correct noun from the exercises on page 99 of UNIT 9. The first letter has been given for you.

a A whole group of related goods is called a p.r.o.d.u.c.t.. r.a.n.g.e...

b Japanese car manufacturers hold an increasing share of the m ....

c The job of the advertising copywriter is the m .... of the minds of the potential buyers.

d The secret of a good advertisement is to find the right s ....

e R............... spend a lot of money on advertising.

f I .... is a more formal word for brainwashing.

g The salespeople were discouraged from using the hard sell approach because c............... feel too pressurised by it.

h Since the traffic was at a standstill on the A 41, I spent a good half hour looking at the advertisements on the h............... by the side of the road.

2 Word formation

Fill in the blanks with a suitable form of the word in brackets. All the words occur in one form or another in READING 2.

a They showed open .... to the project. (*hostile*)

b The far left are as adept as anyone at .... falsehoods. (*manipulation*)

c Many find the attitudes of advertisers............... . (*contempt*)

d In defence of itself, the advertising business can point to the jobs created by the stimulation of .... (*consume*)

e There are a number of .... controls on what advertisers can and cannot say. (*statutes*)

f The passionate arguments some people use against advertising are often rather .... (*excess*)

3 Collocation

a In what metaphorical sense are these phrases often used?

to shed/cast light on something

to see the light

something has come to light

She's a guiding light

She wanted to see her name in lights

b All of the words below can collocate with the word *argument*. Categorise them according to whether they are verbs or adjectives.

get into	settle	rebut	heated
break off	cogent	clinch	valid
irrefutable	convincing	compelling	bitter
refute	spurious	tenuous	
airtight	sound	rational	

Discuss with a partner which of these collocations are the most useful to learn.

4 Link phrases

Give examples of how you would use these link phrases. Decide whether each would be more common in spoken or written English.

a When all's said and done. . .

b Not to mention. . .

c It's as if. . .

d You see. . .

e Not only. . .

5 List as many phrases as you can remember from page 106 that can be used in formal written arguments for:

a drawing conclusions

b refuting other arguments

c defending arguments

6 Reference nouns

Decide which of these nouns you could use to report the following statements. More than one is usually possible.

conjecture	delusion	insight
vision	assumption	finding
notion	theory	viewpoint
view	position	idea
allegation	assertion	boast
declaration	contention	digression
remark	retort	plea
revelation	pronouncement	explanation
excuse	observation	claim

a 'You're a liar!'

b 'I'm going to be rich and famous one day.'

c 'I didn't think you would want her to stay.'

d 'By the way, did you post that letter for me?'

e 'Man that is born of woman hath but a short time to live.'

f 'I don't think the peace negotiations will continue.'

g 'The Porsche cost me £42,000, but then it is *so* much better than your car.'

h 'I think Scotland should be independent.'

i 'I resign!'

j 'I'm really sorry but the dog ate my homework.'

GRAMMAR

So, such, this, that, these, those

Use one of the above words to complete these statements in the most satisfactory way.

a 'I'm sorry to barge in on you like ....'

b 'I'm sorry I barged in on you like ....'

c '................ way, sir, if you'd like to follow me.'

d 'Do you like Chinese food? If .... you should try *The Peninsular*.'

e 'I'm really sorry.'
'................ you should be.'

f '................ a revelation would have destroyed the Conservative Party twenty years ago.'

g 'I really like your glasses. I much prefer them to................ that you bought last year.'

h 'I know the red ones are cheaper but .... are absolutely gorgeous.'

i 'Sarah's getting married.'
'................ I hear.'

j '................ are not the sort of men we should be doing business with.'

Punctuation: *Apostrophes*

In the following sentences, decide whether or not an apostrophe should be added.

a Its a strange sort of advertisement. Its message seems somewhat obscure at first until you notice whats going on in the background of the picture.

b Several of the students complaints centred on the timetable. Its complexities made it practically impossible to follow.

c Stephen Jones mathematics tutor was also a leading novelist.

d Is that your bag or hers? Perhaps its Annes.

e One of the committees resolutions was passed after the chairmans intervention.

Reflexive pronouns

In the following sentences, decide whether a reflexive pronoun can be added for emphasis or to help clarity.

a I wash every morning. Doesn't everyone else?

b He's a university graduate like me.

c They all looked as miserable as I did.

d I'm not particularly fond of his music but I know a lot of people who are.

e There are a great number of people who refuse to have anything to do with computers.

f She had done all the work.

g He insisted on giving the present to Carolyn and not leaving it for her to pick up.

FOCUS

1 'It is better to travel hopefully than to arrive.'

'Travel broadens the mind.'

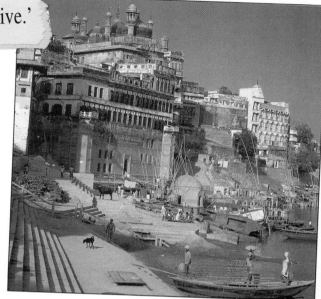

a What do you understand by these two proverbs?

b Do you agree with them?

c How would you translate them into your own language?

2 In small groups, tell each other about a time when:

a you were lost in a strange place.

b you had to rely on the kindness of strangers.

c people laughed at you because they knew something you didn't.

d you really wished you could speak another language well.

LISTENING 1

In this recording, Simon talks about when he and his wife flew to India and then spent eight months returning to England overland using public transport.

1 Listen to the conversation and note:

a what he says about his philosophy of travelling.

b any drawbacks he mentions of this type of journey.

2 Discuss in small groups whether you would like to do a similar trip or whether you'd prefer two weeks in Barcelona. Give reasons for your preference.

3 You will now hear a short section of the recording. It will be played only three times. Listen carefully the first time, note down key words on the second listening, and the third time note down as much as you can.

Now work in groups of three and try to reconstruct the whole section. When you have finished, compare your version with that of another group.

R E A D I N G   1

1 Skim through the following paragraphs from a newspaper article. What is the article about?

A As I rode the Kinki Nippon Railway from Kyoto to Nara, I suddenly understood how Japan rose from the ashes of 1945 to build the most potent economy in the world.

B Like a fool I believed her. The Japanese are always kind when directing lost gaijin. Sometimes they are even accurate.

C 'Nara, kudasai?' ('Nara, please?') I smiled at an Office Lady as Kinki Nippon came into a station that could have been anywhere, and the carriage awoke, <u>the spell</u> broken.

D <u>The long, clean carriage</u> was full of every kind of Nihon-jin ('Japanese-person'). There were high-school kids in their distinctive uniforms – <u>the girls</u> dressed like sailors, the boys in those lapel-less suits sported by the early Beatles. There were shockingly beautiful oh-eru ('OL' – standing for Office Ladies), young women with hair down to their waists who will work for the great Japanese corporations until they meet the 'sarariman' (literally 'salaryman') of **their** dreams. And there were the sararimen themselves, the men in grey suits whose dedication to company and country built the backbone of the economic miracle. All Nihon-jin life was **there**.

E Travelling beyond the borders of Tokyo presents gaijin (literally 'outside-persons' – anyone not fortunate enough to be Japanese) with problems they do not encounter in the capital. Every subway stop in Tokyo has its name written in Roman as well as Japanese characters. But Tokyo is a sophisticated, cosmopolitan metropolis and **this helpful habit** stops at the city limits. By the time you get to the Kinki Nippon Railway, all <u>the signs</u> are in Japanese and it is every gaijin for himself.

The Sunday Times

2 Put the paragraphs in the right order. What helped you to decide on the sequence?

1	2	3	4	5	6	7	8	9	10
A				F					J

F You might learn to speak some Japanese (it's about as difficult as Italian) but you are not going to learn to read Japanese (about as easy as walking on water). There are thousands of different symbols in Japanese writing and three different writing systems, one for words and two for syllables. Basic literacy is incredibly hard work there, and it ingrains an aptitude for learning that helps make the Japanese the most highly educated people on the planet – and so <u>the lost traveller</u> will often find himself relying on the kindness of Nihon-jin.

G What you have to do is look very worried, a little frightened and, if possible, name the location where you would like to be, punctuating your wish with a wistful smile. The Japanese smile all the time. They also nod and bow a lot. <u>The nodding</u> is to encourage the person they are talking to, the bowing is to show respect, and the smiling is for embarrassment, nervousness, happiness – almost anything. It is very easy for an enthusiastic gaijin to overdo the bowing. But **you** can never overdo the smiling.

H And as the Kinki Nippon line rattled south, it was as if a spell had been cast over the train. Because the whole carriage – students, office ladies and sararimen alike – closed their brown eyes and slept: every one of them. It was then I understood their secret. These people just work harder than everybody else.

I 'Hai !(yes)' she said with that glorious briskness that you hear only in Japanese.

J I never did find out the name of **that town**, but you don't wait long for a train in Japan and Kinki Nippon was soon depositing me in the ancient capital of Nara. We disembarked, leaving one lone sarariman on the train, still sleeping like a baby.

3 Now answer these questions on cohesion and coherence.

  a What is the most important sentence in each of paragraphs **2**, **4** and **6**?

  b What is the subject of the first sentence in paragraph **4**?

  c Rewrite paragraphs **4** and **5** so that they include only the information that is essential for understanding the rest of the extract.
  Why do these paragraphs include non-essential information?

  d Can this extract be divided into larger sections than paragraphs?

  e Which words does the author use to avoid repeating the words *train*, *Tokyo* and *people* too often?

  f The following pronouns and nouns are in bold in the extract. What does each refer to?

1	*their*	4	*there*
2	*this helpful habit*	5	*that town*
3	*you*		

  g The following examples are underlined in the extract. Explain why the definite article is used in each case. (For further information, go back to the GRAMMAR section in UNIT 2).

  The long, clean carriage
  the girls
  the signs
  the lost traveller
  The nodding
  the spell

SPEAKING

Negotiating – planning a journey

Work in groups of four or five.

1 As a group, you have £1000 and a free long weekend (Friday to Monday inclusive). Decide where you want to go for the weekend. It can be a place (for example Paris) or a tour, but it must be practically possible and you must all stay together.

2 Now think about the language you have just used in order to reach your decision. Answer the following questions.

  a Did everyone give their ideas or did some just agree with other people?

  b Did any one person dominate the discussion too much?

  c Was an agreement reached amicably or was there a lot of shouting and arguing?

  d Were people more concerned with giving their own views than with listening to others?

  e Was much time wasted on irrelevant argument?

  f Which of these three discussions most closely resembles yours?

1

> *Paul* Paris?
> *Anne* Yeah!
> *Kate* No!
> *Anne* Yeah! Why not?
> *Mary* I want to go to the coast.
> *Anne* Paris.
> *Kate* It's too far.
> *Paul* No it isn't.
> *Kate* How do we get there then?
> *Mary* What about somewhere else?
> *Anne* No!
> *Paul* Paris, then. Agreed?

2

> *Anne* We could go to Paris.
> *Paul* Yeah!
> *Mary* Isn't it a bit far?
> *Anne* Not really. We could fly.
> *Kate* It's not worth it though, is it?
> *Mary* I want to go to the coast.
> *Kate* Anyone else for the coast?
> *Paul* I'd rather not. Anyway, it's freezing.
> *Anne* I still think £1000 is enough to get us all to Paris.
> *Paul* Well has anyone got any other suggestions?

3

> *Anne* We could go to Paris.
> *Paul* Yeah!
> *Mary* No. It's too far.
> *Paul* No it isn't. We could fly.
> *Kate* It's too far for a weekend.
> *Mary* I want to go to the coast.
> *Anne* Nobody else does.
> *Paul* Who wants to go to the sea in the middle of winter?
> *Kate* Well, who wants to go to Paris?
> *Anne* I do!
> *Kate* Well I don't.

g Which of these three discussions provides the best model for how to negotiate? Justify your choice.

3 Work individually. Decide what you personally want to do during this weekend trip to the destination you agreed on with your group. Decide what you definitely do not want to do.

4 Now work together as a group and plan your travel and accommodation arrangements for the trip, and your itinerary for each day. State your preferences, listen to others and, if need be, compromise.

LISTENING 2

1 In small groups, invent a story which includes the following:
- 40 tons of fish
- giant potholes
- a pistol

Then tell your story to another group.

2 Now listen to Bernard telling his story on the tape. Are there any similarities to your stories?

3 Listen to the way Bernard says these phrases. Which words does he stress and why?
  a *Yes, going across Brazil was pretty extraordinary*
  b *. . .we got a lift on a giant lorry, a really huge lorry carrying tons of fish*
  c *I mean big enough to hide twenty people in*
  d *. . .we had one doubtful moment*
  e *We'd better be a bit careful with this guy*
  f *It stank! It was horrible!*

4 What is similar about the intonation of these two phrases?
  a *. . .oh in the roof or something*
  b *. . .oh it was a lorry drivers' hotel*
  Why are they said in this way?

WRITING

Describing a journey

1 Think of a long journey you have been on. Think about how you would tell the story of this journey to a friend. How could you make it interesting and entertaining?

2 With a partner, describe your journeys to each other. Which were the most interesting parts of your partner's story?

3 What difference would it make to the story if you wrote it rather than told it?
  Do you think it is easier to make the story more entertaining when telling it or writing it? Give reasons for your answer.

4 Read the following description of a journey. How has the author tried to make it interesting?

1   I had been on the train for three days and had traversed Europe from north-west to south-east. Interminable delays at borders, further inexplicable stops in the middle of nowhere in Yugoslavia, a

5   succession of different languages passing the window like a radio tuning dial turned at random, lack of sleep due to the impossibility of finding a comfortable position on the hard seats of the crowded compartment: all these had combined in their effect

10 so that now, at half past one in the morning and nearing my destination, exhaustion overwhelmed any sense of excitement.

I stood in the corridor, looking out into the night through the open window. Half an hour to go, I

15 reckoned. The last part of a long journey is always the worst. An Australian I'd talked to briefly in Venice came up to me and we chatted for a bit. He knew the town I was going to.

'What d'you want to go there for?' he enquired

20 incredulously. 'It's a dump.'

'Thanks for the encouragement,' I murmured, and went back to my compartment. I shared it with a Syrian businessman, his Hungarian wife and their seven-year-old daughter who was doted on by her

25 enormous father. She spoke to him in Arabic, her mother in Hungarian and me in English. Husband and wife conversed in Italian. It was like a miniature meeting of the United Nations. Any other passenger would have had to have a set of headphones and a

30 simultaneous translation.

As the lights of the outskirts of the city appeared, the Australian's unflattering description began to seem depressingly accurate. Cement factories, tumble-down shacks, rows of broken goods wagons

35 and even a dead goat made their funeral procession past the window. We shuddered to a halt at the characterless station (I had long since lost count of the number of characterless stations we had shuddered to a halt at) and battled for the door. My

40 polyglot companions were changing trains for the Middle East and I helped them pass their considerable quantity of luggage through the window onto the platform. Rather smugly, I said goodbye to them in their own languages. They

45 looked baffled, and replied in French. I wandered down the platform, barely awake. The strange alphabet gave me no clue where to go. I wondered what the hell I was doing there.

5 Which of the following features are used in the passage?

a	a change of place or focus	e	feelings
b	clear organisation of events	f	images
		g	a conclusion
c	human interest	h	humour
d	dialogue	i	a use of contrast
		j	suspense

Are they used successfully? How?

6 Write an account of your own journey in about 300 words. Your main aim is to keep the reader interested.

LEXIS

Collocation – adverb/adjective

Adjectives, especially **qualitative adjectives**, are often preceded by an **adverb** (**submodifier**) which adds something to the meaning of the adjective. The most common (and least interesting) is *very* as in **very** *good*.

Although many variations are possible (*bitterly disappointed/upset/disputed* etc.), some combinations are more common than others. Some are impossible, or at least sound very odd, for example, *greatly lost, highly depressed*.

Intensifiers

These intensify the meaning of the adjective, for example, *shockingly beautiful* (READING 1). Here are some common combinations:

critically ill	*highly thought of/ praised*
deeply depressed/hurt	*hopelessly lost*
eminently successful/ practical	*infinitely patient/ superior*
extraordinarily beautiful	*radically new/changed*
greatly exaggerated	*wildly original/funny*
heavily underlined/ made up	*wonderfully irreverent*

Some of the most commonly used informal intensifiers in British English are:
dead simple/easy (slang)
really complicated/ill (informal)
bloody stupid/awful (impolite)

1 Find suitable adjectives to combine with these intensifiers:

amazingly	incredibly
dangerously	particularly
dreadfully	remarkably
horribly	seriously

2 Reducing adjectives

Some submodifiers reduce the intensity of an adjective, for example, *slightly damaged*.

a Find contexts in which you could use some of the following:

faintly	quite *
reasonably	rather *
mildly	fairly *
somewhat	pretty (informal) *
moderately	

b Notice that the four adverbs on the right above * can also be used as intensifiers, depending on the context. It also depends on the use of stress and intonation. Practise saying them with an adjective (for example, *good*) as a reducing adverb and then as an intensifier. How does the stress/intonation change?

3 Indicating extent

This smaller group of submodifiers indicates the extent of the quality described by the adjective.

a In what context could you use these examples?

primarily concerned	perfectly ridiculous
largely correct	purely theoretical
partly covered	utterly preposterous

b Think of other submodifiers that might go in this group.

Note that *perfectly, purely* and *utterly* function more colloquially as intensifiers. *Absolutely* and *completely* are the most commonly used adverbs of this sort.

4 Idiomatic intensifiers

Here are some common informal or idiomatic collocations. Match the intensifier on the left with the adjective on the right.

Think of a context in which you could use each one.

bone	naked
dog	idle
red	cheap
freezing	tired
raving	clear
crystal	hot
painfully	obvious
blindingly	slow
stark	mad
dirt	cold

1 Before reading the following text, think about these two questions.

  a Why would anyone want to milk a camel?

  b What practical difficulties might be involved with camel milking?

2 Now read the text in order to see if your answers to the two questions were right.

  What connections can you see between this text and the one in READING 1?

Camel milking

1 Milking a camel is not an easy exercise: the teats are small and almost five feet from the ground, which makes the obvious method of 5 milking into a bucket placed on the ground quite farcical. Instead the Somalis have developed a technique whereby the milker stands on one leg. By balancing a specially shaped milk- 10 ing vessel on his raised knee and supporting its rim between his forearms he can easily squirt the milk into the container with his fingers. This is surprisingly efficient but the 15 success of the milking operation does depend to a large extent on the co-operation of the camel.

If treated kindly, camels are well behaved and even-tempered 20 creatures. As a result of the doting care bestowed upon them by the Somalis, they readily respond to individual names. Approached to be milked, a camel will nuzzle the 25 man's head to establish his identity.

If she recognises him as her owner, she will stand untethered in one spot until the milking is finished and she is reunited with her calf.

30 I had been introduced a few days earlier to the family's herd of thirty she-camels and four gelded loading camels. But despite having herded the animals as a mob, my attempt to 35 milk the camel now before me was my first intimate contact.

Aadan greeted me with disdain. After giving a conciliatory pat, I adopted the milking position 40 (practised earlier without the camel). Everything appeared promising and even my audience of Somalis were impressed to a hush as I began to milk. Unfortunately two 45 squirts was all I achieved. Aadan, obviously feeling that she had co-operated enough, was off. I dropped my raised leg to regain balance, the milking vessel landed upturned in 50 the sand and the Somalis roared with triumphant glee. Aadan came to a halt some yards away and,

determined not to lose face, I approached again. After a second 55 unsuccessful attempt, I finally managed to fill the container with a respectable quantity of frothy milk.

My audience, unprepared for even this small success, sought to try me 60 once more. As a guest I was invited to be the first to drink from the vessel but, having taken the customary mouthfuls, instead of passing the milk to others I was 65 encouraged to drain the contents myself.

Although rich and of strong flavour, camel's milk is fortunately smooth and easily drunk but it has 70 hidden powers. Consumed fresh and in quantity, the milk is renowned for its loosening of the bowels. Unaware of this at the time, for the remainder of the day I was mystified 75 by the constant enquiries as to my 'condition'. Having passed the day unaffected by such problems, my standing amongst the Somalis rose considerably.

World Magazine

3 What is the connection between these two phrases in the article:

to lose face (line 53)

my standing amongst the Somalis rose considerably (last line)

4 Find words in the text with similar meaning to the words below.

a ridiculous	f untied
b edge	g contempt
c pour	h friendly
d loving	i container
e caress	j empty

5 How many adverb/adjective combinations can you find in the text? Do you think these are strong collocations?

6 a What is similar about the sentence structures in the last paragraph?

b How could the four sentences in this paragraph be re-written using different structures?

c Would this revision be an improvement or not in your opinion? Give reasons.

LEXIS

1 Collocation – types of travelling
Match the adjectives on the left with the most appropriate noun on the right.

seasoned	
commercial	
fellow	flight
maiden	journey
safe	cruise
chartered	crossing
reconnaissance	traveller
scheduled	voyage
round-the-world	passenger
rough/smooth	

2 Connotation
a What do all the following nouns have in common?

> outsider   misfit   foreigner   alien   stranger
> eccentric   crank   loner   laughing stock
> outcast   expatriate   refugee   recluse

b Group them into smaller categories of similar meanings. Are there any which you cannot fit into any category?

c Decide which might be potentially offensive in attitude.

3 Add words of similar meaning to this list. Be aware of any differences in context and connotation.

> friendship   hospitality   kindness

GRAMMAR

Perfect aspect

1 Look at these sentences from READING 2 and the WRITING section passage. What do the underlined verbs have in common?

I had been on the train for three days and had traversed Europe from north-west to south-east.

An Australian I'd talked to briefly in Venice came up to me.

Instead, the Somalis have developed a technique whereby the milker stands on one leg. . .

I had been introduced a few days earlier to the family's herd of 30 she-camels.

Explain the reasons for the form used in each of the underlined verbs.

2 Look at the following table which shows the uses of both the present and past perfect. Decide which of the types, 1 a, b, c or 2 a, b, c, fits each of the following examples. The first one has been done for you.

Example

		Type
1	I've owned a Ferrari for 10 years.	1a
2	I'd been on the train for three days.	☐
3	and had traversed Europe. . .	☐
4	There's been a serious accident on the M25.	☐
5	I've lost my glasses.	☐
6	The Somalis have developed a technique. . .	☐
7	He had seen the bank manager before buying the flat.	☐
8	They've returned every year since then.	☐
9	Have you ever had malaria?	☐
10	I'd lived in the same house for most of my life.	☐

1 Present perfect	2 Past perfect
a a state or habitual action begun in the past and extending over a period to the present (and perhaps into the future). Example *I've lived here for three years. She's had that funny walk all her life. She's often been to see him at weekends.*	a a state or habitual action which began before a specified time in the past and continued up to that time (and perhaps beyond). Example *I'd been in the country for several weeks before I met Dimitri. Politicians who had called repeatedly for a full enquiry were furious at the government's refusal to explain its actions.*
b an event that happened at an unspecified time in the past during a time period leading up to the present. Example *Have you been to Somalia? I've heard that you're going to retire.*	b a past event that happened at some point during a time period *leading up to* another *more recent* past event. The time may be mentioned. Example *He mentioned a programme he'd listened to on the radio the previous evening. Before I went on a walking holiday to the Himalayas I'd never climbed anything higher than the stairs to my flat. They'd met in 1982 but it wasn't until five years later that they got together to found the company.*
c an action in the past where the emphasis is on the result in the present. We often use the present perfect to report news. Example *I've broken my leg.* (that's why it is now in plaster) *There's been another bomb scare in central London.*	c an event which happened *just* before another event in the past. Often used to give reasons for subsequent events. Example *I'd spent nearly an hour looking for somewhere to park and arrived hot and flustered. The next morning he came down to breakfast looking awful and complained that he hadn't slept a wink all night.*

b Now look at these contrasting examples which correspond with each of the sentences, 1–10 in part **a** of this exercise. Decide what difference in meaning is caused by the change of tense, or why the second example is impossible in the context.

Contrast

1 I owned a Ferrari for 10 years.
2 I was on the train for three days.
3 and was traversing Europe. . .
4 There was a serious accident on the M25.
5 I lost my glasses.
6 The Somalis developed a technique. . .
7 He saw the bank manager before buying the flat.
8 They returned every year after that.
9 Did you ever have malaria?
10 I was living in the same house for most of my life.

Note 1: The past perfect can never be used without first establishing a past time (using a past simple or continuous). The past perfect indicates a step back further into the past.

Note 2: The past perfect is used only to help clarify the sequence of events or to emphasise them. If context or lexis (e.g. 'before') already make this clear, we can often stay with the past simple. For example, in the two example sentences in **2c** on page 118, the first would still be clear with a past simple (*I spent. . .*) but the second would not (*he didn't sleep. . .*) – this could mean that he never slept on any night.

3 In the following sentences, put the verbs in brackets into the past simple or past perfect. In how many examples is it possible to use either tense while still keeping the sequence of events clear?

a When we finally .... (*return*) home, we .... (*do*) a couple of hundred miles.

b When the time for our appointment .... (*pass*) and he still .... (*not arrive*), someone .... (*suggest*) that perhaps he .... (*have*) an accident.

c The sun .... (*set*) and the tourists long since .... (*disappear*) from the beaches when Simon slowly .... (*push*) his bicycle home.

d They .... (*buy*) a new car after they .... (*win*) some money.

e I eventually .... (*sell*) my stamp collection. I .... (*cease*) to be interested in collecting since I .... (*be*) at University.

4 Say whether the following sentences are correct, as they stand, in their use of tense. If they are wrong, explain why.

a I've seen her this morning.
b I'm living here since last month.
c I was starving. It was days since I had a good meal.
d He had come in after he knocked.
e It's a good few days since I last saw you.
f He told me he had been blind ever since an accident when he was a child.
g The Greek philosophers, notably Plato and Aristotle, have had a lasting effect on the way we view the material world.
h Shakespeare has written a number of poems as well as the more famous plays.
i I've just sold my old computer. She gave me £200 for it.

Present perfect continuous

The difference between perfect simple and perfect continuous is similar to that between other simple and continuous verbs (see UNIT 7 GRAMMAR page 84).

However with the present perfect, it should also be noted that the difference between continuous and simple is often one of emphasis rather than a radical difference in meaning.

Example
I've lived here all my life.
I've been living here all my life.

LEXIS

1 Adverb/adjective collocation

Supply a collocating adverb to intensify the adjectives in the following sentences.

a He was hurt by her criticisms.

b Many were able to walk away from the accident but those who were injured were taken to the nearby hospital.

c Mark Twain claimed that reports of his death had been exaggerated.

d I'm sorry.

e The interior of the theatre has been redesigned.

f After wandering around for what seemed like hours, they realised that they were lost.

g Although a(n) successful lawyer, his personal life was a mess.

h As a journalist, she always feels it is her duty to avoid stating obvious facts.

2 Match the adverbs on the left with a collocating adjective on the right.

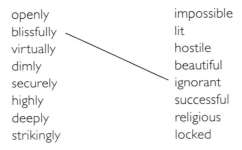

openly	impossible
blissfully	lit
virtually	hostile
dimly	beautiful
securely	ignorant
highly	successful
deeply	religious
strikingly	locked

3 Verb/noun collocation

Use your dictionary to find collocating verbs for these idiomatic pairs of nouns.

a in dribs and drabs

b hammer and tongs

c heaven and earth

d hook, line and sinker

e ifs and buts

f life and limb

g man to man

h every nook and cranny

i rack and ruin

4 Synonymy

It is often argued that there is no such thing as a **synonym**: every word is different from its apparent synonyms on account of collocation, connotation, register, etc. Use a dictionary to help you find differences between the following sets of words.

a farcical, ridiculous, absurd, preposterous

b edge, rim, border, margin, verge, brim

c container, vessel, box, tin, carton, packet

d caress, nuzzle, stroke, pat

e pour, spill, squirt, sprinkle, slop

5 Idiomatic intensifiers

Use a suitable intensifier to complete the following passage.

She looked at her husband contemptuously, 'You're [1] .... idle,' she said. 'It's [2] .... cold outside, I've been working hard all day, I'm [3] .... tired and I come home to see you sitting there as if you haven't moved a muscle since I left you this morning!'

He looked at her, hurt and confused, and then something inside him suddenly snapped. 'Are you [4] .... mad, woman?' he snarled, 'I've only just got back from town where I was looking for a heater for YOU!'

'Oh, so where is it then?' she enquired, a little less sure of herself. She looked around the room in expectation and caught sight of a small box next to her husband's chair. 'It surely can't be that tiny little thing there, Ron?'

'What's a matter with it? The larger ones were far too expensive,' he said, somewhat sheepishly. 'Ron, I checked the prices on Saturday. They were [5] .... cheap – there's a sale on at the moment ... Now I understand – it's all becoming [6] .... clear to me where *you've* been. You've been to the betting shop, haven't you, spending all my hard-earned money!'

---

6 Select the correct word from those given to complete each of these sentences.

1 Graham Greene, the novelist, has often written stories about English people who have chosen to live abroad. The novel *The Heart of the Matter* tells of one such .... living in Sierra Leone.
a) foreigner b) expatriate c) eccentric

2 In the later years of her life, Greta Garbo fulfilled her desire 'to be alone' and lived as a(n) .... in her apartment block, rarely going outside her door.
a) refugee b) recluse c) eccentric

3 The film E.T. tells the story of a(n) .... from outer space who comes to earth and befriends a young child.
a) alien b) outcast c) foreigner

4 The plot of most Westerns shows a mysterious but benevolent .... coming to town to take on the forces of evil, often in the form of a corrupt sheriff or wealthy landowner.
a) outsider b) stranger c) outcast

5 The film director Roman Polanski was a Jewish .... during the war. He fled the ghettos of Warsaw and escaped to freedom as a young boy.
a) outsider b) outcast c) refugee

6 Quentin Crisp is often seen as the archetypal British................ . He lives in New York, he has mauve hair and an unusual, flamboyant taste in clothes.
a) eccentric b) laughing stock c) crank

GRAMMAR

Perfect aspect

1 Put the verbs in brackets into an appropriate tense. Justify your choices.

a I .... (buy) this CD last year and I only ....(listen) to it once.

b I just .... (read) a wonderful book by Mario Vargas Llosa. You .... (hear) of him?

c It .... (be) wet and windy for the last few days.

d The dreadful condition of the railways in this country often .... (criticise – passive).

e I always .... (feel) that more competition between the airlines would lower fares. Recent experiments with this .... (prove) me right.

f Many people .... (lose) their jobs since the recession .... (start).

g Inflation .... (fall) to 4% in December since

when it .... (remain) fairly static.

h I .... (not go) to the dentist since October when he .... (give) me a clean bill of health.

i Ever since I .... (see) that film I .... (be) interested in boxing.

j He................ (work) on this project for twenty years, during which time he .... (make) an outstanding contribution to our understanding of the subject.

2 The perfect continuous

Decide what difference in meaning or emphasis is conveyed by the change in tense in the following pairs of sentences.

a I've been writing a letter to the bank manager.
I've written a letter to the bank manager.

b I'd been walking for nearly two hours when I finally reached the garage.
I'd walked for nearly two hours when I finally reached the garage.

c The English team has been playing well this season.
The English team has played well this season.

d How have you been getting on?
How have you got on?

e I've been living in Banbury for the last few months.
I've lived in Banbury for the last few months.

f It's been snowing overnight.
It's snowed overnight.

g Sharon's been spending all her money on John again.
Sharon's spent all her money on John again.

h What have you been doing?
What have you done?

i I've just been watching a rather strange programme.
I've just watched a rather strange programme.

j Who's drunk my coffee?
Who's been drinking my coffee?

FOCUS

> ' *Doctors pour drugs of which they know little, to cure diseases of which they know less, into human beings of whom they know nothing.*'

Voltaire

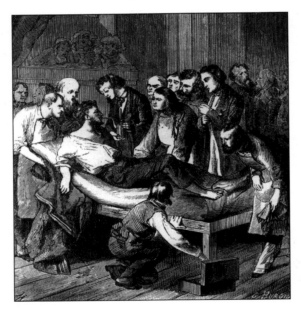

1 Do you think the statement above is as true today as it was when Voltaire wrote it? Give reasons for your opinion.

2 Countries which have a state health service spend billions of pounds per annum on it. Do you think this is money well spent? Why (not)?

3 In small groups, answer these questions. If you can answer 'yes' to any of them, tell the others about it. Have you ever:

   been in hospital?
   tried homeopathy or herbal remedies?
   watched an operation?
   visited a hospital or health centre in a poor country?
   wanted to be a doctor/nurse?

LEXIS

Disease and treatment

1 Look at the words in the box below and sort them into four categories:
   a diseases
   b causes
   c treatment
   d prevention

virus	typhoid	physiotherapy
malaria	injection	cholera
leprosy	inoculation	blood-transfusion
tuberculosis	polio	contagion
anaesthetic	amputation	germ
immunisation	bacteria	carcinogen
first aid	measles	

2 What is the difference between *a surgeon, a pathologist, a GP (General Practitioner), a physician* and *a consultant*?

3 What do these verbs have in common?

treat	cure	recover	heal
revive	convalesce	resuscitate	

How are they different? Use your dictionary to help you. What changes, if any, are needed to make them nouns?

4 In what medical circumstances could you use these phrasal verbs: *pull through, come round, patch up*?

READING 1

I Read the following extract which refers several times to 'the JR'. What is 'the JR'?

1 A look at the John Radcliffe points up the problems. The JR is widely considered an efficient but chilly machine for medicine, huge, complex, impersonal and apparently not much liked by the staff, many of whom
5 hark nostalgically back to the cramped county hospital feel of the old Infirmary. [1] .... it seems oddly topsy-turvy, with its entrance at one end and car parks at the other. [2] .... a major airport in all its comprehensive variety, it contains
10 shops and restaurants, an industrial block and art studio, sports facilities, a bank, a hairdresser, several social workers and, underneath, a miniature road system. [3] .... it also has something of the atmosphere of an international airport, its broad
15 corridors dotted with padded seats like those in departure lounges and that same sense of distant bustle and repressed anxiety.
     [4] .... on the lower levels are the blood and guts – the hospital's ten operating theatres.
20 [5] .... all is bright, ticking intensity under the scrutiny of cameras; many of the twenty or so daily operations are filmed for research purposes. Cloth-bound surgical instrument packs ('the big ones to get you in, the others for detail,' the orderlies
25 bluffly tell you), are sent in sharp and shiny, emerging bloodied in canisters to be dunked, shaken ultrasonically and steam-sterilised before being flung back once more into the fray. But this is the grim old sawbones side of the hospital. [6] .... its
30 new high tech face gleams down – the giant body scanner into which patients are fed as if into the drum of a huge washing machine, or the new Institute of Molecular Medicine, a kind of hotel for research in whose suites specialist teams plumb the cellular levels
35 of disease.
     [7] ...., almost everything seems represented here, from the sprains and smashes of accident and emergency to the haggard recovering suicides on the Barnes ward, from the comfy
40 contiguity of Maternity's mother-and-child cubicles to the bright, sad colours of the children's wards. The JR

is in fact three hospitals – maternity, general and cardiac – and will in the course of time become more. It has virology and haematology, it has histopathology
45 and cytology and a mystification of other -ologies. It houses ten university departments, a suite of lecture halls and the prestigious Cairns Medical Library. It even has a Bereavement Officer, a warm-hearted lady in a cosy bower of cushions who counsels up to thirty
50 grieving relatives a week.
     Its statistics are staggering. [8] ...., if you include students and outpatients, some 3,000 will go to work there and 8,000–9,000 be treated. In the course of a year it will patch up 54,000 accident
55 victims and deliver 6,000 babies. Each week its seven kitchens dish up 190 lbs of frozen peas, 42 kilos of dry jelly crystals, 313 lbs of potatoes and 294 lbs of Smash. [9] .... its pipes stream 26,000 gallons of water every twenty minutes. It holds
60 thousands of sheets and blankets and literally millions of medical records (mostly microfilmed and tended round the clock by 236 staff). 'If this is a hotel,' commented the hospital's Head of Hotel Services, 'it is one hell of a hotel.' [10] .... too are its
65 costs: currently it gets through over £35 million a year, nearly a quarter of the local area health authority budget. And here we come to the nub of the problem. The JR is chronically short of cash. In spite of the most careful trimming and balancing, the hospital's
70 spending has invariably surpassed its income in recent years.

2 Fill the gaps in the text with these words:

Externally	Staggering
Down	Like
Through	Medically
Internally	Here
Elsewhere	Every day

3 How could you describe the style of this extract? Choose from the following or use adjectives of your own.

formal	academic	ironic	humorous
literary	chatty	sensational	

Find passages from the text to support your answer.

4 Work in pairs.
   a Decide which aspects of this text would be most useful for you to study further. Consider the following:
   - sentence structure
   - cohesion and coherence
   - vocabulary (which?)
   - metaphors and comparisons
   - the writer's aims

   b Work on your chosen area together. Decide on the best method of studying.

   c When you have finished, report back to the rest of the class on what you have learned.

5 With your partner or group, say if there are any parts of the text which you particularly like or dislike. Give reasons.

GRAMMAR

Fronting

1 What is similar about the word order of these sentences?
   a In the garden, the flowers were starting to bloom.
   b Staggering too are its costs: …
   c One of the letters he sent immediately. The other he kept for a while in case he changed his mind.
   d What I like to do on my days off is sit and read a good book.
   e It is waiting around in the cold that I hate most about this job.

2 **a** What do you think is the purpose of this particular word order?

   b Do any of the examples in exercise 1 sound strange to you?

   c Rewrite the examples in exercise 1 in what you would consider a more usual word order.

3 In the following short passages, decide whether the underlined item is in an appropriate position in the sentence. Consider register, the relationship with surrounding sentences, and the focus of attention within the sentence itself.
   a Recordings by Pavarotti have become best-sellers. <u>Popular</u>, <u>too</u>, are his rare live concerts.
   b It was a tall, grey building. It was surprisingly small <u>inside</u>.
   c <u>What you do next is</u> add a pinch of salt and a handful of chopped parsley.
   d Don't talk to me like that. <u>Never</u> have I been so insulted.
   e 'She's always buying *Cosmopolitan.*'
      'No, it's <u>*Woman's Own*</u> that Caroline buys.'

4 In the following examples:
   - what do the fronted items have in common?
   - what happens to the subject/verb word order?

   a *At no time must these children be allowed near the road.*
   b *Scarcely had I started when there was a terrific noise.*
   c *No longer will animals be able to roam freely in this area.*
   d *Seldom did a week pass without a request for information on the matter.*

5 Rewrite the following sentences starting with the words given.
   a He left school and immediately got a job at a hospital.
      No sooner…
   b He got home late. Then he realised he'd left his keys at work.
      He got home late. Only then…
   c She not only worked longer hours than her father but also earned considerably more.
      Not only...
   d You won't find a better health service than this.
      Nowhere…
   e You seldom find two such dedicated workers in one place.
      Seldom...

6 Read this passage and decide if 'fronting' any items, or changing the word order in any other way, would make it clearer.

> The many arguments about 'alternative' medicine rage back and forth. Is 'alternative' the right word, looking at terminology, for example, or would 'complementary' be better? Can the different traditions learn from each other or are they all mutually exclusive? Unqualified practitioners can be another problem, from the point of view of reliability, since so many 'alternative' medicines do not have universally recognised qualifications or professional representation. The problems do not end there, either. Should the 'alternative' methods, financially, receive state funding in the same way as traditional western medicine? And should, if this is agreed, doctors be free to send their patients to an acupuncturist as part of their treatment? If not, why not? Legion are the questions and legion and complex the answers.

LISTENING 1

1 What do you know about *acupuncture*? In groups or as a class, find out how much you know about the following points.

  a What is acupuncture?

  b How does it work?

  c What medical problems can it be used to help?

  d Is it an alternative to Western scientific medicine or can it be used to complement it?

  e How can you prove it works?

2 Listen to this interview with a practising acupuncturist.

  a How many of the questions in exercise 1 does she answer?

  b How fully does she answer them?

3 Listen again in order to answer these questions.

  a What is the point of her comment, *when we catch a cold we don't generally die*?

  b What are *meridians*?

  c What does *psychosomatic* mean?

4 Has your opinion of acupuncture been changed by listening to this interview? If so, how?

LEXIS

Idioms on health

1 Divide these idiomatic phrases into those that deal with good or improving health, and those that deal with bad or deteriorating health.

	Good/ Improving Health	Bad/ Deteriorating Health
a She's on the mend.	☐	☐
b I feel on top of the world.	☐	☐
c I'm in pretty good shape these days.	☐	☐
d You look a bit below par.	☐	☐
e She went home because she felt a bit under the weather.	☐	☐
f What happened? You look in a bad way.	☐	☐
g I think I'm coming down with something.	☐	☐
h She's over the worst now.	☐	☐
i He's getting over it.	☐	☐
j I think I'm running a temperature.	☐	☐
k You look a bit run down.	☐	☐

2 How many of these idioms are metaphorical?

1 Skim through the following text in order to find out what the author thinks of acupuncture. What other types of 'fringe' medicine does he mention?

Nonconformists, Mystics, Charlatans and Cranks

1 There is a marvellous variety of fringe medicine theories and techniques, offering wildly disparate explanations for our human ills, and for the 'efficacy' of the many and widely differing cure-alls available.
5 ....¹ *any* of them contain some element of truth, they can't *all* be right. Your migraine or asthma *might* be due to an imbalance between the Yin and the Yang, as the acupuncturists would have us believe, or it *might* be the result of 'pressure on the nerves'
10 caused by a misalignment of a strangely rickety spinal column (as a chiropractor would maintain). Both hypotheses are fancy-bred, ...², even to a believer in the absurd, both can't be true. ....³, practitioners of fringe therapies achieve remarkably
15 similar success rates, whatever the nature of their beliefs. ....⁴, this logical dilemma doesn't prevent a fair proportion of unorthodox healers using, ...⁵, acupuncture, and homeopathy, and naturopathy, or whatever – anything, ...⁶ it
20 isn't in the official rule book. They like to make a great play of treating the whole person, ...⁷ not just the disease, emphasising their superiority, in this respect, over your average proper doctor. The best proper doctors.............⁸ adopt this
25 approach, recognising that a living organism is greater than the sum of its parts, but the term 'holistic medicine' has recently been hijacked by the fringes as a blanket term to categorise their peculiar brand of thinking about disease. It has
30 overtaken 'fringe' and 'alternative' as the preferred epithet for dissident doctoring.

All this suggests that all fringe practitioners and all 'unscientific' therapies exploit a shared and powerful healing force which is quite apart from
35 the particular theories and procedures involved, and to which needling, backslapping, and other ceremonies are merely ritual ornaments. ....⁹, there is a strong bond of sympathy between all kinds of unorthodox healers, based upon an 'us'
40 against 'them' communion (.............¹⁰ in the case of osteopaths and chiropractors, who hate each other's guts because, like Protestants and Catholics, they only differ in the details of their beliefs).

A majority of healers, just like their customers, have
45 sincerely espoused the ideas and practice they sell. A substantial minority know full well that they are preaching rubbish and exploiting credulity and fear for vulgar gain. ....¹¹ they are accomplished actors, the members of the second category benefit
50 their clients just as effectively as the members of the first.

The Black and White Medicine Show

2 Put these words in the appropriate gaps in the text. You may use each item more than once.

however	say	but	moreover	and
so long as	also	indeed	except	even if

3 a What adjectives in the text collocate with these nouns?

    rates (line 15)   minority (line 46)   gain (line 48)

   b What adverbs collocate with these adjectives?
   • differing (line 4)
   • similar (line 15)

4 What words does the author use to indicate the strength of his feelings about 'fringe' medicine?

5 What other linguistic means apart from strong vocabulary does he use to show his opinions?

6 What attempts, if any, does he make to present a balanced view?

7 Do you agree with the view expressed in this text?

LEXIS

Discourse markers

One way of guiding a reader around a text, or helping a speaker understand the relevance of what you are saying, is to use words or phrases which explicitly indicate the purpose of what you are about to say. These are often called **discourse markers** since they act as signposts, or markers, in the discourse. You looked at some of these in UNIT 9 (page 103 and 106).

1 Put the discourse markers seen in exercise **2** on page 126 in the appropriate places in the chart below, according to their function in the reading passage. Decide if each one is used mainly in written or spoken English or both.

Function	Examples	Spoken/Written
Showing cause or effect		
Introducing a contrast or alternative	however, but	Spoken + written
Qualifying a statement	but	
Giving an example		
Introducing conditions		
Correcting other statements	however, but	
Emphasising the truth of your statement		
Adding new information		
Making exceptions	but	
Indicating a change of topic		
Indicating that something will happen despite problems		

2 Categorise the discourse markers in bold in the following text according to their function. Put them in the chart above.

¹**Whilst** Henry knew exactly what I had done, I was ²**nevertheless** unconvinced by his assurances that he would never reveal our little secret. ³**As a matter of fact** he made me even more nervous when he tried to be nice to me. ⁴**Apart from** him, nobody else knew and ⁵**furthermore**, nobody could ever get to know if he were not around. I thought about it for months, I began to study his movements obsessively so as to know exactly where he would be at any given moment. ⁶**In fact**, the more I watched him, the more I came to realise how incredibly easy it would be to get rid of him. He seldom departed from his routine and ⁷**provided** he continued in the same way, it would be plain sailing.

⁸**Anyway**, eventually the day I had been waiting for came, it was bright but windy and the sea was quite rough: perfect conditions.

'I shall be in Lymington all afternoon,' Henry announced. 'Oh and ⁹**by the way**, Paul has invited me round this evening.' He smiled as he spoke, 'You don't mind Sheila, do you?'

I smiled and shook my head. ¹⁰**On the contrary**, I was delighted. Paul was ¹¹**indeed** a friend, he could not have done more to assist me in Henry's demise had he been a knowing accomplice. Paul's cottage was conveniently placed on the cliffs overlooking White Head Cove, and ¹²**whereas** our bungalow was on lower lying land which gave way gently to the sandy ridges of the beach, his had a much more spectacular view.

Paul and Henry were old school friends who often ate together and chatted about the old days. Henry infuriated me because he was always so shy and predictable. Paul, ¹³**on the other hand**, was something of an older brother figure, mischievous and jolly, ¹⁴**yet** at the same time highly astute.

I phoned Paul's cottage about 8.00, under the pretext of having lost something, to ensure that Henry was there. He sounded loud and in good spirits and assured me that he would return around 12.00, ¹⁵**thereby** confirming to me that there would be no problems and that I could proceed as planned.

3 In the sentences below, decide whether the right discourse marker is being used. If not, correct it. Consider whether an appropriate register is being used, as well as thinking about the meaning of the sentence.

a 'I bet Cambridge won the boat race this afternoon.'
'*As a matter of fact*, they lost again.'

b You have now reached retirement age and *yet* qualify for a pension.

c Computers, VCRs and so on have become much easier to produce since the invention of the microchip and *on the other hand* cheaper.

d The government said that it would provide greater health care services *whereas in fact* the number of people not being treated promptly has grown.

e Doctors should only prescribe drugs *provided* they are convinced there is no simpler treatment available.

f I'm very short of money this week *whilst* you owe me £30.

g Many people vigorously support the provision of 'alternative' medicine on the National Health Service. *On the contrary* this is opposed with equal vigour by many doctors.

h She was caught cheating in the semi-final, *thereby* forfeiting her place in the final line-up.

i He spent the night sleeplessly. *Nevertheless*, he was up and ready to go at dawn.

j 'It's a lovely morning, isn't it?'
'It is *indeed*.'

LISTENING 2

1 How far has medical science improved in the last one hundred years? In small groups, list as many advances as you can.
Example
open heart surgery

2 Listen to this argument about how far medical science has advanced. What are the main arguments on each side? Which point of view do you most agree with?

3 Listen again to the first part of the argument and this time fill in the following flow chart by noting the main points of what is said. The main spoken discourse markers are given.

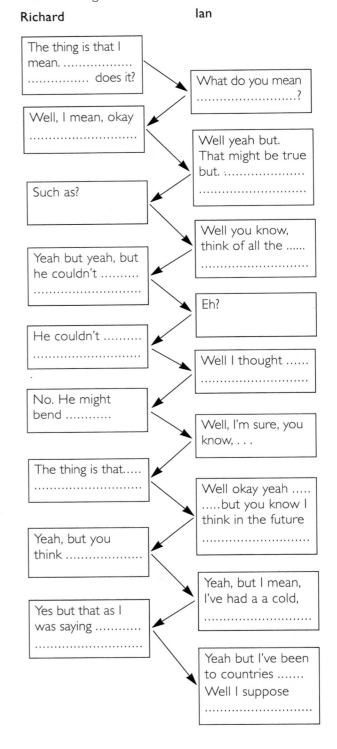

Richard   Ian

The thing is that I mean. .... does it?

What do you mean ....?

Well, I mean, okay ....

Well yeah but. That might be true but. ....

Such as?

Well you know, think of all the ....

Yeah but yeah, but he couldn't ....

Eh?

He couldn't ....

Well I thought ....

No. He might bend ....

Well, I'm sure, you know, . . .

The thing is that..... ....

Well okay yeah ....but you know I think in the future ....

Yeah, but you think ....

Yeah, but I mean, I've had a a cold, ...

Yes but that as I was saying ....

Yeah but I've been to countries .... Well I suppose ....

4 Now using your notes and the given discourse markers, re-enact the argument in pairs. Try to achieve the same argumentative tone and pace as the recording.

SPEAKING

1 Working in small groups decide which of the two speakers in LISTENING 2 you agree with most. Look at the arguments used and decide in your groups how they could be improved and what other arguments you could use to improve the point.

2 Now get together with a group which has prepared the opposing point of view. Try to persuade them that you are right and they are wrong.

3 When you have finished, answer the following questions.

   a How polite were you when disagreeing?

   b Did you simply contradict people or did you try to persuade them?

   c Did you listen to the other's points or did you simply try to make your own?

   d Did you interrupt a lot?

   e Did you ever feel frustrated during the discussion? If so, when and why?

   f Was anyone too deferential or too assertive?

4 Listen again to the recording.

   a How good were the two people at listening and arguing?

   b What language did they use to disagree?

   c How well do you think they know each other?

Pronunciation of unstressed words

5 Look at this extract from the argument in LISTENING 2.

   a Mark the stressed words. Then check with the recording to see if you agree.

   Yes but that as I was saying this is this is because of improvements for example in diet. People are so much more healthy. The more healthy we are then the better your chances are of fighting the disease and the disease not taking over.

   b How are the underlined words pronounced? Why do you think words are underlined in pairs or groups and not individually?

   c Practise saying the phrases a few times as they are said on the recording.

6 In the text below, most of the unstressed words have been omitted.

Chiropractor ....[1] term applied ....[2] person ....[3] practises chiropractic. This ....[4] system ....[5] adjustment ....[6] hand ....[7] minor displacements ....[8] spinal column. These ....[9] displacements, ...[10] subluxations ....[11] spine, chiropractors contend, affect ....[12] associated or neighbouring nerves. ....[13] claim ....[14] chiropractic is ....[15] manipulating ....[16] affected part ....[17] spinal column ....[18] patient's complaint, whatever ....[19] may be – ....[20], backache – is relieved.

a Fill the gaps with appropriate words. (There may be more than one word per gap.)

b Listen to the recording and fill in the remaining gaps.

c Practise reading the whole text a few times, paying careful attention to stressed and unstressed words.

WRITING

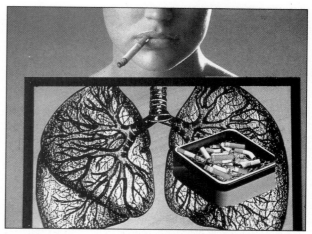

The following text contains no grammatical errors but its style, organisation, register and sentence structures are far from ideal.

Rewrite it as part of a government leaflet aimed at encouraging people to stop smoking. This leaflet would be read, for example, by people waiting in doctors' waiting rooms. The style should therefore be direct and to the point, neither too chatty nor too formal.

'Reasons of health. That's why you should give up smoking. It's the best reason. If you smoke you're twice as likely to keel over from coronary heart disease (heart attack) as somebody that doesn't smoke. Here are some statistics. Of 1000 young men who smoke regularly, the average works out at something like this. One will be murdered. Six will be killed on the roads. 250 will be killed by tobacco-related diseases. Not only this heart attack business either. There's strokes, cancer (e.g. of the lung, mouth, throat, bladder, pancreas, and other bits) and emphysema. Impotence, moreover, in men and infertility in women. They've also been linked to smoking. And bronchitis, by the way. What happens if you give up is this. Oxygen instead of carbon monoxide is what your blood gets. Thus your blood is less likely to clot. Thus your heart isn't having to strain so much. Your body, gradually, gets back to normal. In maybe as little as five years. And you don't smell like an old ashtray.'

LEXIS

1 Medical vocabulary

Fill the gaps in the following encyclopaedia entry with the words in the box.

infection	immunity	antibodies
cough	debilitating	fatigue
common cold	subside	epidemics
illness	outbreaks	chills
respiratory	symptoms	brought on
sore	virus	

Influenza

A viral [1].............. of the respiratory tract (air passages) that causes fever, headache, muscle ache, and weakness. Popularly known as 'flu', it is spread by [2].............. infected droplets coughed or sneezed into the air. Influenza usually occurs in small [3].............. or every few years in [4].............. . Outbreaks tend to occur in winter, rapidly spreading, especially in schools and institutions for the elderly.

Causes

There are three main types of influenza virus, called A, B and C. A person who has had an attack caused by the type C virus acquires [5].............. (proteins made by the immune system) that provide [6].............. against the type C virus for life. Anyone who has been infected with a particular strain of the type A or B viruses acquires immunity to that strain. Both the A and B type viruses occasionally alter to produce new strains that may be able to overcome immunity built up in response to a previous attack, thus leading to a new infection.
The classic [7].............. of flu ([8].............., fever, headache, muscular aches, loss of appetite, and [9]..............) are [10].............. by types A and B. Type C causes only a mild [11].............. that is indistinguishable from a [12].............. . In general, type A is more [13].............. than type B.
The general symptoms described, which are more common in adults than in children, are usually followed by a [14].............. (often accompanied by chest pain), a [15].............. throat, and a runny nose. After two days, fever and other symptoms start to [16].............. and after, five days, these symptoms have usually disappeared. [17].............. symptoms persist, however; the sufferer may feel weak and sometimes depressed.

The British Medical Association Complete Family Health Encyclopaedia

2 Medical Quiz

1 Name three diseases which you are advised to be inoculated against if you go to India.
2 What are you given to make you go to sleep before an operation?
3 Which disease is transmitted by some mosquitoes?
4 What is the general name for a substance which can cause cancer?
5 Which disease, also known as *consumption*, affects a person's lungs?
6 What is *acupuncture*?
7 Which illness, common amongst children, covers the skin with red spots and is also known as *rubella*?
8 Which acute intestine infection, often fatal in nineteenth century Europe, is caused by drinking infected water or eating infected food?
9 What is the name of the treatment given to someone to help them to regain their ability to move, especially by the use of exercise?
10 What is a *chiropractor*?

3 Discourse markers

Use a dictionary to find the differences between the following sets of discourse markers. Differences may involve register, position in the sentence, meaning, strength and punctuation. Try to write an example sentence for those you are not sure about to check whether you have fully understood.

a even if	provided that	so long as
b thus	thereby	so
c however	but	though
d even so	nevertheless	and yet
e on the contrary		on the other hand

4 Insert these discourse markers in the text below as appropriate. Not all of them may be necessary. Aim to make the text clearer: the use of too many such markers can obscure the sense. Change the word order of the sentences if necessary.

although	while	however
even if	moreover	furthermore
above all	in fact	nevertheless
on the contrary	thus	so
and	yet	apart from
on the other hand	so as to	thereby

It is widely believed that medical science has been gradually and systematically reducing civilisation's diseases. People believe that ignorance and superstition combined to allow epidemics like the medieval plagues to take place. People think that during the 19th and 20th centuries scientists finally managed to discover what caused infectious diseases and began to cure them with drugs and immunisation. Improved technology and advances in anaesthesia enabled surgeons to carry out sophisticated operations. Penicillin and antibiotics helped complete the advance. Some people disagree. They point out that more credit ought to be given to social reformers who campaigned for purer water, better sewage disposal and improved living standards. The drugs and antibiotics merely speeded up the process. Their contribution was valuable. It did not lower the level of disease in general. Increasing numbers of people depend on drugs and doctors for meeting the ordinary problems of everyday life.

5 Explain the meaning of these words and phrases from the two reading texts in UNIT 11.
a *hark nostalgically back* (text 1)
b *a sense of distant bustle* (text 1)
c *under the scrutiny of cameras* (text 1)
d *flung back once more into the fray* (text 1)
e *tended round the clock* (text 1)
f *the nub of the problem* (text 1)
g *wildly disparate explanations* (text 2)
h *a blanket term* (text 2)
i *the preferred epithet* (text 2)
j *exploiting credulity* (text 2)

GRAMMAR

Focus

1 Change the word order of these sentences in as many ways as is possible in order to achieve a change of focus. You may also use the cleft sentence structure (see UNIT 3 page 33) or the structure prefaced by 'What …' ('What I am going to do is. . . '). Use the passive if you think there is a context for it. Make any other changes that are necessary.

Example

The doctor gave him a thorough examination.
What the doctor did was give him a thorough examination.
It was a thorough examination that the doctor gave him.
It was the doctor who gave him a thorough examination.
He was given a thorough examination by the doctor.
Gave him a thorough examination the doctor did.
What the doctor gave him was a thorough examination.

a I rarely take the car into town.
b I find the loud music from next door particularly annoying.
c Mark takes his children out every weekend.
d I want to fix the car before we go away next week.

2 In these examples, decide if a better focus could be achieved by fronting or by using a cleft sentence structure, and alter the sentences accordingly.

a Progress continued throughout the century. The basics of human anatomy were established by the end of it.
b Surgery remained at a very primitive level. Pathology was also rather limited. It wasn't until the discoveries of bacteriologists that things began to improve.
c Galen knew about muscles in the second century AD from his dissections of apes. His knowledge of the brain was good too.
d He was mean, cruel and selfish. I shall ignore his lack of hygiene.
e 'I want to make an appointment with Dr Clubb.' 'Dr Clubb is away this week. You will have to see Dr Brice.'
f 'Now watch carefully. I'm going to make a small incision here, avoiding any major blood vessels.'

FOCUS

1 a Would you consider all of the following to be forms of sport? If not, what are they?

synchronised swimming	motor racing
ice dancing	jogging
fox hunting	aerobics
caving	

b What makes something a sport?

2 In what sports are the following involved?

racket	wicket
pits	baton
bat	paddle
scrum	shuttlecock
pole	oar

3 Do you agree or disagree with these statements? Why?

a Most sports at international level are unfair.

b Sport is essentially an amateur pastime and to have professional sportsmen and women is ridiculous.

c Top sportsmen deserve all the money they are paid.

d Professional sport owes its existence almost entirely to television.

LEXIS

Sporting idioms

In what situations could the following idioms be used?

a Give him a sporting chance.

b The ball is in your court.

c Once again, it looks as if I've backed the wrong horse.

d I think we should lay all our cards on the table.

e That's just not cricket!

f Let's see if she'll rise to the bait.

g Oh, come on! Be a sport!

h If we play our cards right, we should get a good deal.

i I'm not really on the ball this morning.

j She's keeping her cards very close to her chest.

k He's rather a dark horse.

l Let's beat them at their own game.

READING 1

I Skim these extracts and say where you think they were taken from.

1 'Some athletes don't know what we are talking about when we say it is wrong. So far as they are concerned, athletics is about elite performances, to be as good as you can be and therefore if a chap takes substances to be as good as he can be, that is no big deal.'

Radford complained about a general lack of morality in society but thought athletes had specific problems. They could get sponsorship and had no need to work, as Radford himself always worked as a teacher. They could go to warm climates to train and some could go to high altitudes which improved long-distance runners' performances.

'They don't see the moral difference between that and a tablet,' he said. 'They go on intensive training month after month. What steroids have done is to give them the capacity to recover from that intensive work more quickly than we could so they can do more of it.'

2 Negative drugs tests show only that an athlete was not taking anything illegal at the time of the test, although the beneficial effects of many months of drug-enhanced training will largely remain.

3 Johnson is officially banned for life by the International Amateur Athletic Federation, although after two years he can appeal for reinstatement. All athletes who have done so have been brought back into the sport.

4 On the track, the purest moment came at the end of the 20-kilometre walk. A Czechoslovak, Joszef Pribilinec, finished first and collapsed. The second man, Ronald Weigel, a 29-year-old East German journalism 'student', knelt over Pribilinec, attempting to congratulate him. But the winner was spent, a prone image of total exhaustion. Unable to elicit a response, the East German silently kissed the Czechoslovak's chest, got up and left.

In Pusan, Lawrence Lemieux, a Canadian yachtsman, spotted a Singaporean in the sea as he raced. The Canadian stopped, took the victim on board and finished 21st. Lemieux was awarded second place in that particular race and, much to his surprise, was given a special International Olympic Committee award.

5 Such is the nature of competition and human self-esteem, that even without any promise of financial reward many competitors will risk death, cancer and other horrific side-effects in order to win. In 1984, when more than 100 Olympians were asked if they would be prepared to die within five years in return for winning a gold medal, 50% said they would. And the promise of monetary reward, sometimes amounting to millions, the aiding and abetting of unscrupulous doctors and coaches, even pea-brained propositions that chemical aids to performance might be studied and encouraged, have accelerated progress towards an athletic Armageddon.

6 Birgit Dressel, the West German heptathlete, moved from 33rd in the world rankings to sixth within the space of a year. Then, aged only 26, she collapsed and was dead within 72 hours from the horrifying number of drugs she had taken. The post-mortem revealed that her dizzy 12-month rise had been stimulated by 400 injections of various drugs.

An amateur body-builder in Essex died with four tumours of his liver, caused by anabolic steroids. The Belgian world champion weightlifter Eric Coppin was caught by Norwegian customs with 28,000 anabolic steroid pills in his luggage.

7 'Johnson has pushed back the limits of human achievement,' he said. 'He has the right to choose what he does with his body. Man has laid down arbitrary rules that man can't use medical science. People must have the freedom of choice.'

8 'Drugs are spreading into the lower level of sport, especially in American football, ice hockey and other track and field events. It is spreading to schoolkids and to people who want to do better than they ever did before. It is crazy. It even gets into fun runs,' says Beckett.

2 Now scan the extracts in order to answer these questions.

a Which one is the odd one out? Why?

b Which one quotes from an ex-athlete, now psychologist?

c Which one quotes from an ex-athlete turned drug smuggler who condones drug-taking in sport?

d Which two show the ineffectiveness of current methods of enforcing a drugs ban?

e Which talk about the attitudes of athletes?

f How many give examples of the physical risks of taking steroids?

g Which give reasons for the growth in the use of drugs?

h Which refer to the money athletes can earn?

3 Use the context to help you explain the meaning of these phrases:

a *her dizzy 12-month rise* (extract 6)

b *he can appeal for reinstatement* (extract 3)

c *Man has laid down arbitrary rules* (extract 7)

d *aiding and abetting* (extract 5)

e *pea-brained propositions* (extract 5)

f *a prone image of total exhaustion* (extract 4)

g *drug-enhanced training* (extract 2)

4 Are suggestions that chemical aids to improve performance should be studied and encouraged misguided? Give reasons for your answer.

LISTENING 1

1 You will hear two people discussing the use of drugs in sport. As you listen, list the arguments used on each side under the following two headings:

Drugs are acceptable	Drugs are unacceptable

2 Which person do you think argues most effectively? Why?

3 Look at the transcript on page 177.

a Read it through aloud in pairs, paying careful attention to stress and intonation. Discuss any parts of the transcript which seem unclear.

b Listen to the recording again. Make a note of any places where the stress or intonation is not what you expected.

c Read the transcript aloud in pairs again, this time including the stress and intonation you noted in **b**.

d Finally, read it again at the same time as listening to the recording. Try to imitate what you hear exactly.

4 Do you think the above exercise is useful? Give reasons for your answer.

SPEAKING

Informal argument

1 Look at these phrases that might be used to disagree with someone. Were any of them used in the argument above?

On the other hand. . .	Yes, but. . .
Only because. . .	Rubbish!
On the contrary. . .	That's because. . .
All right, but. . .	That's just not true!
I don't agree. . .	I can see your point, but. . .
I agree with you, but. . .	But aren't you forgetting. . .?
No way!	Are you seriously suggesting. . .?
That's true, but. . .	The thing is. . .

2 Organise the phrases in exercises **1** into two columns: those which are used to express total disagreement and those that are used to express partial disagreement.

Total	Partial
On the contrary	*On the other hand*

3 Put the phrases into approximate order of strength of feeling from the strongest to the mildest.
Example
Rubbish! = **strong**

4 Are any of these phrases particularly formal or informal?

5 Here are a list of suggestions on how to argue successfully without being offensive.

In groups, decide which are good suggestions and which are not. Put them in order from the most important, 1, to the least important, 12.

You must all agree, so you will have to put an argument forward for some of them. Use some of the phrases you listed above to argue with if they are appropriate.

a Never lose your temper.
b Always listen carefully to the other person's view.
c Find points on which you both agree and work from there.
d Don't bulldoze your opponent: let him or her feel they've won at least one point.
e Use examples and analogy to illustrate your point.
f Never answer a question directly if you think it might damage your own standpoint.
g Always part amicably.
h If the other person appears to be winning, keep interrupting them to put them off their stride.
i Saying things like *'That's typical of your boringly conventional attitude!'* or *'That's a pathetically weak argument!'* makes your opponent feel insecure and helps you win.
j Always compromise.
k Try to answer your opponent's objections before they get a chance to mention them.
l Try to get your way while letting the other person think that they've got theirs.

LEXIS

Collocating prepositions

One problem with learning dependent prepositions is deciding whether the preposition collocates with what goes before it or what goes after it. Some collocations are better learned as whole prepositional phrases.
Example
*Radford **complained about** a general lack of morality* = verb + preposition collocation

*. . .took the victim **on board*** = preposition + noun collocation

*They **go on an intensive training course** every month* = verb + preposition + noun collocation

1 The following sentences contain collocations with *'on'*. Decide whether *'on'* collocates with the preceding or following word(s) or whether it would be better to learn the collocation as a whole phrase.
a I'm afraid we charge interest on all loans.
b I went to the library but the book is on loan at the moment.
c The film is said to be based on fact.
d The bill must be settled on demand.
e We stopped off for a short while on the way.
f The miners went on strike because of threats to close the pit.
g You just cannot rely on her anymore.
h I'll be on my best behaviour. Don't worry.
i We can do either. It depends on you.
j How many teachers have you got on your staff?
k I'll just check on that for you.
l I'm on the lookout for a cheap pair of training shoes.
m It seems to me you're on to a good thing there.

2 Say which dependent preposition usually follows these verbs.
a His style of running has been likened .... that of a cheetah in full stride.
b I'm accustomed .... doing things a bit faster than this.
c With his distinctive hair style, he couldn't possibly be mistaken .... anyone else.
d His years of hard work culminated .... a dramatic victory.
e He has been gravitating .... the left of the party for some time.
f That performance is one which would be difficult to improve ....
g He dissociated himself .... the corrupt practices of his team mates.
h The deal is set to go through, subject .... the approval of the Managing Director.
i I really believe that she's entitled .... some sort of apology.
j It is vital that you believe .... yourself.

3 What do you think is the best way to learn collocating prepositions?

READING 2

1 Have you ever been *caving*? Can you understand why people enjoy it?

2 Would you be more likely to suffer from *claustrophobia* or *agoraphobia* when caving?

3 The following article is about somebody's first caving experience. Which of these words would you not expect to find?

squeeze	darkness
rope	miserable
pressing	subterranean
cathedral	dustbin
wriggle	waterfall

Now read the first extract to see which words are used.

Extract 1

The Wretched Rabbit and me

Julian Champkin gets down to some deep, damp adventure

Beauty of the deep: A moment of wonder underground

1 'It's not a proper squeeze,' they said, with my belly pressed against one slab of rock and a few thousand tons
5 of another pressing on my back.

I couldn't see where I was wriggling to, because turning my head would have
10 involved another three inches of space that just wasn't there. 'It's not a *proper* squeeze. A *proper* squeeze, you have to hold your breath.'
15 That wonderful life-enhancing experience was called The Cheese Press, and it was kids' stuff. Proper caving happens much further
20 underground, in places that are much darker, much wetter, much more mud-filled and exhausting and miserable. Like down
25 Lancaster Pot, which was where they took me for my first day's caving.

To enter Lancaster Pot, they take what looks like a dustbin
30 lid off a bit of Yorkshire moorland and lower you

150ft down a rope into total emptiness and a cavern that, at a guess, is about the size of
35 St Paul's cathedral. I say at a guess, because the rather powerful lamp on your helmet illuminates only a very small patch of very distant
40 cave wall, and that indistinctly.

Splashing time: Mailman Champkin tackles the torrent.

Add to which, swinging halfway down a rope in pitch darkness you have other
45 things to worry about. Such as that this is nine-millimetre rope, and nine millimetres is really rather thin.

When you do get to the
50 bottom, you find that a major subterranean waterfall is pouring down the back of your neck.

At the bottom they point
55 out that it is quite impossible for anyone to climb 150ft of nine-millimetre rope. Consequently we can't get out this way. So equally
60 consequently there is little point in leaving the rope there. As the once top end of the rope hit the floor of the cave, it all seemed a little
65 final.

The Daily Mail

4 Now answer these questions.
   a What exactly is happening in the first two paragraphs?
   b What does the entrance to the Lancaster Pot look like?
   c How did he know that the cavern was huge?
   d How do you think they are going to get out?

   e Which of these words would you not use to describe the author's attitude?

self-deprecating	wry	macho	disbelieving

   f How many examples of understatement or irony can you find?

5 Read the second extract. When you have finished, say if caving seems more, or less attractive to you as a sport.

Extract 2

The exit, they say, is that-a-way – though how they can tell is a mystery. It is about two miles, though not as the crow flies. It is two miles as the worm, or caver, crawls, or wriggles, or scrambles, or splashes on his belly through black water, or now and then walks upright.

And so, after a brief side excursion to admire the stalactites and stalagmites of The Colonnades, and to experience the absolute, utter, and impenetrable blackness that you get when you all turn your lights out at once, we proceed.

These guys were experts. They had discovered caves in Mexico, 32 kilometres of caves and passages that no one knew were there. . . . 'But the real heroes are cave divers,' they said. 'Their mortality rate used to be 50 per cent. Two dives and a death.'

It is not a sport for the claustrophobic. 'Actually, I got agoraphobia, fear of open spaces, in Mexico once.' said Bob. 'I'd been crawling through a tunnel and suddenly it all opened up into this immense cavern; huge, you couldn't see the end of it. Just you, alone, where nobody else had ever been before.' The shivers were quite understandable.

I would have shivered down Lancaster if I'd had the time and energy. There was this torrent, you see. Sometimes we clung above it, sometimes we clung to one side of it, and sometimes we splashed through it.

Not when we could avoid it, though, because you needed one hand on either rockwall, and your feet wedged well out of the main current to remain upright at all. Making any sort of progress against it was another ball-game.

6 Now answer these questions about extract 2.
a What point is the author making in the paragraph starting on line 67?
b What are *The Colonnades*? (line 80)
c What are *cave divers*?
d Why does the author say *The shivers were quite understandable.* (line 108)
e Explain the author's position in the final paragraph.

7 Read the last extract. What do you think the author's opinion of caving will be by the time he gets out?

Extract 3

Friction seemed rather an important element. Faced with two utterly smooth walls and either torrent or, worse, bottomless black holes between them, you had to press your backside against one smooth wall and your feet against the other and do a sort of bottom-shuffle to move at all.

Exhausted.

'Use your whole body,' said Debbie and Jane. I think I must have. Caving reaches muscles that other sports don't know exist. And makes them ache.

'We could have used the upper passage, which is dry,' said Howard, our leader. 'But it's a bit boring.' On the non-boring route we heard the surface river roaring above our heads.

And we saw needle-shaped stalactites covering a roof, and waist-thick stalactites that grow at an inch in a thousand years; and The Minarets, which is a corridor whose head-high roof is onion-shaped; and chokes where half a million boulders were wedged above our heads by a single fist-sized stone that looked as though it would fall out if you touched it – and I don't think appearances were deceptive.

They would all have been wonderfully impressive had I not been so exhausted. We never did see daylight.

By the time I crawled out of a hole they appropriately call Wretched Rabbit, four hours and a lifetime older, and filthier than I have ever been, which is saying something, it was dark. And raining.

The way back to the cars was through a bog. Tim fell into mud up to his waist. He didn't seem overjoyed, though it was no filthier than the stuff he'd been hurling himself into for fun ten minutes earlier. A perfect end to a perfect day. I thought, falling over in the dark and clutching a thistle to save myself. Anyone who goes caving must be stark, staring mad.

I went again the next day.

The Daily Mail

8 Now answer these questions about the third extract.
a Explain how the author moves in the first paragraph.
b What exactly is a *choke*? (line 157)
c Why is it appropriate that the hole is called *Wretched Rabbit*?
d Explain what the author means by *which is saying something.* (line 174)
e How many examples can you find of exaggeration, understatement or irony in the article?

9 a Choose five or six items of vocabulary from the whole article which you think would be useful to learn.
b Compare your choice with a partner. How far do you agree over the definition of 'useful'?
c How would you categorise the items you have chosen?
Example
verbs of movement, compound adjectives

LISTENING 2

1 You will hear part of an interview with a British Olympic swimming coach about her work with synchronised swimmers.

In pairs write down three or four questions that you would like to ask her. Compare your questions with those of other pairs.

2 Now listen to the recording. How many of your questions are answered?

3 Listen again and take notes on what is said about the following. (You will need these notes for the WRITING section below).

a Similar sports

b Different components in competition

c Skills involved

Compare notes with your partner.

4 Having heard the recording, discuss your opinion of synchronised swimming in small groups.
- Is it interesting to watch?
- Is it a sport?
- Should there be different competitions for men and women?
- What motivates someone to do it?
- Do you think the competitors would be better employed doing something more useful?

WRITING

Use the notes you took in the LISTENING section above to write one of the following:

a A report to a sports committee of an annual swimming championship setting out your reasons for recommending that a synchronised swimming competition should be included in future championships.

b A short, humorous newspaper article mocking what you see as the absurdities of synchronised swimming at a recent championship.

Think about the form and style of your piece.
- How do you introduce the topic?
- What sort of conclusion is needed?
- Is paragraphing necessary? Why?
- Do you need to include all the information given in the LISTENING section?
- Do you need to add anything extra? If so, what?
- Do you want to refer directly to the interview? Example: 'According to an experienced coach. . .'
- How personal/impersonal should you be?
- What sort of register is appropriate?

LEXIS

Collocation – *run* and *get*

1 Decide whether the following nouns collocate with either of the verbs *run* or *get* or both.

a chance	somewhere
a country	your life
a bus	a bath
a mark/grade	help
a course	a risk
a car	a race
a joke	an experiment

How many different meanings of *run* and *get* are illustrated in these examples?

2 Both *run* and *get* can be used in combination with an adverbial particle to produce a large number of different phrasal verbs.
Example
run away, get off

a In pairs, list as many of these as you can. Make sure you know what they mean and when to use them. Compare your list with that of another pair.

b Using a dictionary, add three or four other phrasal verbs to each list. Decide in what contexts you could use each example.

3 Use the dictionary to find three or four idiomatic expressions which use *get* or *run*.

4 a What is the purpose of question **2a**?

b Why in questions **2b** and **3** has the number of new items been limited to three or four?

c How could you extend this exercise?

GRAMMAR

Using modal verbs to express the past

1 a Look at this list of modal verbs. Use each one to provide an example sentence referring to the present or future.

can	may	must	shall	will
might	would	ought to	should	could

b Write another sentence for each verb, where possible, referring to the past. Do not use reported speech.

2 Modals in reported speech

Rewrite the following statements as though you were reporting what Sue told you. Think about what changes, if any, the modal requires. If there are two possible answers, explain the difference between them.

Example

'I can run 100 metres in about 11 seconds.'

1) Sue told me she could run 100 metres in about 11 seconds.

2) Sue told me she can run 100 metres in about 11 seconds.

(The second example stresses that she still can at the moment of speaking.)

a 'I may go out this evening, I'm not sure.'

b 'I could give you a hand, if you like.'

c 'You ought to try taking breaks more frequently.'

d 'You will marry a tall, dark stranger.'

e 'You really must stop eating so much chocolate.'

f 'He might succeed, but I doubt it.'

g 'You shall go to the ball!'

3 *Could* and *would* are the only modal verbs which can be used, without perfect infinitives(*might have done, should have done*, etc .), to express the past.

Match these sentences, (a-e), with the function of the modal verb below.

a We couldn't leave the school unless we had good reason.☐

b Travelling long distances could get pretty dangerous in those days.☐

c I couldn't swim until I was 9 years old.☐

d Every morning, he would get up at the crack of dawn and light the fire.☐

e I wouldn't go with her so she had to go alone.☐

1	*refusal*	*4*	*possibility*
2	*ability*	*5*	*permission*
3	*regularity in the past*		

Modal perfect

Using the perfect infinitive *have done* after certain modals moves the main verb (rather than the modal itself) into the past.

Example

I may have made a mistake = making the mistake is in the past. '*May*' shows the speaker's attitude (that it is possible) towards the past event.

4 Explain the differences in meaning between these pairs of sentences. The first sentence has been done for you.

a You should have got in touch with them. = *You were wrong not to have got in touch with them.*

You should get in touch with them. = *It would be a good idea for you to get in touch with them.*

b It must have been raining.

It must be raining.

c He ought to have arrived by now.

He ought to arrive now.

d You could have done some serious damage like that.

You could do some serious damage like that.

e I may have given her my number, I can't remember.

I might have given her my number, I can't remember.

5 a Explain what happened in these sentences.

Example

I could have been an actress but I wanted more job security. (*I had the opportunity to be an actress but chose not to.*)

1 I would have lent it to him but I forgot.

2 You should have kicked him.

3 I ought to have been more grateful.

4 We were lucky: it could have been a real disaster.

5 It's just possible that I could have left it here by mistake.

6 She may have phoned the office after I left.

7 He can't have said that, surely?

8 It must have been a very close race from what I heard.

b What conclusions can you draw about the difference between the modal verbs used with the perfect infinitive in sentences 1–4 (*would, should, ought to, could*) and those used in sentences 5–8 (*could, may, can, must*)?

6 🔲 Stress and intonation can change the meaning of modals considerably. Listen to the sentence below being said in two different ways. How does the meaning change?

Example

He couldn't have got in that way. . .

• could he?

• it's always locked.

Now listen to each of these sentences being read once and add a suitable following comment as above.

a She should have got there by now.

b She can't have been in this morning.

c You might have found it difficult.

d You might have told me.

7 What sort of modal verbs and structures are used to express the past in READING 2. How are they used?

LEXIS

Dependent prepositions

I Add a collocating preposition to the verbs in these sentences.

a Your decision is based .... a misreading of the evidence.

b The task has been entrusted ....a junior member of the firm.

c Members of the public must be prevented .... entering this area.

d The festivities culminated .... a firework display.

e The book can be divided .... four sections.

f I owe everything .... my first teacher.

g I'm unaccustomed .... public speaking.

h Publication of this material is subject .... certain legal restrictions.

i You are entitled .... full compensation in the event of a cancellation.

j The outbreak has been confined .... a small area so far.

2 Now add collocating prepositions to the verbs in these sentences.

a That is a goal worth striving ....

b He began to despair .... ever reaching an Olympic final.

c I wouldn't bet .... that horse if I were you.

d The whole story stems .... an apparently unconnected series of events.

e This is a result that can't be improved ....

f I don't want to detract .... his achievement but the results are in some doubt.

g I insisted .... her following us immediately.

h I am unhappy about being associated .... such a project.

i They would never stoop .... such childish behaviour.

j As a writer, he occasionally indulges .... passages of purple prose.

3 Say what prepositions commonly follow these verbs.

hint	react	invest
contend	spy	opt
care	long	grapple
clamour	suffer	listen
refer	shrink	wallow
yearn	resort	sympathise

GRAMMAR

Modal verbs

I Rewrite these sentences using a suitable modal form.

a I was capable of running very fast when I was young.

b It is possible that I misunderstood her point.

c My opinion is that an immediate apology was required from you.

d Every morning I used to go for a swim in the sea before breakfast.

e She refused to accept my offer without certain preconditions.

f We weren't allowed to leave the school grounds during morning break.

g It's simply not possible for him to have got there so soon.

h I can't think who did it. The only remaining possibility is my mother.

i I wish you had told me.

j He found it impossible to be an authoritarian figure.

2 Respond to these statements or questions with an explanation using a modal perfect. The first one has been done for you.

a The bus is a long time coming this morning.
   It may have got caught in the traffic.

b Catriona didn't come to the party last night.

c Why didn't she leave me the keys?

d He never said anything to me about going away.

e I haven't seen Simon for ages.

f They should have been here half an hour ago.

g Their response to my request was extremely prompt.

h I thought they said they were going to go to Spain this summer.

i Angela completely ignored me at lunch time.

j Caroline looks a bit sleepy this morning.

3 Complete these conditional sentences with a suitable modal clause.

a If I hadn't warned her about the one-way system. . .

b . . . , unless she already knew about it.

c If he gave that report to the director yesterday, . . .

d . . . , if they hadn't stopped her in time.

e . . . , provided I was paid full expenses.

L E X I S

Phrases with *get*

'Get' is very commonly used as an informal alternative to other verbs.
Example
He got dressed. = he dressed
I only got a glimpse of him. = caught a glimpse
They got drunk. = became drunk

1 In the sentences below, decide if another verb could replace *'get'* and, if so, what effect of register or meaning the change would have.

a She soon got better and went back to work.

b They got married in the autumn.

c My elder sister always used to get the better of me in arguments.

d Try and get hold of the rope.

e I think Andy's going to get the sack.

f Can you get the BBC World Service on your radio?

g Get lost!

h I don't get the joke.

i She really gets on my nerves.

j Ah! Now we're getting somewhere!

k We had to use a rope bridge to get across the river.

l Where do you want to get to?

m She always gets her own way in the end.

n This room gets a lot of sun in the afternoon.

2 Use a dictionary to add to the list of phrases in exercise 1 using *get*.

Phrasal verbs: *away*

3 Add more phrasal verbs with *'away'* to this list.

keep away	throw away	talk away
pack away	wash away	give away
take away	run away	blow away
break away	put away	

4 Make any connections you can between the verbs in the list above.
Example
put away and *pack away* have a similar meaning.

5 Categorise the meanings of the phrasal verbs with *'away'* listed above into those:

a involving distance or separation

b involving lessening or disappearance

c involving continuous activity

6 Categorise the phrasal verbs in these sentences.

a He kept *hammering away* at the lock until it broke.

b The tree got some disease and started to *rot away*.

c Attendance at the meetings started to *fall away* during the summer.

d He *swept away* any lingering doubts with a wave of his hand.

e If you do that you'll *frighten* everyone *away*.

f If you park there the police will *tow* your car *away*.

"I can tell you one thing right off—you can't solve your problems by running away."

141

FOCUS

1 **'Children begin by loving their parents; after a time they judge them; rarely, if ever, do they forgive them.'**

Forgive them for what? Is there any truth in this saying or is it just trying to be clever?

2 Who is involved in the following dialogue? Have you ever been involved in an argument like this?

> X – You can't go.
> Y – Why not?
> X – Because you wouldn't get back till late.
> Y – But *everyone* else is going.
> X – I don't care what everyone else is doing.
> Y – But it's not fair.
> X – You're not going and that's final!
> Y – You're always stopping me doing things I want to do. You don't care about me!
> X – That's not true.
> Y – Yes it is.

3 a If your 15-year-old daughter wants to go to a party at a friend's house that doesn't finish until late, would you set any conditions in allowing her to go? Discuss your actions with a partner.

  b Would your reaction be different if it was your son rather than your daughter?

4 Add to this list of phrases that might be used in a family argument. Would they be used by the parent or the child?

> That's absurd!
> I'll say it once and for all. . .
> You're always saying that.
> I'm not going to argue about it.
> I've made my decision and it's final.
> But why not?

READING 1

1 Read the headline and introductory paragraph of the article below.
Who does the author want the reader to sympathise with?

I'll Go to Jail Before I Let My Runaway Son Set Foot in My House Again

by Karen Capuano

1 I'm mad as hell and I'm not going to take it anymore. For six long months I've been living a 5 nightmare at the hands of a teenage son who's suddenly turned into a monster.

I've been terrified by 10 threats of violence and reduced to tears by the mental torture inflicted on me by a child who's chosen drugs and drink over love 15 and security.

And each time he decides to come home after running away again, I'm supposed to welcome him with open 20 arms and act as if nothing has happened? Hell, no! Not anymore. I'll go to jail before I'll let him darken my doorstep again.

25 Countless nights I have sobbed myself to sleep, praying to God to end my nightmare.

My horrible ordeal began 30 last September. My husband Alfred and I were watching TV with our three other children, John, 13, Alfred Jr., 10, and Jeanne, 35 9. Gary, 15, was out that evening.

When he came in, we immediately noticed something was wrong. He 40 was stuttering, his eyes were blinking and his mouth seemed dry. My husband asked him what he'd been doing, and Gary 45 just shrugged his shoulders and muttered, 'Nothing.'

Then he walked into the wall. It was obvious he had been taking drugs. We had 50 a big argument and my husband sent him to his room.

The next morning he had vanished – packed his 55 clothes, climbed out the bedroom window and run away. I was panic-stricken.

My husband and I searched all over town. I 60 spent two sleepless nights – then he called. He was alive and safe, 200 miles away in Fort Lauderdale. We sent him the airfare to 65 come home.

Gary promised never to do it again. But two weeks later he vanished again. No warning, no note ... 70 nothing. The heartache began again.

Again, he was found in Fort Lauderdale. And we had to cough up the airfare 75 to return him home again. We don't have a lot of money. It's difficult enough for my husband, a truck driver, to keep up 80 with the regular bills and to put food on the table.

This time when he got home my husband whipped his butt and sent him to his 85 room. I was heartsick. Almost overnight, Gary had been transformed into a degenerate drug-addicted slob.

90 He seemed to have a big chip on his shoulder. He rarely spoke to us except to snarl 'do this or that.' When he did talk he used 95 the foulest language. He never smiled. He had become almost a zombie.

Gary began to pick fights regularly with his younger 100 brothers and sister. And he began to threaten me. Once he raised his fist in my face and threatened to beat me up. I was terrified. He's 105 five inches taller than I am, and I knew he could really hurt me.

Three counselling sessions, costing us $60 110 each, did no good. And then Gary point-blank refused to go back again. I tried to see a juvenile court judge, but none would talk 115 to me. I felt so alone ... helpless. Later, Gary ran away again. But this time when police found him, I 120 refused to let him back in the house. The officer said if I didn't, I could be arrested and charged with child neglect.

125 But I made up my mind that the only way for me to help Gary was to get arrested and tell my story to a judge. I was 130 handcuffed, searched, fingerprinted and thrown in jail then released on $250 bail.

Two weeks later I stood 135 before a judge and told my story.

'My boy needs help,' I told him. 'We've got to act now – before he gets 140 deeper into drugs and deeper into delinquency.'

All the judge did was order Gary to undergo psychiatric counselling. 145 And before any counselling could take place, Gary ran away again.

It makes me so angry. Counselling doesn't work. 150 Off-the-track teenagers need to be shaken to their senses. My son needs a dose of real punishment. That's the only thing these 155 teenagers understand.

A lot of other parents feel the same way. That's why I've formed an organisation called 'A 160 Mother's Cry for Help'. My first objective is to make repeated running away a crime, so authorities will have the 165 power to slap these kids in a detention centre to shake them up.

I hate having to talk publicly like this about my 170 own flesh and blood. But if all parents with the same problem would pull together, we could salvage the lives of many many 175 youngsters.

It's time we stood up and declared 'Enough's enough.' Give these kids the punishment they 180 deserve to bring them back in line – before it's too late.

National Enquirer

2 Read through the article. Of all the people involved (Gary, his mother, his father, the judge), who do you feel most sympathy for and why?

3 In pairs, note:

a all the things Gary did wrong.

b all the measures his parents took to punish and/or help him.

Do you think the measures his parents took were adequate and/or appropriate? Why (not)?

4 Who does Gary's mother blame for her son's continued bad behaviour?

5 a How would you describe the style in which this article is written? Find words or phrases to support your answer.

b How could these phrases be expressed less emotionally?

let him darken my doorstep

sobbed myself to sleep

I was. . . thrown in jail

slap these kids in a detention centre to shake them up

c Rewrite this paragraph in the style of the article. Choose suitable vocabulary and pay attention to the length of the sentences.

'Gary's behaviour rapidly deteriorated and became aggressive and abusive, forcing us to take steps to punish him. These measures, however, proved ineffective and the situation worsened until eventually we sought the help of the courts in controlling our wayward son.'

WRITING

Summary

1 A social worker involved in the case has to write a brief summary for a colleague of what Gary has done wrong, explaining what measures his parents have taken.

Using the notes you took in question **3** (READING 1), write a coherent paragraph of about 120 words.

Consider these things:

- register
- omitting any irrelevant information
- organising the information within the paragraph
- sentence structure
- revising your first draft

2 When you have finished, compare your summary with the version on page 165. Can you justify any differences between the two?

LISTENING 1

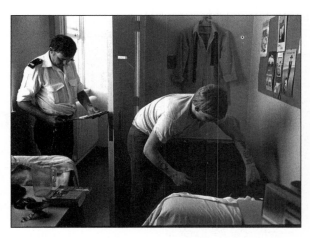

In this recording you will hear Mary Piggot of the Youth Justice Resources Team for Oxford Social Services. She is responsible, among other things, for interviewing young offenders and recommending to the courts what sort of sentence they should be given. Listen to what she says about Gary.

1 Which of the following statements best summarises her view of Gary's behaviour?

a It's impossible to comment because there is not enough information in the article.

b He seems on the whole to be perfectly normal.

c It is unlikely that this behaviour started suddenly.

d His behaviour is a fairly typical preliminary to more serious offending.

2 Read the transcript on page 178 carefully.

a How many mistakes can you find?

b Can you account for why each of these mistakes was made?

Example

The speaker changed her mind about what she was going to say.

c Listen to the recording again. Is it easier to understand why the mistakes were made when you hear them than when you read them? Why (not)?

d Much of the transcript is unpunctuated because that is how it was spoken. Choose the section beginning *'The other thing. . .'* and write it as coherent and cohesive written English with punctuation.

SPEAKING

Role-play

The situation

At a preliminary counselling session with Gary involving his parents and a social worker, a decision has to be made about what the next steps in dealing with Gary should be.

The social worker acts as chairman and should steer the discussion towards a final decision about Gary's future.

Preparation

Role-play the meeting in groups of four. Students A and B should study their role profiles on this page and students C and D look at page 165. Spend five minutes preparing what you are going to say.

> **Student A**
> You are Gary's loud and outspoken mother. Try to dominate the discussion, making sure your husband always agrees with you. You don't trust the social worker and should prepare reasons as to why Gary should go to a special school. Your language is informal and emotional.

> **Student B**
> You are Gary's father, a timid man, frightened of his domineering wife and of the social worker's professional competence. Prepare what to say if asked for an opinion. Your language is full of hesitations and you tend to agree with whoever spoke last.

LEXIS

Slang

1 The text on page 143 contains a number of examples of slang. Match each of the slang words, 1–3 below with a neutral equivalent:

1 butt	a pay
2 cough up	b bottom
3 slob	c lazy, unpleasant person

2 To which of the above slang words are the following groups of slang phrases connected?

lazybones	to pick up the tab
layabout	to put it on the slate
bone idle	to fork out
couch potato	What's the damage?

3 Describe the situation in which each of the following slang phrases might be said.
   a You are driving me up the wall.
     Two people having an argument, the speaker becoming exasperated.
   b I've got a bone to pick with you.
   c He gives me the creeps.
   d He gave me the cold shoulder.
   e Put it there!
   f I'm in the doghouse again.
   g I'm absolutely over the moon.
   h That bloke's a complete nutter.

'I now declare this juvenile secure unit open'

READING 2

I a Would you agree that for children obedience is a virtue? Give reasons for your opinion.

b What do you understand by *authoritarian parents*? Do you think the word *authoritarian* has positive or negative connotations?

2 Tick the appropriate box according to whether you think the following statements are true or false. Then compare your answers with a partner.

	True	False	Don't know
Children of domineering parents:			
a often can't cope well in difficult situations	☐	☐	☐
b are motivated by religion	☐	☐	☐
c value obedience	☐	☐	☐
d are very independent	☐	☐	☐
e are less likely to leave home	☐	☐	☐
Authoritarian parents:			
a consult their children	☐	☐	☐
b lack self-reliance	☐	☐	☐
c depend on their children	☐	☐	☐
d expect conformity	☐	☐	☐
e pay no attention to their children	☐	☐	☐

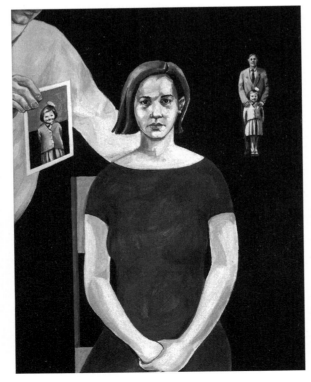

3 Read the text below and find out if it corresponds with your opinions of the statements in exercise **2**.

Parents who are authoritarian and who favour physical punishment to enforce their rigid set of rules (in which the adolescent has no voice) tend to have more dependent and, at the same time, rebellious adolescent offspring. Restrictive, authoritarian parents attempt to shape, control and assess the behaviour and attitudes of the child according to a set code of conduct, usually an absolute standard, which is often motivated by religious considerations. Obedience is valued as a virtue, and punitive, forceful measures are usually favoured in order to curb self-will at those points where the child's (and later on, the teenager's) actions or beliefs conflict with what parents think is correct conduct. They believe in indoctrinating – as opposed to educating – their offspring into such values as respect for authority, respect for work, and respect for the preservation of traditional order. Verbal exchange is discouraged because the teenager should accept the parent's word for what is right.

The children of domineering parents often lack self-reliance and the ability to cope realistically with their problems; later they may fail, or prove slow, to accept adult responsibilities. They are apt to withdraw from situations they find difficult, and they tend to be the people who later make up most of that part of the adult world which has never left home, psychologically and, much of the time, physically as well.

4 Is there anything you find surprising about the analysis of such families? Is there anything you disagree with?

5 Style

a Where might this extract have come from? What factors help you decide this?

b Are the following features more characteristic of formal or informal language?

- Impersonal, objective language (example *use of the passive*)
- Technical terms
- Complex sentences
- Full written forms (example *would not* rather than *wouldn't*)
- Clear logical argument and/or enumeration of points
- Words used carefully with close attention to their exact meaning

c Which of these features are illustrated in the text? Find examples.

GRAMMAR

Complex sentences and discourse

1 Work in pairs.
Put the clauses, a–q, into the table below in the correct order to form a coherent and cohesive paragraph.
Pay careful attention to:
- punctuation
- lexical discourse markers (*thereby, however* etc.)
- reference words like *this, these, which*
- singular/plural agreement (*has/have*)

Five of the clauses have been done for you.

✓ a The way in which we understand adolescence
b as well as a more sophisticated,
c over the last few years.
d Equally important, however,
e has been changing slowly but perceptibly
✓ f many of which have had a direct effect on young people,
g is the fact that new and valuable research is being carried out,
h To some extent this is as a result of the major social changes
i view of the teenage years,
j These advances have led to a more realistic,
k which have occurred in western countries,
✓ l within developmental psychology.
m and thereby focused attention
✓ n much of it linked to and inspired by
✓ o on this particular group within society.
p major advances in theories of human development.
q and brought the study of adolescence to a more central place

	Letter	Clause
1	a	The way in which we understand adolescence
2		
3		
4		
5		
6	f	many of which have had a direct effect on young people,
7		
8	o	on this particular group within society.
9		
10		
11	n	much of it linked to and inspired by
12		
13		
14		
15		
16		
17	l	within developmental psychology.

2 Now read through the complete paragraph below and answer the following questions as a class.

  a Is there a clear logical connection between the sentences?
How does the author try to make it clear?

  b Which sentence did you find the most difficult to put together? Why?

  c Which sentence do you think is the most complex? Why? Which is the most straightforward?

  d One sentence has two relative clauses. Do you think this is unusual?

  e What is the function of the commas? Are they all essential?

  f What problem does the author have with prepositions in the third sentence? In what other ways are prepositions used to make the text cohesive?

  g The sentences can be broken down into smaller 'chunks' than in this paragraph. The chunks may be seen as the bricks which build complete sentences.

  Example

  The way in which/we understand adolescence/has been changing/slowly but perceptibly/over the last few years.

  In pairs, do the same with the next two sentences in the paragraph. Then compare your breakdown with another pair. Pay careful attention to which 'chunk' the preposition belongs to.

> The way in which we understand adolescence has been changing slowly but perceptibly over the last few years. To some extent this is as a result of the major social changes which have occurred in western countries, many of which have had a direct effect on young people, and thereby focused attention on this particular group within society. Equally important, however, is the fact that new and valuable research is being carried out, much of it linked to and inspired by major advances in theories of human development. These advances have led to a more realistic, as well as more sophisticated, view of the teenage years and brought the study of adolescence to a a more central place within developmental psychology.

3 a Look at the following paragraph. Where there is a choice of words or phrases in the text, choose which you think fits best.

> The term 'juvenile delinquent' is merely an administrative term, not a clinical diagnosis. It has to be recognised that relatively minor delinquent activities (e.g. petty thefts, vandalism) are surprisingly common in the teens. Such/These activities tend to be transitory. Additionally/However, there is a small but hard core of adolescents who habitually break the law. Delinquency is perhaps the most noteworthy of all activities as an adolescent manifestation, reaching a peak at 15 years for boys and 14 years for girls. By their twenties most of the former offenders have gradually become broadly law-abiding members of the community. But/So there is nothing to be complacent about.

b Find examples of the following and justify their use:
- the passive
- fronting
- a non-finite clause
- the author being tentative about generalising
- the author giving his personal reaction to the facts

LISTENING 2

You will hear three people discussing how they deal with their children when they are difficult.

I Before you listen, what methods do you think would be most effective in dealing with a child who behaves very badly?

2 Now listen to the recording.
 a What methods are mentioned?
 b What advantages and disadvantages of these methods are mentioned?

3 In Catriona's story about her daughter Emily,
 a what exactly did Emily do wrong?
 b what was Catriona doing at the time?
 c why did Catriona react as she did?
 d who lost their temper?
 e what exactly did her mother do?
 f who do you think Jim is?

4 Would you have done the same thing as Catriona? Give reasons for your answer.

5 The phrase *things tend to blow over fairly fast* is used at least twice in the conversation. What do you think it means?

LEXIS

Synonymy

I Put the following words into groups of four with similar meanings.

authoritarian	penance	pinnacle
trivial	intermediate	dogmatic
strict	aggression	penalty
strait-jacket	youthful	severe
defiance	punishment	peak
petty	transitory	insolence
rebelliousness	chastisement	climax
trying	insignificant	restraint
unruly	temporary	minor
restriction	suppression	juvenile
immature	maximum	adolescent
troublesome	tiresome	provisional

2 a Choose the three or four groups that seem to you the most useful to learn.
 b Use a dictionary to find the differences and similarities between the words in your groups. Think about register, collocation and connotation.
 c Choose a few of the most useful words you have studied and teach them to other people in the class.

LEXIS

Discourse markers

A Indicating your attitude

There are a number of words or phrases that can be added to sentences to show your opinion of what you are talking about. These are often used at the beginning of the sentence or clause.

Alas, the relationship was not to last.

Naturally, he didn't like being told off.

Paradoxically, bullies often feel threatened by their victims.

I **a** Add words to this list which can be used in a similar way.

surprisingly	luckily
admittedly	remarkably
ironically	of course
predictably	understandably
sadly	

b Write five sentences using some of the discourse markers in the box above.

2 **a** What effect do the words and phrases in bold in these sentences have on what is said?

*I agree with what you're saying **up to a point**.*

*He was **to all intents and purposes guilty** of fraud.*

*They were **more or less** bound to get lost.*

*It's **virtually** certain that we will win.*

b These discourse markers can be used with the same effect. Write some example sentences to illustrate their use.

almost	in a manner of speaking	in a way
to some extent	practically	in effect

B Changing the subject/Emphasising

Changing the subject in the middle of a conversation can sound abrupt or can confuse the listener. Changes therefore tend to be introduced by a word or phrase.

***Anyway**, let's forget about it.*

***So** how are the children?*

***Right**. Let's get down to business.*

The following set of phrases can be used to emphasise the truth of what you are saying or to stress how serious it is.

*He's a pain in the neck, **to put it mildly**.*

*You'll never do it like that, **believe me**.*

***Above all**, remember to take plenty of water with you.*

I Divide the following words and phrases into those that introduce a *change of subject* and those that *emphasise* what you are saying. One of them can be used for both. Which one?

at all	really	without exception	now then
by the way	well now	positively	actually
to say the least		incidentally	anyhow
surely	whatsoever	indeed	

2 **a** Which two emphasising markers above can only be used with negative statements or a statement using *any*?

Example

Have you done any work .... ?

They've never offered me the slightest help ....

b Which emphasising marker can be used at the beginning of a sentence when you want someone to agree with you?

Example

.... you don't want to go out with that idiot?

c Which change of subject marker seems to you the most assertive?

d Which markers could you use in these sentences?

1 It was a very large room ....

2 The whole place was .... crawling with police.

3 That .... was the best meal I've ever had.

4 ...., you owe me £10.

5 I don't like her ....

GRAMMAR

Complex sentences

Choose one of these sentences and expand it as much as you can by adding other words and clauses. It must remain as one sentence and must not become obscure or meaningless.

Think about the following:
- punctuation
- the position of the subject in the clause/sentence
- subject/verb plural/singular tense agreement

Example

She didn't feel loved.

When the girl was eventually stopped by the police, who were suspicious when they saw her alone late at night, she told them that she had run away because **she didn't feel loved** *by her parents.*

a The girl ran away from home.

b Her father was a taciturn man.

c Grandparents are crucial in the upbringing of children.

LEXIS

Slang and idioms

1 Decide for each of these sentences whether they describe someone who is (or is being at that moment) clever or stupid.

a She's nobody's fool.

b He's really on the ball this morning.

c He is really dumb.

d That man's not got a lot between the ears.

e He's solid muscle from the neck up.

f She's a brainy child.

g He knows what's what.

h That kid's very quick on the uptake.

i He really knows the ropes.

j Most of her ideas are half-baked.

k He's totally clueless.

l Don't be thick!

2 Say whether the following phrases express approval or disapproval.

a Everything appears to be *hunky-dory*.

b He's a really *special* person.

c He's a really *dodgy* character.

d This programme is really *naff*.

e I had a really *brill* time! *Out of this world*.

f This smells really *foul*.

g He's a very *iffy* looking character.

3 Match the following slang expressions with the definitions below.

a *Let's get down to the nitty-gritty.*

b *On your bike!*

c *For some reason she completely flew off the handle.*

d *Did you get out of the wrong side of bed this morning?*

e *Stop taking the mickey!*

f *Those two are as thick as thieves.*

g *He's kicked the bucket.*

h *I'd give him a wide berth if I were you.*

i *It's time we jacked it in.*

j *He's round the bend.*

- mad
- deal with the basics
- teasing
- go away
- stop work
- avoid
- be in a bad mood
- lose one's temper
- very close friends
- die

"Oh , she's <u>very</u> attractive. . .
I don't like her at all."

FOCUS

1 The whole aim of setting up a business is to make money. Do you agree? Why (not)?

2 Imagine you are given the money and the opportunity to set up your own business. Which of the following types of business would you choose? Explain your choice to a partner.

Retail	Advertising agency	Consultancy
Manufacturing	Computer services	Private school
Finance	Travel agency	Estate agency
Agriculture	Theatre company	Design
Restaurant	Funeral services	Hotel

3 In which of the businesses listed above do you think English is most useful? In what ways might it be used in each case?

Example
Theatre company
   • *booking hotels abroad on the phone*
   • *performing plays in English*
   • *touring in English speaking countries*

4 If you were the managing director of a large company, which of the following statements would best reflect your attitude towards employer/employee relations? Tick as many as you like.

   ☐ Employees do not need to know more about the company than is necessary for them to do their job.

   ☐ Managers should mix socially with workers and make every effort to get to know everyone personally.

   ☐ Managers make decisions. Workers carry out orders.

   ☐ There is no need for the managing director to know everyone in his/her company.

   ☐ Managers should always be paid more than workers, regardless of the number of hours worked.

   ☐ It is important in all companies that the management hierarchy is understood by everyone.

   ☐ Workers should always be consulted before management decisions are taken.

   ☐ The ideal working environment is when everybody knows a little bit about everyone else's job.

LEXIS

Business vocabulary

1 Put the following words and phrases under the most suitable heading (1–8). Use each item once only.

fixed assets	merger	down payment
cash reserves	recession	hire purchase
consignment	backlog	balance sheet
conglomerate	invoice	unique selling point
overheads	audit	parent company
brand name	capital	advertising campaign
by-product	slump	sleeping partner
break even	boom	a buyer's market
assembly line		

1 Company property   5 Making Payment

2 Working together   6 Marketing

3 Economic climate   7 Production

4 Accounting   8 Distribution Cost

2 Add further words of your own under each of the headings above.

3 What is the best way of learning these words?
   a Which words did you know already?
   b Which words looked familiar but you weren't sure about their use?
   c Which words did you think you knew which actually meant something else?
   d Which words had you never seen before?
   e Which do you think are the most useful to learn?

READING 1

1 Many universities and other institutes of higher education teach *Business Studies* or *Management Studies*.

  a What do you think these courses involve?

  b How useful do you think such courses are?

  c Would you consider following this type of course? Give reasons for your answer.

2 Read the following extract from a book on management skills. Does it change any of your answers to the questions in exercise 1?

1　The Harvard Business School, on the east coast of America, is one of the best respected centres for management education in the United States.

5　Robert Heller gives his view of its success rate in his book *The New Naked Manager.*

Executives, the most intensively educated group of adults in society, are very possibly educated to the least effect. The teaching of executives has been the 10 best-paying branch of education, and by a very long way. It has also been a soft market; only a few heretical voices have ever questioned whether you can really teach executives, that is, make them better at their jobs by any general course of 15 instruction, short or long.

Although executives should be numerate (and many are not), they don't require skills in higher algebra, and many great businesses have been created by men who all but count on their fingers.

20　A story tells of two schoolboy friends, one brilliant at maths, one innumerate to the point of idiocy, who meet much later when the first is a professor and the second a multi-millionaire. Unable to control his curiosity, the professor asks the figure- 25 blind dunderhead how he managed to amass his fortune. 'It's simple,' replies Midas. 'I buy things at a dollar and sell them for two dollars, and from that 1% difference I make a living.' The business world is full of successful one-percenters who live, not by 30 their calculators, still less their personal computer, but by knowing the difference between a buying price and a selling price. It is also full of clever fools who work out elaborate discounted cash flow sums to justify projects and products that a one-

35 percenter would laugh out of sight.

The clever fool syndrome would explain why one controversial study of Harvard Business School students found that, after a flying start, the alumni (presumably among the ablest young men of their 40 day) gradually slipped back to the general level inside their chosen management hierarchies. A Harvard graduate has no reason at all to suppose that he will manage more effectively than a less instructed contemporary. The Harvard man can 45 only claim that he is more highly educated; and high education and high achievement in practical affairs don't necessarily go together. John F Kennedy found that assembling America's brightest brains in Washington neither got bills through 50 Congress nor avoided the Bay of Pigs; and many companies have discovered that business-school diplomas are a thin defence against incompetence.

An overwhelmingly large proportion of the highest and best American executives did study business. All 55 this proves is that an overwhelmingly large proportion of business-minded undergraduates got the real message, which is that a diploma will be good for their careers, starting with starting salaries. It does not follow that the education was of any other 60 direct benefit either to the executive or his firm. Nor does it follow, of course, that the schooling was wasted. As a general rule, the wise man recruits the finest intelligence he can find; and good minds are far better for good training. The question is only whether 65 academic training in subjects that seem to have some connection with management is the best education for managing, and that is something that nobody can prove either way.

3 Think of a suitable title for the extract.

4 Answer these questions.

  a What point is the author making when he tells the story of the two schoolboy friends?

  b How successful does the author feel that graduates of the Harvard business school are when they actually work in business?

  c Did J F Kennedy choose his political advisers wisely, according to the author?

  d What point is the author making in the final paragraph?

  e Which phrase or sentence in the extract best illustrates the author's overall argument?

5 From the context, explain what each of the following means:

    soft market (line 11)   *heretical* (line 12)

    dunderhead (line 25)   *amass* (line 25)

    successful one–percenters (line 29)

    alumni (line 38)

6 Choose four of five phrases from the extract that you think would be useful to learn. Compare the phrases you have chosen with those of a partner and explain why you selected them.

LISTENING 1

In this recording, you will hear part of a conversation with a tutor at the Henley Management College, which has been running management training courses for many years.

1 Listen to the recording once. How far do you think the speaker agrees or disagrees with the author of the text you have just read?

2 Look at this edited version of the transcript. Fill in as many words as you can, from memory and from your general knowledge of business and English.

Then listen to the recording again to check your answers.

> Yeah that's a good question, isn't it? Somebody's been in here for a week's (1) .... or whatever. They've had the latest (2) .... of knowledge, has this in fact in some way improved their (3) .... performance? If you were working in a training (4) .... you can sometimes do that. You can say 'well I taught this person this and now let's see if that person can (5) .... that'. This works very closely in a skills area where (6) .... skills are important for example. What we are more concerned with here is not so much (7) .... training as (8) .... work. So Henley puts an (9) .... into a person's longer term (10) .... development. In that sense it's not quite so easy to see a (11) .... between input of training experience and (12) .... of job performance. You can't quite measure it in that way. And I don't say that in a dismissive sense to (13) .... or minimise the problem of dealing with that question because it is a question that we (14) .... with quite a bit here because if companies can't see an improvement eventually then they will clearly stop sending their people to places like Henley or anywhere else. The (15) .... that we are grappling with in that area are no different than the similar issues in (16) .... organisations.

3 What do you think is the difference between *skills training* and *development work*?

4 Do you feel more in agreement with the tutor you have just heard or with the author of READING 1? Discuss your opinions.

WRITING 1

1 Imagine that you work for a small stationery business. If a customer is late with their payment, what should you do? Choose from the following:

  a phone them to find out what has happened.

  b write a threatening letter.

  c write a respectful reminder.

  d send them another invoice.

  e send somebody round to make a personal enquiry.

2 Now read the extract below from a guide on how to collect money you are owed. Do you agree with its recommendations?

Sending a letter

A letter, subject to its contents, is less threatening than a phone call and gives the recipient time to think and do some checking. It is therefore more courteous and friendly to write first. Many, perhaps most, of your customers will respond to a well written letter and this reduces the list of stressful telephone calls that you must make. If no reply is made to the letter then you will have a ready-made excuse to phone later.

Rule number one is that the letter should be a letter, not a pompously worded routine circular with 'Dear Sir' at the start and 'Yours faithfully' at the end. Dickensian expressions should be avoided, as should accounting jargon. These will make the letter sound as if it has been produced by an antique accounting machine.

```
Dear Sirs,
    We beg to remind you that your
account is now overdue. We
respectfully request that you
put steps in hand to regularise
the position at your earliest
convenience.
    May we take this opportunity
to respectfully remind you that
our terms of trade are payment
in full within 30 calendar days
of the date of our invoice.
    Thanking you in anticipation
of an early response,
we remain,
Yours faithfully,
DINGLE, DOYLE AND DANGLE
```

So, avoid letters like this:

To obtain a response from the human being who will read the letter it should sound and look as if it is written by a human being and is being sent to one. The basic requirements for your letter are. . .

*   *   *   *

The resulting, typed, letter might look something like this:

```
Dear Sarah
    I would be grateful if you
would let us have a cheque for
two overdue payments.
    The items concerned are:
i  Invoice No. 123 for £1000.00
dated 1st January (Sales order
no. 6789).
    and
ii Invoice no. 161 for £800.00
dated 3rd January (Sales order
no. 6788).
    As you will see, these amounts
are now about a month overdue.
    If there is any problem with
either of these items, please
let me know before the end of
this month.
Yours sincerely
```

3 What do you think the *basic requirements* omitted from this extract might be?

Example

The letter should be sent to a named person rather than a company or department.

4 The letter above still receives no reply so another letter must be sent.

a In small groups, consider these points:
- Is it now time to be threatening?
- How polite should you be?
- How long should the letter be?

b If you receive no reply to this letter either, what will your next response be?

In your group, write some phrases that you think would be suitable for this letter.

Compare your phrases with those of another group. Which are more likely to achieve the desired result?

c In groups or individually, write the letter.

155

SPEAKING 1

Telephoning

I'm here to engage you in light conversation while you're on hold.

When phoning large companies, the initial task is to make sure you're talking to the right person. Before you launch into a long explanation of your problem, check that the person you are speaking to is the person who deals with that area.

1 Divide the following phrases into those that might be used by the caller, those used by the switchboard operator, and those by the receiver of the call.

Which one phrase would never be used?

	Caller	Switchboard operator	Receiver of call
Can I speak to somebody about . . . , please?	☐	☐	☐
Hello, is that accounts?	☐	☐	☐
Extension 248, please.	☐	☐	☐
Who's calling?	☐	☐	☐
I'll hold.	☐	☐	☐
I'm afraid she's in a meeting at the moment.	☐	☐	☐
Putting you through.	☐	☐	☐
Still trying to connect you.	☐	☐	☐
Hello, I am George Tavridis.	☐	☐	☐
I'm getting no reply from her office. Shall I try her secretary?	☐	☐	☐
Can I take a message?	☐	☐	☐
Can I leave a message?	☐	☐	☐
Can I speak to Sarah Colyer, please?	☐	☐	☐
Perhaps you could get her to ring me back.	☐	☐	☐
Speaking.	☐	☐	☐
Number's ringing for you.	☐	☐	☐
Can she ring you back? Is it urgent?	☐	☐	☐
Is there somebody else in the department I could speak to?	☐	☐	☐

2 You have still not received any reply to the letter you wrote in WRITING 1 asking for payment of an invoice. You now decide to ring the accounts department of the company concerned to find out what's going on and if necessary, to put some pressure on them.

In pairs, think of phrases that could be used :

a to ask for the money. (Be polite, not aggressive: there may be a very good reason why you haven't received it.)

b by an accountant explaining why the invoice hasn't been paid. (Your company has financial problems, but for business reasons it must appear that money is no problem.)

3 Work in groups of three. One person is the caller, another the switchboard operator and the third the accountant of the company concerned. Use your own names. You have not met before. Read the instructions for your part below. Then role-play the phone call.

> **Caller**
> Be polite but insistent. Don't let the switchboard operator keep you waiting. You suspect he/she has been told to put you off (i.e. prevent you from speaking to the people you want to). You insist on payment by next Friday, but are prepared to compromise if there is a real problem.

> **Switchboard Operator**
> You have been told to put this caller off by pretending the accountant is in a meeting. Offer to take a message. If the caller is very insistent, you will have no alternative other than to put him/her through.

> **Accountant**
> You've been on holiday and the junior clerk has been in charge while you were away. You can blame some of the trouble on him. However your company is badly in debt and cannot afford to pay the entire amount at the moment. Offer to pay half now and half later. Be very apologetic.

WRITING 2

1 Business letters can contain a number of standard phrases. Put the phrases below under the appropriate function heading in the table. Say whether the phrase is more likely to appear at the beginning or end of the letter or in any other position.

STANDARD PHRASE	FUNCTION
a With reference to your letter of July 12th. . .	**Stating subject of letter** **Confirming** a (beginning)
b With regard to your recent enquiry about. . .	
c We would like to draw your attention to. . .	**Acknowledging receipt** **Apologising** of letter, etc.
d Thank you for your letter of January 14th.	
e Thank you in advance for your assistance. . .	**Requesting** **Thanking**
f We are pleased to inform you that the goods have been received.	
g We regret to inform you that. . .	
h Following our recent telephone conversation, I would like to confirm the appointment on 6th June at 2.30.	
i We would like to offer our apologies for the delay. . .	**Answering queries** **Offering Help** a (beginning)
j May I take this opportunity of thanking you for your assistance.	
k We have pleasure in enclosing payment for invoice no. . .	
l Should you require any further information, please do not hesitate to contact us.	**Endings** **Listing enclosures**
m We would be grateful if you could send us a copy of your catalogue.	
n As regards your recent proposals to supply. . .	
o Please find enclosed two copies of. . .	**Pointing something out**
p We look forward to doing business with you.	

2 Answer the following letter. Take care with the layout and paragraphing.

George Tranner
Cambridge Processing Technology Ltd
12 Bedford Road
Cambridge

Data Systems plc
14-25 Queen Street
Newbury
N12 4PT

16 June 1993

Dear Mr Tranner

On 2nd May I sent you an order for eight computer programs from your catalogue. Although the order form specified delivery within 28 days, we have received neither the programs nor acknowledgement of the order. I notice however that the cheque for £127 enclosed with the order has been debited from our account.
Would you please look into this for me and let me know at the earliest opportunity what steps you are taking to despatch our order?
Yours sincerely

Kostas Popadopoulos

Mr K. Popadopalous

LEXIS

Collocation

1 Match the word on the left with a collocating noun on the right.

early	chain
introductory	offer
cash	retirement
private	profits
take-over	salary
starting	enterprise
retail	bid
limited	flow
pre-tax	liability
share	index

2 Complete the following extracts using a suitable phrase from those in exercise 1.

a

> **20% off all designer goods at J J Shorts!**
> This ...., valid until 9 November only, gives you the chance to discover the designer outfits of your dreams at a dream of a price ...! To save £s,£s,£s, all you need to do is apply for one of our money saving J J Shorts instant credit cards, allowing you to spend up to £500!!

b

> The government today reiterated its support for small businesses by relaunching the .... scheme, giving loans at preferential rates to those wishing to start their own company.

c

> despite Morris' involvement in the $20 million loan deal which led to the collapse of Source Kemble Ltd., it is believed that he will have .... for the company's debts and that his family will remain multi-millionaires, leaving those who bought Source Kemble kitchens with little chance of seeing either their kitchens or their money.

d

> Chromalin plc, the York based photographic company, announced massive staff cuts today which their managing director attributed to the slump in consumer spending. Although 587 people have been laid off, 65 accepted voluntary redundancy and another 18 opted for ....

e

> **............. Rejected**
> Petrochem UK plc were today unsuccessful in their attempt to buy the pharmaceutical giant Ryder-Caplin. Shares in Petrochem fell by 4p when news broke of the

f

> Trading resumed quietly on the floor of the US stock exchange after yesterday's excitement. At the close of trading today the Dow Jones .... showed a rise of

3 Four of the collocating phrases seen in exercise 1 were not featured in the exercise above. With a partner, write clear definitions of these phrases and compare them with those of another pair. Which definitions do you think are the clearest?

READING 2

1 What do you know about *The Body Shop*? What do you think it sells?

2 The following case study comes from a book called *The Green Business Guide.* What do you think a *Green Business* is?

3 Read the case study on *The Body Shop* and write notes to fill in the chart on the right.

CASE STUDY:
THE BODY SHOP INTERNATIONAL
Body and Soul

THE COMPANY

The Body Shop, the franchise-based green cosmetics retail chain, has been a phenomenon. For over a decade, sales and profits grew by an average 540 per cent a year. There are now more than 580 stores in 38 countries. For the year to February 1990, the company reported pre-tax profits of £14.5 million on sales of £84.5 million, despite a major retailing recession. The company is known as much for its environmental campaigning as for its profitability.

THE STORY

'I've just taken what every good teacher knows,' *Body Shop* founder Anita Roddick told *Business* magazine in 1990. 'You try to make your classroom an enthralling place. When I taught history, I would put graphics all around the room and play music from the period we were studying. Now I'm doing the same thing. There is education in the shops.'

Employees are bombarded with lively newsletters, brochures and posters, and encouraged to take part in broadly based training programmes. Throughout, the purposes is to expand employee horizons – and sales. 'I see business as a renaissance concept,' Roddick explained, 'where the human spirit comes into play. How do you ennoble the spirit when you are selling moisture cream? Let me tell you, the spirit soars when you are making products that are life serving, that make people feel better.'

Macho manufacturing companies would writhe at some of the things said in the *Body Shop Charter*. For example: 'We care about each other as individuals; we will continue to endeavour to bring meaning and pleasure to the workplace.' But the result is a level of employee commitment that would turn most other companies green with envy.

So seductive is the *Body Shop's* business formula, that franchisees, employees and managers talk about the difficulty they would have going back to work in an 'ordinary' company. And when the company was building up in the US, some 2500 people applied for franchises before it had even started operating.

THE LESSONS

Green companies depend on green-minded employees. Employees, in turn, often take their cues on environmental quality – and their employer's environmental commitment – from the surroundings in which they work. Our workplaces can be seen as part of the front line in the battle to save our communities and planet. If they are safe, healthy and pleasant, we will be that much more interested in greening the rest of the world.

Type of Company:	
Size:	
Financial Performance:	
Business Philosophy:	
Attitude to employees:	

4 How do you account for the phenomenal success of *The Body Shop*?

5 *Macho manufacturing companies would writhe at some of the things said in the Body Shop Charter.* What do you think this means?
Could Anita Roddick's business philosophy be used successfully in other businesses such as banking, food processing, the textile trade, the construction industry, etc.? Explain how.

6 Some businesses now commission a 'green audit' of their workplace and production methods to find ways in which they can function in a more environmentally friendly way. In small groups, list all the ways you can think of in which businesses can improve their environmental record. Compare your list with another group.

LISTENING 2

In this recording you will hear John Eckersley, principal and owner of the *Eckersley School of English* in Oxford, talking about the business of running a language school.

1 Before you listen, discuss the following questions in small groups.
   a Do you think running a language school is different from running any other sort of business?
   b What other considerations might there be other than maximising profits?

2 Listen to the recording and answer these questions:
   a How fully does John Eckersley answer the above two questions?
   b How does he explain the difference between his point of view and that of the accountant?

3 How do you think this conversation will continue? How could computers or video be cost effective in running a language school?

GRAMMAR

Future forms

Grammatically, English does not have a future tense. Instead it has a number of alternative future forms.

1 Use the examples in the chart on the right, 1–9, to help you put the functions of the future forms, a–i, in the appropriate places. Although there may be more than one alternative on occasions, try to choose the most suitable function in each case.

FUNCTIONS

a making general predictions about the future
b making predictions after observing present events
c saying what you intend to do in the future
d making instant decisions now about the future
e talking about definite, timetabled events
f making promises and threats
g talking about future events completed before another time in the future
h talking about future events which have already been arranged
i talking about a future event that will happen as a matter of course, without the explicit intention of the speaker

STRUCTURE	FUNCTION
'will' + infinitive	
1 I bet that his company will be bankrupt within a year.	1 a
2 That report will be on your desk first thing tomorrow morning.	2
3 If you wait a moment, I'll go and get the file from my office.	3
'be going to' + infinitive	
4 We're going to step up production by 15%.	4
5 If we continue to increase sales as we have been doing, we're going to be in a position to launch a take-over bid.	5
Present simple	
6 The first presentation starts at 9.30 tomorrow.	6
Present continuous	
7 The new board of directors is meeting next week.	7
'will' + continuous	
8 There is no point going to Hong Kong on business at the beginning of February because they'll be celebrating Chinese New Year there.	8
'will' + perfect	
9 By January next year, we will have implemented all the recommendations contained in this report.	9

* Note: The present simple is also usual in *If*-clauses and after certain time adverbials: *when, after, before, until, once, as soon as,* etc. . The present perfect can also be used.

2 Discuss the differences between these pairs of sentences.
   a I'll be seeing him later on today.
      I'll see him later on today.
   b The investment group meets at 2.00 on Thursday.
      The investment group is meeting at 2.00 on Thursday.
   c I am going to send a circular informing our clients of these decisions.
      I am sending a circular informing our clients of these decisions.
   d We'll let you know if there are further developments.
      We'll be letting you know of any further developments.
   e The project will be reviewed at frequent intervals.
      The project will have been reviewed at frequent intervals.

f   Will you be coming to the meeting on Thursday?
    Are you coming to the meeting on Thursday?

3 Put the verbs in the following interchanges in a
    suitable future form. More than one answer may be
    possible. Justify your choices.

a   'You .... (go) to the conference next month?'
    'Well I was going but it looks as though I
    .... (have) too much to do here.'

b   'You .... (finish) that by this afternoon?'
    'I .... (do) my best but I can't promise
    anything.'
    'Can you finish it for three o'clock? George
    .... (go) to the Post Office then and the last
    post .... (be) at three thirty.'

c   'What you .... (do) about these sales figures?'
    'I ....(show) them to Tony. After he
    .... (see) them I .... (give) them to you.'
    'What do I do with them?'
    'I .... (let) you know when I .... (decide).'

d   'The meeting .... (start) in ten minutes.'
    'I may be a bit late, I'm afraid. A client
    .... (phone) me back about the deal we
    .... (make) next week.'

4 In small groups discuss your predictions, plans or
    arrangements for some of the following:

a   The place you live in the next century
b   The future of English as a world language
c   Your future career plans
d   Your arrangements for tomorrow morning
e   The role of computers fifty years from now
f   The role of religion in international affairs
g   The future of medical science
h   Next year's fashion trends

SPEAKING 2

Giving a presentation

Business people sometimes have to give presentations to
other companies or other company employees about new
projects, the aims of the company, financial reports, etc. .

1 Look at this list of guidelines for giving presentations
    and decide which are good rules to follow.

a   **Keep your voice deep and slow**
b   **Try to vary the pace**
c   **Use short sentences and simple vocabulary**
d   **Keep your hands in your pockets or fold your
    arms to hide nerves**
e   **Tell a couple of jokes to liven things up a bit**
f   **Address the most important people in the room
    and ignore the rest**
g   **Pause occasionally to give your audience time to
    think**
h   **Give a summary of what you are going to say at
    the beginning of your presentation and again at
    the end**
i   **Use visual aids such as an overhead projector or
    flip chart**
j   **Read straight from a prepared script**
k   **Steer clear of jargon, abbreviations and statistics
    as much as possible**
l   **Make sure both you and your audience are clear
    as to the purpose of the presentation: decide
    what you want them to know or do as a result of it**
m   **Structure the talk carefully and make sure the
    audience follows your stages**

2 Give a short presentation to the class on a subject of
    your choice, for example your country, your
    business, your academic studies, etc. .
    Structure the talk as follows:
    • opening/introductory remarks
    • summary of contents of talk
    • main substance
    • conclusion
    • invite any questions

You may find some of these phrases useful:

The purpose of this presentation is. . .
As far as. . . is concerned,. . .
. . .is of secondary importance
Let me give you a broad outline. . .
Perhaps I should start by refreshing your memories as
to . . . , in particular. . .
This may give you some indication of. . .
This chart details some encouraging/depressing
trends. . .

To sum up. . .	May I begin by. . .
Finally. . .	Our priorities are. . .
Secondly. . .	As you know, . . .
I'll now move on to. . .	As a whole. . .
In other words. . .	
First of all	
Next	

LEXIS

1 Find words from the exercise on page 152 (LEXIS: BUSINESS VOCABULARY) which correspond to the meanings below.

a the place on the factory floor where things are produced = <u>assembly line</u> .

b a time when things are going well for the economy = ...

c something extra that is produced as a result of producing something else = ...

d when two companies join together to become one company = ...

e an examination of a company's accounts to ensure they are legally in order = ...

f a trade name which people have confidence in and will set out to buy = ...

g an expense not directly related to producing a product; regular essential costs of a business (i.e. telephone, rent) = ...

h when the amount the company spends and the amount it earns are equal = ...

i a quantity of goods for delivery = ...

j a company which owns another one = ...

k the amount of work that has gathered over a period of time and still needs to be done = ...

l the one thing about a product which differentiates it from other similar products. = ...

m things owned by the company which are required for the company to operate over a long term e.g. buildings, land, machinery = ...

2 Use collocations from the exercise on page 158 to fill the gaps in these sentences.

a They launched the product with a(n) .... of two for the price of one.

b *Lloyds Bank* launched a hostile .... for *Midland Bank*.

c During the 1980s, the British government strongly encouraged .... and many people started up their own businesses.

d At the age of 55 he decided to take ....

e *The Financial Times* .... fell 23 points in trading this morning.

f A .... company is one where the shareholders cannot be asked to pay debts beyond the value of their shares.

g Increased capital expenditure soon resulted in a .... crisis.

h *Williams Ross*, the accountancy firm, offers university graduates a .... of £18,000.

i She was the area manager for a .... of clothes shops.

j This year the company has made .... in excess of £1.2 million.

3 Say what these abbreviations mean and where you would use them.

a PLC

b Corp. or Co.

c c.c.

d enc. or encs.

e a/c

f misc.

g p.a.

h M.D.

i c.i.f.

j P.R.

k Ltd. or Inc.

l rec(d).

m i.e.

n cf.

GRAMMAR

Future forms

In the situations below, choose the most suitable response.

1 You have made an appointment to see a prospective customer this afternoon. When someone asks you about him, you reply:

a) I'll see him this afternoon.

b) I'm seeing him this afternoon.

c) I see him this afternoon.

2 Someone needs a letter posting. You are on your way out to lunch so you say:
   a) I'm posting it for you.
   b) I'll post it for you.
   c) I'm going to post it for you.

3 You're not feeling 100% so you decide to go home now. You say to your secretary:
   a) I'm going to go home.
   b) I'll go home.
   c) I'll be going home.

4 You are likely to be away from the office for a while. A polite secretary asks you:
   a) How long are you going to be away for?
   b) How long are you away for?
   c) How long will you be away for?

5 You are going to meet a client in town. Your secretary asks you:
   a) When will you come back?
   b) When are you coming back?
   c) When will you be coming back?

6 You are going on a business trip and are late leaving the office to catch the flight. A friend who is driving you to the airport says:
   Hurry up!
   a) The plane leaves in an hour and a half!
   b) The plane is leaving in an hour and a half!
   c) The plane will leave in an hour and a half!

7 On the flight, the pilot announces:
   a) We will be flying at a height of around 30,000 feet.
   b) We will fly at a height of around 30,000 feet.
   c) We are going to fly at a height of around 30,000 feet.

8 You arrive at your destination. You look out of the aeroplane window. The sky is looking rather black. You say:
   a) It will rain.
   b) It's going to rain.
   c) It will be raining.

9 Someone asks you what you think about the recession. You say:
   a) I think it will get better by the end of the year.
   b) I think it will be getting better by the end of the year.
   c) I think it is getting better by the end of the year.

10 Someone asks you about your plans for the evening. You say:
   a) I'm sitting at home watching television.
   b) I'm going to sit at home and watch television.
   c) I'll sit at home and watch television.

"I'll wait for him one more year, I keep telling myself he may be having engine trouble somewhere."

Communication Activities

UNIT 2

READING 1

3 A point related to the preceding one is that the Japanese are for all practical purposes incapable of debating with one another. In order to debate, the second speaker must grasp all the particulars of the first speaker's statement, question what needs to be questioned, and offer a complete rebuttal of the points of disagreement. The first speaker must listen carefully to this rebuttal, discern where the differences of opinion lie, and address them in an attempt to persuade the second speaker. By repeating this process the debaters move toward a conclusion. But a debate between Japanese usually ends after only one round; either one party yields to the other, or both give up, thinking, 'That one's impossible to talk to'.

4 The Japanese dislike specifying things down to the last detail. This has led some Westerners to conclude that Japanese speech is like Japanese ink painting: ink painting creates an effect by the use of blank spaces, and unless one is able to read those empty areas, one cannot understand the work. The same is true, they say, of Japanese speech. One always has to figure out the parts that have been left unsaid.

Because the Japanese prefer not to state things clearly, they get little practice in doing so. As a result, they are unskilled at using words to report facts accurately or to express their opinions logically.

UNIT 4

READING 1

Gatwick Stopover
Gatwick Moat House
£60 to £100

1 At the Moat House I slept, fitfully, in a narrow, dimly-lit corridor of a room where the distance between the bed-end and the wall was a bare two feet, and where the air-conditioning unit contrived to make as much noise
5 as the aircraft would have made if they'd left the windows single-glazed and had me open them for fresh air.

Indeed, the whole room seems to have been designed by an architect who has no idea why people stay in hotels. I
10 give you the storage facilities as an example – or at least I would if there were any. The Moat House storage concept is two short hanging rails with six hangers. Those sartorial types who like to keep a spare set of socks or a second shirt will find nowhere in a Moat House
15 room in which to store them. The bedroom fitment, into which the mission control panel had been set, was drawerless and there was no shelf or drawer space elsewhere in the room. The bathroom contained two tiny cerise tablets of the brand of soap that smelled of
20 the sort of air freshener hospitals use in terminal wards.

Room service was, by the time I arrived at 11 pm., not available, but for £3.50 they took 25 minutes to send me up a dryish ham sandwich and a glass of beer. The continental breakfast was from apparently the continent of Antarctica: cold, mean and unappetising.
25 The public areas are rather grubby, although the medium-sized restaurant (which I didn't have a chance to try), looked reasonable enough.

The slogan of the Moat House is, according to the notepaper, 'The Service You'd Recommend'. Not me, I
30 wouldn't.

Text B
a single-glazed window
b sartorial types
c bedroom fitment
d terminal wards
e a continental breakfast

UNIT 6

READING 2

Text B

Report on reinvestigation of shooting in 1952 stirs hopes of clearing hanged man's name

Family awaits pardon for Bentley

Duncan Campbell
Crime Correspondent

1 Iris Bentley will tomorrow lay a wreath at the gate of the prison where her brother Derek was executed, amid family hopes that an announcement of a posthumous pardon is imminent.

5 Last week the report of the reinvestigation of the circumstances of the death of PC Sidney Miles was passed to the Home Office by the Metropolitan Police. Kenneth Baker, the Home Secretary, had ordered a fresh inquiry into the case in August.

10 The Home Office said the report would be given full consideration, but there was no indication as to its conclusions. A spokesman for the Metropolitan Police said they were unable to comment on its contents. It is understood that surviving officers who were present at the shooting were reinterviewed.

15 Derek Bentley was hanged in January 1953 at Wandsworth prison for the murder of PC Miles. He was shot by Mr Bentley's companion, Chris Craig, during an attempted break-in at a warehouse in Croydon, south London. Mr Craig was, at 16, too young to hang.

20 Despite pleas for clemency, Mr Bentley was executed. His death lead to disturbances in London and helped in the eventual abolition of the death penalty. His sister, Iris, from south London, has campaigned for his posthumous pardon, and has attended death penalty debates in the House of Commons

25 to dissuade MPs from ever bringing hanging back.

Ms Bentley said yesterday she had not been informed of the findings of the report.

'I'm still in the dark,' she said. 'It's just like when they sent the letter saying that his appeal had been turned down. We 30 have heard nothing at all.'

She is hopeful that evidence that has emerged recently will finally clear her brother. She had contacted Angela Rumbold, the Home Office Minister of State, she said, and was awaiting further information.

35 She believes that the film of the case, Let Him Have It, released last year, and the continuing controversy about the hanging, will finally vindicate her campaign. There have been three books, a play, three songs and numerous documentaries on the case.

40 Mr Craig, now aged 55 and living in Bedfordshire, appeared on the television programme, Thames Report, last year to say that Mr Bentley had never uttered the words 'let him have it', as the prosecution had alleged at their trial.

'The man was innocent,' said Mr Craig, who was released 45 after serving 10 years in prison.

'I was doing my own thing. I was running amok,' he said. 'I was guilty as charged. . . as equally Bentley wasn't.'

The only precedent for a posthumous pardon is the case of Timothy Evans, who was cleared in 1966, 16 years after his 50 execution, of the murder of his baby daughter at Rillington Place. Like Bentley, Mr Evans had the mental age of a child.

The Guardian

UNIT 13

WRITING

Gary has been involved in taking drugs and alcohol and has run away from home on three occasions. His behaviour at home is anti-social and abusive and he has threatened violence. His parents have on different occasions sent him to his room, beat him and argued. When he ran away they sent him the airfare home. They have also paid for three counselling sessions. The mother also tried to see a juvenile court judge to discuss the issue. Now the mother is refusing to allow Gary back in the house. She has been arrested for child neglect and has formed a parental lobby group aimed at toughening the law dealing with juvenile crime.

SPEAKING

Role-play

Student C

You are Gary. You disagree with everyone, often loudly and abusively and show contempt for your parents. You are a little frightened of the social worker, but often sulk and refuse to answer questions.

Although you hate your home, you do not want to go to a special school and should prepare reasons for not going.

Student D

You are the social worker and must remain in control of this discussion, eliciting everyone's opinions and steering things towards a conclusion. You are a professional and have had this sort of discussion many times before, so your language should be polite but firm. Try to control Gary and his mother and allow the timid father to give his opinion. Prepare arguments to persuade people that Gary should stay at home and that both he and his parents should receive professional counselling.

Tapescripts

UNIT 1 LISTENING 1

1 (*Ewa*)

Do you get bored, when you're learning English? I mean, are you always interested or are there times when you think 'God, this is boring'?

Yeah, well, sometimes it's boring, but most of the time it's interesting.

Is there anything in particular you find boring?

Er, it's difficult to say. Maybe sometimes, if I know something and some other students don't know and the teacher is explaining it a lot. Then I might find it boring. But most of the lessons I think are very interesting.

I mean, if you're still learning after six years you must find it interesting. I'm just interested in how someone can study a language for six years and still be interested in it.

Yeah but there's so much to learn and I want to be able to speak it. . . I want to be able to say what I want to say in the way I want to say it. Not just make myself understood barely but I want, you know, to be able to say exactly what I want to say. *Right.*

2 (*Jan*)

The most difficult thing is to understand people. And it's still a difficult thing because you have to concentrate a lot upon what the other one is saying. I think it's not so, so difficult to read something or to write something, even to speak something, but I think it's very difficult to understand. When you're sitting in front of the television for example I'm really trying hard to understand everything and I have to say to myself, 'Come on! Concentrate yourself!' It's really, it's really difficult.

3 (*Maria*)

The most difficult thing is to speak like an Englishman. Because you can speak like a foreigner. You can learn English like a foreign, you can write like a foreign, everything like foreign but no, like real English.

What's difficult to get it like real English? What exactly in the language. . .?

You know is something like er, I think it's a style or, I don't know really what it is, but. . . is something really difficult to get.

What about grammar? Do you like grammar?

Oh, well I don't really like it.

Why not?

Because. . . is sometimes is irrational. It's nonsense er, you know is. . . it could be easier if you can follow some rules and regulations but in English grammar everything is possible sometimes. Sometimes something is not possible and you don't know why. . . is not possible. But there is no real reason. . . it's just 'Nobody say that'. And 'wow' how can you know if people say that or they don't say that?

UNIT 1 LISTENING 2

Richard = R Helen = H

R: How many students have you got in the class?

H: Nine.

R: Do they all have different problems or I mean, are there any general problems that you could abstract out?

H: Erm, linguistically? (Yeah.) Erm, no I think they tend to be more individual problems, erm, partly just because they come from so many different countries, you know. (So one of. . .) Scandinavians and. . .

R: Problems are related to their first language?

H: Yes, and to the exposure that they've already had to English. Some people have . . . have learnt English formally erm at school erm then other people like the Scandinavians – I think they haven't had such formal teaching of the language but they've had it around them all the time, on the TV, that sort of thing. . .

R: So what sort of problems linguistically do they have? Can you give me a few examples?

H: Well the Scandinavians can't. . . can't relate to when you're dealing with complex areas of grammar, they can't relate to any overtly grammatical explanations if you like and they can't work things out.

R: What, you mean they don't know the sort of the terminology?

H: Yes, the terminology is a big problem. Erm, the other students who, er, are just not as fluent don't know as many colloquialisms, idioms, that sort of thing. The ones that have the more formal teaching and and haven't been listening to films and watching TV programmes in English.

R: So you think that being advanced, the more exposure they have to the language, that that definitely rubs off; that they should be reading lots, listening. . .

H: Yes, because they have more of a feel for the language and they can usually sense whether something is right or wrong. They know it sounds right or sounds wrong but they can't explain why. Whereas another student will take a more analytical approach to a piece of language.

R: That's fine, that's fine as far as grammar is concerned. What, what other. . . Is there anything else apart from grammar?

H: Pronunciation. Again, that, the students who have been taught more formally tend to have, don't tend to have as good a pronunciation. Again, particularly the Scandinavian students seem to be, to pronounce English quite well. . .

R: Um. Is that a problem? I mean as long as you can understand what what they're saying?

H: Er, no. It's not a big problem. No. It's more to do with when they have to produce certain intonation patterns. It comes naturally to some students more than others.

R: Yeah. Why, why, I mean, do they need these intonation patterns? Why can't they just keep their own?

H: Erm, I think at an advanced level you do need them. I mean, it's part of, of being advanced in English for register and you know . . .

R: Um, to avoid perhaps their attitude being misunderstood.

H: Misunderstood. Yes. Very much so.

UNIT 2 LISTENING 1

Catriona = C Bernard = B

C: Something which I think a lot of people find difficult when they go to other countries is the problem of greetings.

B: I agree, yeah . . .

C: I suppose in Britain we're terribly informal, I mean, much too informal perhaps, but I find that whenever I go to France or Italy I never really know who I should shake hands with, who I should maybe kiss . . .

B: It's very difficult.

C: . . . on one cheek, maybe two cheeks. I think in parts of France it's three cheeks, I mean, how do you know (three times)?

B: That's right. Well, Belgium it's three cheeks, I mean, er, if you think of Marie-Louise, I mean, she comes along and sees us and says bang bang bang on three cheeks straight away, doesn't she? But erm, I can remember when I first went to Thailand I had a bit of a problem because, erm, you really didn't know who, who was who and in the end I discovered you had to watch the height of the erm, hands if er, because they have a way of bowing to each other which I think they call is 'waiing' – you 'wai' to somebody. You put your hands together and you bow, and, according to the height of your hands. So you are more or less important erm, if your hands go very high to your head, it means the person you're speaking to is much more important than you are, but if you hold your hands like this, sort of chest height sort of thing, you're more or less equal. Er, interesting . . .

C: And when do you start doing this? Do children bow or is it just as you get older?

B: Erm. I don't know, I just don't know really but, erm. . .

C: I wonder how you get to know.

B: But I'll tell you another place that's er, a bit of a problem with greetings. If you go er, go over the ocean to Peru, er, that's where I started off as a teacher, erm, the Peruvians really are very, very good at er, hugging you and embracing you and even people who you don't know awfully well – you sort of meet them in the street and immediately they hold out both their arms and they, they put them right round you and they go slap slap slap slap slap and it's really a bit of a joke, because I mean you can't see their head, because you've tucked your head sort of behind them and sometimes you can't even remember who's actually slapping your back, you know, but the great thing is it gives you time, because you go, '¡Hola! ¿Qué tal? how are you?' erm, 'We haven't seen each other for such a long time, have we?' slap slap slap slap slap and you think, 'Oh my gosh yes, I remember who this is. I met him at a party a few nights ago. . .'.

C: Is this generally men to men? This wouldn't be women to women?

B: Ah, that's a very interesting question. I expect probably it's the men. Yes, it's probably the men greeting each other.

C: 'How are you, old boy?' slap on the back kind of thing.

B: That sort of thing, yeah, I expect so.

UNIT 2 LISTENING 2

1 Hi there!
   Alright, then?
   Not so bad.
   Goin' down the local. Fancy a pint?
   Why not?

2 Come in.
   Good morning.
   Ah. Morning. Come in. Have a seat. How are you?
   Good journey?
   Not bad at all thank you.
   Coffee? Tea?
   Er. . . a cup of coffee would be very nice. Thank you.

3 'Scuse me. How much is this?
   One pound thirty eight.
   Ooh, that's dear.

4 Excuse me. Could you tell me how much this is?
   One pound thirty eight, madam.
   Thank you so much.

5 New jacket Matt?
   's right.
   Dead smart. How much?
   45 quid.
   You're joking!
   No. Honest.

6 Comin' down town?
  Wha' for?
  I dunno. Bit of shopping.
  No. Can't be bothered.

UNIT 3 LISTENING 1

Pat = P Richard = R

R: Are they dangerous? I mean. . .

P: No, not really. Erm

R: 'Cause they're big. It has to be said.

P: They're big. That's it. It seems the bigger they are the gentler they are. When you think of the big Shire horses. . . (Yeah). Their temperaments are amazing 'cause I mean when you think how they let us control them. Erm, (This one's trying to eat my tape recorder) they they're so strong, and there's over a ton of horse there, you know (Yes) but because they're work horses and they're steady and you know through generations of breeding they seem very docile. (Yeah) Even the unbroken ones are very friendly.

R: Because I mean I know nothing about horses. I've never ridden horses and and I've always been very nervous about sort of walking round behind one, for example, or. . .

P: Yes, I think you want to have a healthy respect for them. (Yes) Because if you creep up behind them and they're perhaps half asleep (Yes) and you don't say 'Hello old chap. How are you getting on?' (Right) and they don't go like that, you see like he knows we're here now.

R: This one's enormous.

P: Well, he isn't really, he's just rather fat.

R: Oh I see!

P: Er, he erm, he might sort of, in self-defence, because that's their natural, erm, attack is with their heels because flight is their, is their idea of safety, you see, (Yes) whereas a bovine animal with horns will turn around and attack, won't run away (Right) and isn't very speedy anyway. (Yes, yes) But these have nothing to attack with except their heels.

R: It's a gorgeous coat.

P: Well he's rather elderly again. I know you want to talk . . .

R: He's going going grey.

P: Oh stop it, I don't want my ears nibbled off. Erm, they erm, yes well, he always was, he's what you call a roan (Ah right) so he had a, had a white fleck in a black coat, anyway but. . . Nature seems to, when they get older erm, provides them with more woollies.

R: He seems remarkably trusting. I mean there you are sticking your, sticking your fingers in its nose.

P: Oh yes.

R: He likes that, does he?

P: Yes. Oh, he likes that, yes. He's sort of likes, they like fuss. (Yes) They like being talked to. You can teach them words, which they learn like a parrot fashion.

R: Right. So they they obey commands.

P: Like walk or trot or halt or whatever you like to call it you know.

R: Yes. This, this one's waving his head around

P: This little person: . . . Yes, getting very agitated because he's thinks I should come and feed.

R: Extremely hungry. Right.

P: There. Yes. Sort of, yes.

UNIT 3 LISTENING 2

Richard = R Susannah = S

R: Can you tell me about the job 'cause, I mean, as I said I don't know much about ACIS. . . What is it?

S: Well I can tell you what we do, which is we're in, I'm involved with the hiring of couriers and all the things that the couriers would do, which is what that advert's all about. Erm, and so we employ couriers to act as, well they're tour guides. Erm, and to act as guides to American students and their teachers who come on educational trips round Europe and so as a guide you'll be responsible for absolutely everything: from the logistics of the trip, getting people into hotels and onto buses and all that sort of thing, to giving them road commentary on the bus and telling them all about the sights and that sort of thing. Erm, and also filling their free time so whenever they have free time on their agenda, on their itinerary of things to do, erm, you're there taking them to Covent Garden or the theatre, or whatever, just filling their free time so it's 24 hours a day, every day.

R: How do you, I mean, people apply to you from this advertisement, telephone you. How do you decide from their application whether to interview the person or not, or do you interview everybody?

S: Erm, we do interview everybody unless their application looks, you know, if they've got no languages at all and, erm, you see part of the job, it's important that the courier has quite a, the personality side, that's what I'm trying to say, is really important because you're running this trip and the idea's to keep everybody jolly and happy and the energy going, and all that sort of thing, so that side is, you know, sometimes if somebody has got the most incredible personality and they're good fun and you know that they're going to be a great courier but they don't have many languages or their knowledge of the countries and so on isn't so wonderful, we still might employ them because they can swot up in those areas, erm, because their personality is so important erm, and their attitude. Attitude can make or break the trip or make or break us employing them really, erm.

R: So they send you a written application?

S: They send us a written application with a photograph and generally we do see most people (Right). Yeah, I mean 99% erm, and er, what was the question again?

Exercise 5

S: Some of them. . . generally they're quite short, you know, they just say, 'Thanks for coming along and good luck in the future' or something awful like that. You know one of those. . . We've all had the rejection letters. (Diplomatically expressed) Yeah, erm, so we have two or three. (Right) Do you want the exact wording? I can't think of the exact wording. You, it's 'Thanks for coming along. Unfortunately you weren't successful this time.' Cause when people ring up on the phone, that's the sort of thing I say, is 'Unfortunately this time we won't be using you' and quite a lot of the time, especially towards the end, it was because we've got so many people, and this year we've got a lot of trips to Italy and Spain and we've got so many people that if they didn't speak Spanish or Italian, they had. . . or they weren't absolutely brilliant and they didn't speak Spanish or Italian, we had to say no.

R: Right. Do you find it difficult to say no? So, so that that was quite . . .

S: Yeah it kills me 'cause I've been in that position. Erm, but er, so if they didn't speak Spanish or Italian that was good, we'd have their application form there and that would be the reason, 'cause it's nice to have a reason. But we have plenty of people ring up and saying 'Why?'. . . you know. . . and people who weren't very good 'cause their personality or, or whatever, that their personality wasn't right, we'd have them ringing up saying, 'Why didn't I get the job?'

R: And what do you say?

S: Erm, you lie. We lie. You have to don't you? (Yeah.)

UNIT 4 LISTENING 1

1 Well, there's two large windows in the front. Then there's a side gate and I go through the side gate, it takes me onto a very small area of garden which is surrounded by borders of daffodils at the moment.

2 Well Sheffield's a really interesting place you know, they say it's built on seven hills just like Rome. And especially at night you're standing on you know, you know, on top of some of the hills and you can see the whole sort of panoramic view of the place. It's absolutely fantastic with all the street lights erm, making that place look really beautiful.

3 It's a modern place built with plenty of red brick, with a good open space. Erm, iron, black painted ironwork and er, a little bit fanciful. It was called a bit romantic, I think, when it was originally designed.

4 Right, well it's a lot bigger than you'd think from looking at it from the outside erm. It's got a couple of erm, standard doors on the outside and the steps leading up to it. Inside it's, quite frankly, it's massive erm, there are about three or maybe four

floors. It's usually full of smoke.

5 North Uist's an incredible place. It's erm, it's a bit like one of those Scandinavian islands. It's erm, treeless, it's, it looks pretty barren when you see it for the first time. Especially if you see it in a rainstorm. It's covered with water. Hundreds and hundreds of lochs in every direction. Erm, it's not really very much like the mainland because it's so flat and barren.

6 Well, it's a typical terraced street really and it's got that, a real atmosphere about it. Lots of cats hanging around and er, tatty gardens interspersed with nicer ones, more municipal flower arrangements.

UNIT 4 LISTENING 2

Richard = R Colin = C

R: Now. This is looking at a building. And you write just half a sentence here. 'He stopped in front of a rangy three-storied stuccoed building set back from the street behind bright yellow railings.' Now that's quite a detailed description of the building.

C: Probably a bit too detailed, in this.

R: I wasn't I wasn't trying to sort of pull it to pieces. I was wondering what processes went through your mind. Why you . . .

C: Where was that? Was that in St Ebbes?

R: That's in St Ebbes. It's a fictional building, isn't it?

C: Yes, well. . . No, no, I think, I think that virtually all of those are specifically real. Now if I was writing, I can't remember, but certainly when I was writing that book, I think, I remember exactly where it was, it was the vicarage of er, of of, one of the. . . St Aldates, if I remember rightly. And what I would have done is to have gone along and er, walked as we were saying earlier, through the streets. And for me I've always felt much more at home if, if I can visualise, and therefore earlier have seen, a particular place. I somehow feel erm, much more at home if for example a girl comes in and she's wearing an elegant suit, she's a much more real girl to me if I can visualise her in an elegant red suit or something like this. It's as if er, if I have seen things, buildings or people or places or rooms or whatever it is. Some visual, specifically visual aspect helps me, I think, in er, er, as a, I suppose one would say imposing a sort of spurious reality onto this very unreal business of writing whodunits. So I know that er, quite a few, say, North Oxford, the last one I wrote. *The Randolph.* I would go in there and of course you miss an awful lot out; you wouldn't say that er, the stairs were 16 feet wide but you might well say that they were a particular shade of, you know, maroon carpeting or something because for me if I do that I feel very much as if I'm there. And this does help me.

Unit 5 Listening 1

Richard = R Noel = N

R: What about other measures? Erm, have you thought for example of er, bringing trams in rather than buses? Because the pollution problem of all these buses piled up in the centre of the city is horrific, especially at rush hour.

N: Yes, erm, there's actually er, two policy erm, studies going on at the moment. The City Council's reviewing its local plan which is (actually document?) has to do and it's coming forward with proposals in, which are coming into consultation fairly soon. The County Council has also erm, appointed transport consultants to look at Oxford and they are busy working at the moment, so both of these things will be developing during this year. And er, certainly the idea of trams has been suggested but in my personal view, I think its scope in Oxford is limited. I think we haven't got the size of a city and the density of passenger flows that will make it commercially viable. Erm, in a large city where you've got very dense heavy flows on particular corridors you can fill a large articulated vehicle of two or three hundred erm, people every few minutes and provide a very good level of service. We haven't got that sort of intensity of use of the bus system in Oxford. It is a smaller city, obviously, than others er, but the other factors I suppose are the huge costs in investment terms of establishing it. We're talking about many millions of pounds. And what Oxford needs more than anything, what the public transport in Oxford needs, is dedicated routes for the buses to run on where they're separated from congestion. And obviously you can't set a rapid transit system, system up whether it's trams or whatever form, unless you actually do that.

R: Sorry. What do you mean by 'dedicated routes'?

N: Well, actually separating from other traffic. Whether you actually go to the extent of knocking buildings down to provide routes, erm, or you actually clear traffic off the other, off the roads. So they er. . .

R: Knocking buildings down would be a bit of a problem in Oxford, wouldn't it? Historic buildings. . .

N: Oh, I think, I think there'd be tremendous opposition. Well obviously the city centre, I think is very heavily constrained and it's one of the reasons why the city adopted its shift towards transport policy 20 years ago. It recognised that road building in the city centre was not tenable as a solution. I think more and more people have accepted that it doesn't solve the problems anyway with the continual pressure for increased erm, use of vehicles. Erm, but obviously in Oxford it's a particular constraint. But I was thinking not just the city centre; I was thinking Oxford-wide. Wherever these vehicles run they've got to be able to run up and down freely and not be stuck in traffic jams obviously. Erm. And I think the point I would make is that if you create conditions whereby you can provide dedicated routes on the road networks then I think the conventional bus, which has the flexibility of being able to move off the route at any point and into the residential areas in Oxford, will actually provide, has the potential to provide, a much better service than going for any sophisticated tram system. Erm, I recognise the comment about pollution and the diesel engines and there's no reason why the technology can't be provided so that buses in the city centre couldn't run either on battery power or obviously erm, from overhead supplies. But that raises another problem whether in Oxford we'd want to see overhead catenaries erected er, through the historic streets like the High Street.

R: Right. It'd be another eyesore. Yeah.

N: That's right. In other parts of Europe obviously this sort of thing has become accepted. You know they don't think twice about having this sort of thing. They, if you drew their attention to it they probably wouldn't have realised the catenary was there. . . it's, they, just it's become life in a way. But I think if you tried to establish something like that in Oxford there'd be great opposition to that.

Unit 5 Listening 2

Sharon =S Dominic = D

S: So how do you come in in the morning then Dom?

D: Well I drive.

S: Eugh! How. . .

D: 20 miles all the way from Faringdon, erm, you know. . .

S: What's the average length of the journey then?

D: Well it's. . . basically between Faringdon and Oxford it's about 20 minutes, 25 minutes. (On a good day?) But door-to-door it's going to take 50, 55 minutes.

S: It's a fair long time, though.

D: Because, well yes it's the. . .

S: What, to be in your car, stuck? (Yeah) I don't know if I could handle that really.

D: Well, I always say that I, I think perhaps 'cause when I was at school, I lived just up the road from the school. And erm I. . . I, I'm not saying it's always been my ambition to be a commuter, I wouldn't say that, but I, I actually quite enjoy the drive.

S: What, it gives you time to think?

D: Er, because it's a very it's a lovely drive actually, between Faringdon.

S: The A420?

D: A420 (Yeah) yeah. It's a nice road and erm in a way especially for teaching it is, it's a sort of way of getting yourself in gear a little bit.

S: Yeah I find that on my bike when I'm sort of riding along, I'm often sort of mulling ideas over, and, yeah. . .

D: Yes just sort of preparing yourself (Yeah) erm, and. . . and that's what I find really. How about you how do you come in?

Exercise 3

S: Well, on good days and if I'm feeling fit and healthy

etcetera I try and cycle. It's about (All the way) well, to make the round trip it's about 14 miles (yeah) which is far enough definitely on hot days. When I'm home I'm whacked. You know.

D: Is it uphill or downhill?

S: It's quite flat really (Yeah) which is lucky, you know, being Oxfordshire, but there's a cycle track you see along the A40 which I take now (Yeah) 'cause I used to come in on the A. . . along the Botley Road there, but I dunno, I just got the feeling it was getting too dangerous; so many people I knew were having accidents (Yes) and I sort of clicked, 'Oh yeah, there's this cycle track, why don't I use that?' And it added about two miles.

D: It's about time they put these cycle tracks in. . .

U N I T   6   L I S T E N I N G   1

So what are you actually looking for when you go to these places? You're, you're trying to find people to talk to or you're just looking at what the situation is?

No, no. The basic things is you're actually. . . it's very much the basics of who, what, why, when. In a war both sides, and both sides particularly in this war, lie to you like mad and they try to pretend that you know they held out against the whole platoon. Erm, so what you're really going in for is, is finding out exactly how many people died, what happened, when. And the only way you can do that is to go very very much to the local people on the ground. Er, and that was a question of going into and through another physical, if not, mental jurisdiction. As soon as you walked up to someone who was manning er, a post from the Croatian side you had to basically go through this whole thing of re-establishing your identity. You had to hold the passport and a white flag. You had to say, take me to your leader. And everyone calmed down as soon as you were accepted by their system. If you walked back into Croatia exactly the same thing would happen to you. Almost. Erm, there were, there were differences depending on which group of people you landed with because this wasn't a homogenous army. There were not two homogenous armies facing each other. Er, there were, there were small autonomous groups er, there were, I can remember one lot which were very hostile er, if they thought you were remotely German or Austrian and that would be . . . so you had to establish immediately that you were English and at that time to be English or American er, in Serbia, in the Serbian controlled parts of Eastern Croatia and Slovonia, meant that you were all right. If you were German they would literally shoot at you. In fact that's what they did, I mean they did, they did. We had TV and Press put all over our cars, you know. 'Don't shoot', you know, 'We're the Press', but in fact they did begin to erm, target cars which had TV and Press written all over them erm, because erm, in their view we were

spies, we were, er, we were sending back reports to Croatians as to where their positions were and what strengths there were. You know, we were the free agents going round a war zone.

At which point, who makes the decision whether to carry on or whether to pull out? Is it you, or. . .? I mean, generally speaking do you stay in this area or is it time for you to get out if you're being shot at?

Well if, if the, the way communications work in that sort of situation is that erm, you make all the decisions about your own safety and you make all the decisions about filing as well. Because there's another problem, there's the technical problem attached to er, straying too far away from a telephone. And that is that, that you don't know what. . . In a situation like that where not only communication is fragmented but news is fragmented you simply do not know what is happening two kilometres down the road. There could be the biggest firefight going on and you wouldn't know about it because you don't. All you know in a situation like that is actually physically what's in front of you er, so you have to make extremely selective decisions about where you're going to put yourself er, you can, you've then got to make sure you can get back to your hotel in time in order to file.

U N I T   6   L I S T E N I N G   2

The Home Office is being pressed to launch an urgent enquiry into how an Australian drug smuggler escaped from an open prison in Buckinghamshire. It's been revealed that Murray Stewart, who was serving a five-year sentence for a £40 million computer swindle, just walked out of Springhill Open Prison in Aylesbury seven weeks ago. Conservative MP and law and order campaigner Geoffrey Dicken says Stewart should have been more heavily guarded.

A 15-year-old boy who tackled a gunman during a raid on a South London off-licence has died. Mavid Sadiq was shot in the chest as he struggled with the raider on Saturday night. A 27-year-old man has been charged in connection with the raid.

The sister of Derek Bentley will today lay a wreathe at the gates of the prison where he was hanged 39 years ago. Iris Bentley will also hand in a letter to the Home Secretary calling for an immediate decision on the long-awaited posthumous pardon. James Bays reports:

'Derek Bentley was 19 when he was sent to the gallows in 1953 at Wandsworth prison for his part in shooting dead a policeman. A fresh enquiry has cast doubts on claims that Bentley shouted, "Let him have it!" just before the officer was shot. His sister, Iris, is praying a decision on a pardon will come today.

"Even though it is 39 years, when I go there each year I always feel that I am going to see Derek. And if it comes in, I shall feel that I want to go in to get him, bring him home. And I know I can't."

But she says even if the decision goes against her brother she's vowing to fight on.'

171

UNIT 7 SPEAKING

That's rather odd, isn't it? (rising intonation)

That's rather odd, isn't it... (falling intonation)

UNIT 7 LISTENING 1

Dominic = D Bernard = B

D: Well it is, it is a very arresting beginning, isn't it? Erm, something slightly kind of er, macabre about it. I mean, it does raise a lot of issues, doesn't it?

B: Certainly does, yeah. Erm...

D: Relationship with the father. Obviously there's going to be, I should think some sort of death described. Erm...

B: Yeah. I think there's a lot written between the lines there, in a way. (Yeah there is.) I think, you know, 'I sometimes felt I had helped him on his way'. How, how had I helped him on his way? What exactly was the situation? I rather like that.

D: Yes, and also his attitude. You know it doesn't seem... (Yes) he's not exactly maudlin or he doesn't seem terribly er, er, miserable about it, does he?

B: What about three, I mean that's erm, I find that quite intriguing. I think I'd like to read that: 'He had, romantically, a bad reputation.' Now that sounds fun, don't you think?

D: Yeah. Yes, that's true I mean, a bad reputation is always going to be fun to read about, isn't it? Er...

B: Well especially if it's 'romantically' a bad reputation, yeah.

D: Do you think that could be ironic, that 'romantically'?

B: Er. Dunno. Well, you see, if you look at two and four you've both got qualifying words. You see number two, you see, 'I sometimes felt I'd helped him on his way' and then in four you've got erm, 'he didn't precisely decide to murder his wife.' (Yes) It's these little little bits of colour that well I suppose an artist would give a painting, isn't it?

D: That's it, and perhaps it's rather English, the sort of irony, slight wry humour about it.

B: I, I actually I quite agree, now you talk about irony, the second time, I quite agree. I think it has, it is quite er, erm, ironic, yes.

D: Whereas the first one is rather conventional. It's almost the type of thing that I might have erm, er, put in...

B: Written yourself!

D: Well no, I wouldn't say that. You know, it could almost be a sort of, rather an immature start you know. 'Oh he was running as fast as he could and then the people were chasing him' some erm, rather exciting story like that. (Yeah) I'm sure there are probably, it, you probably find it's some really heavy, serious novelist here (Yeah) who's being deliberately unpretentious perhaps.

B: Well just on its own it doesn't give much away, does it? It doesn't give much away that first one.

D: No, apart from the name.

B: It could, it could... Lok. What sort of erm, country do you think that name comes from?

D: Well, it could be Oriental, couldn't it?

UNIT 7 LISTENING 2

Richard = R Colin = C

R: What about revising? Do you, you, you keep going back over what you've written and rewritten?

C: No. I always write in exactly the same way. I write from a sort of blank page, which has got to have lines on it and I just write and write and write, a chapter at a time, not quite knowing, not quite knowing where I'm going sometimes, but I have to do that I have to write a book in a very rough and ready way from beginning to end and maybe about, let's say, 60 or 70 chapters and just keep going on. And then when I get to the end of that I'll feel that that is the plot as it were really. I've worked it through and that is the hard work for me and I do that in long hand. And then I go back to the beginning and re-write the whole of this and of course kick most of it out. Especially all the er, the fine pieces of writing and so on that you've done at the time. And then re-write the whole thing again in long hand. So I always do it and then get it typed. And each process is a bit of a filter but above all it's the, for me, the difficult business is just the first part. Getting it down. In any way or form really. That's the hard work. It's much easier once you've got, got a story there. And you change bits of it. And of course you write it again and er, as I say you tend to cut out all the adjectives and adverbs and so on or of course on the other hand, you put them in. Tart it up a bit but...

R: So you're aiming for a consistent style. I mean the actual process of revision is looking specifically at at your prose style?

C: Yes. I'm never very worried who it's for. The only thing I'm trying to do is to write a few sentences or a few pages which to me sound er, as if they would be pleasantly read in somebody's mind. I mean that's what I really look for. I'm not conscious of an audience at all. I do try to write in a way which I find is pleasing to myself, that's all. That's all you can do really, I think, as soon as you start writing for an audience you've almost had your chips. Especially if you write for youngsters. It's very difficult to know how you ought to talk to different people anywhere. I think the only thing to do is to feel I am, certainly on the page, this is a reasonable sentence, you know. It's er, it doesn't contravene the rules of English grammar too much and it's pleasantly structured and it reads easily, and I think that sort of thing is, is er, something that pleases you as a writer or not. That's all you can do. It's all I do anyway.

UNIT 8 LISTENING 1

1 (*Robbie*)
Do you like working with girls?
Erm, sometimes, yes.
You do? You don't mind it?
Not much.
Yeah?
But sometimes it, it, it gets a bit erm, well, not very nice, because erm, they keep on saying, 'No it isn't that, it's that', and I think it's that and they don't think that but then John, John, the person I work with doesn't say that at all and he just goes straight ahead and he some. . . he sometimes, he says the answers, sometimes I say the answers. And things like that. We're especially good at doing Maths as well.

2 (*Henry*)
Do you go to school yet Henry? You do?
But. . . go to a different one now.
Yeah? Where do you go?
I don't know now.
You don't know? Is it a nursery school?
Yes.
Yeah.
It's a bit, bit like playgroup.

3 (*Edmund*)
What do you. . . What do you do at school? Do you play? Or do you draw pictures?
I usually sort of work.
Sort of work?
Hey, what is this?
It's a microphone. What sort of work do you do?
I don't know actually . . .
You don't know!

4 (*Neil*)
Tell me about your school.
Erm, my teacher's called Mrs Simpson and I do sums sometimes and I'm good at them.
You're good at sums?
Yeah and. . .
What else do you do?
And I do writing about the weekend and. . .
Yeah.
Well, those sort of things, you know. We do P.E. .

5 (*Brent*)
Tell me about your school.
My teacher's called, my teacher's called Mr Naylor.
Yeah.
And he's erm, he's quite mad at me and. . .
He's mad at you?
Yeah.
Why? What've you done?
I keep er, make fun, I keep making funny, make, I make impressions of him.

6 (*Sophie*)
There are 27 people in our class and not many people in my class actually like me. Well, they do like me but it's kind of like they've all got their own friends. When they want me I can be with them and when they don't want me I'm just left out so I'm usually working on my own. But I enjoy working with people when I can.

(*Naomi*)
I usually work erm, together.

7 (*Sophie*)
Well sometimes what boys do, they're kind of, like they're saying. . . They're always causing trouble. Every boy in my class has been sent to Mrs Powell more than twice. And they're always singing rude songs about the teachers, always being horrible to the teachers and I just don't like them.

(*Naomi*)
This, this boy in my class – I think he's called Craig – and he's been to Mrs Prescott, the Head Teacher, I think about 7 times.
What does he do wrong?
He's being silly.

UNIT 8 LISTENING 2

Richard = R   Jenny = J

R: What about the curriculum? Do all all students do all the same subjects? There's . . .

J: Yes.

R: Yeah. Regardless.

J: Yeah.

R: Are there any subjects that are perceived by the, by the pupils themselves as being either er. . . more interesting for the girls or more interesting for the boys? Or maybe not at this level.

J: Not really at this age. No. I mean it's very rare that I find that any of them say, 'Oo I'm not doing that 'cause it's a girl's thing' or 'I'm not doing that 'cause it's a boy's thing'. And you you do find a difference in reaction in some subjects. Like technology. The way they approach technology is completely different. Erm, like, you know, you'll start a topic and I'll say: 'Right (y'know) make your plans, make your initial drawings'. And all the girls will actually do that and they'll be fairly logical about it and the lads are straight away hands-on. The girls stand back a lot more. It's. . . the same applies to science. You have to actually push the girls to get in the group and and deal with science experiments. You know, you'll always find you'll wander round and if you've got them in mixed groups, the girls will be writing all the results down and the lads will be fooling around with the cars and the ramps and things and. . . It's irritating!

R: The lads are irritating or the girls are irritating or does it. . .?

J: It's, it's just, I mean, it's irritating. It's almost like learned helplessness on the part of the girls, that they can't. So I'll swap them round all the time. Or else do them single sex groups. In some cases I think there's quite a lot of justification for doing single sex groups in subjects like that.

R: So you you would actually manipulate the groups to make sure that, I mean, do it yourself, make sure they're working in separate sex groups rather than allow them to do it themselves?

J: Yeah, but if you usually say to them get yourselves into a group of four they will get themselves into a single sex group. Whereas if I want them in mixed groups I'll say: 'get yourselves in pairs,' and then I'll say 'get yourselves in a four that's mixed'.

R: You consciously. . . How do they react to that when you do it?

J: Erm, well if you do it all the time they don't think anything of it particularly. It's only if you suddenly introduce it.

R: But why would you do that anyway? Why would you force them to work in mixed groups? Just to sort of shake up the class a bit?

J: Well. Yeah, and because it's important that they do, they do work together and they don't see each other as sort of completely separate. They must work together and I think it gels the class better as well. And when you get them working in mixed groups you get different qualities out. They see each other's qualities and the way of thinking is sometimes slightly different. I think it gives you more variety. You don't want them either working in single sex or mixed sex all the time. I think you've got to give a balance.

UNIT 9 LISTENING 1

So how would you how would you design, set about designing an advertisement? You had to place an advertisement in the trade press or whatever. Erm, presumably you would sit down and decide what, actually decide what that advertisement's going to look like. What sort of decisions would you would you be making at that point?

Well the most important thing is to understand the market niche that they're going for. Many companies don't understand what niche they're going for at all and as a result they really fritter their money away in a sort of shotgun approach. We strongly advocate a much more focused approach to make a better use of limited resources. So first of all you understand the niche (and) what it is that motivates that customer in the niche. You have to understand the target audience. Who they are. What their sort of, what their habits are. What they like and dislike. What motivates them. And then you have to decide what the, what the strategy is, what you're going to sell on as the unique selling point. I mean this is all classic sort of advertising stuff. Nothing innovative here. So you then basically decide on your strategy, what the selling point is. And the selling point may be erm, for example in the soap powders or take *Head and Shoulders* as an example, is simply that is specifically focused on the fact that it clears dandruff better than anybody else. That is the single line of selling proposition. It clears dandruff better than anybody else. Erm, or *Fairy Liquid*: it lasts longer. It's better value 'cause it lasts longer. So once you've decided on that, you have to try and visualise that. Erm, I suppose the golden rule is that a picture is worth a thousand words. So you have to try and create a visual image which puts across the single proposition which is the key selling point erm, in a very impactful way. So in a way which you take one glance at and they understand instantly what it's about. That is the ideal. It, it and some classic takes would be the sort of side by side demonstration. Erm, you know. . . we. . . the before and after or like er, on *Head and Shoulders*: we washed, we washed this half, half this man's head in *Head and Shoulders* and half in a cosmetic shampoo and Hey Presto! he's got dandruff on this side!

It must be very difficult to wash half someone's head actually.

So there are a number of sort of fairly standard techniques. The side by side demonstration. Before and after. Torture Tests are a good example, you know, we, we erm, subjected this battery or this er, this car was sent to the North Pole and it survived all this (you know).

Oh right, yes.

It's been up and down mountains like the latest er, *Range Rover* ads or *Discovery* ads. You know that's the torture test.

UNIT 9 LISTENING 2

1 *La Piazza!* Quality Italian pizzas and pasta! Look out for our free menu and discount voucher coming through your door, offering 20% off. *La Piazza*, in Park End Street.

2 You know a drinks machine from OGV will save you time, mess and money, whatever your size of business. But to make certain of the high quality of our drinks, why not arrange a free, no obligation demonstration and tasting. Simply dial 100, ask for Freephone OGV and find out about your free first 2000 drinks, microwave or colour TV. The call is free, the gift is free. What can you lose? Make it OGV for your coffee and tea: your local vending experts. Freephone OGV now!

3 As you can no doubt ascertain, Hobson here is somewhat excited. He thinks he's about to be fed with his favourite *Pedigree Chum*. But he's in for a surprise. It's got all the nourishment of *Pedigree Chum*, but it's different. New *Pedigree Chum Select Cuts*: tasty, wholesome, meaty chunks covered in delicious gravy. Now, what do you think of that, Hobson? Hobson? *Pedigree Chum*, and *New Pedigree Chum Select Cuts*. Now Hobson has a choice.

Exercise 4

Ladies and gentlemen, boys and girls: it's here, it's big, it's on for a limited time. It's the great bike sale at the *Banbury Cycle Centre*. Everything must go! There's savings of up to 30% on all the quality guaranteed bikes as well as accessories. *Banbury Cycle Centre*, 54 Bridge Street.

Call Banbury 259349.

This urgent message has just been received from *Johnsons*: this Saturday and Sunday only there's extra special discounts off these stock items – 10% off paint, 20% off tiles and 25% off wall paper. For the widest choice and lowest prices, hurry to *Johnsons Building and Home Improvement Centre*, Watlington Road, Cowley. Don't miss the extra discounts, this weekend only.

February's here and it's that depressing time of year. So cheer yourself up with a visit to the *Suite Shop*, Newbury. We've now got new stocks of over one hundred sofas and chairs in soft and leather upholstery. And we're still offering three years' interest free credit on selected suites, sofas and chairs. Ask for written credit details. There's also one hundred pounds part exchange for your old suite, whatever the condition. Hurry to the *Suite Shop* now! Open 7 days a week on the London Road, Newbury, just off the A34. Phone Newbury 37717. *(Song: Suites from the Suite Shop sofas and chairs.)* Also the *Suite Shop* is now at The Ideal Home Superstore on the A4 between Slough and Maidenhead.

UNIT 10 LISTENING 1

Richard = R Simon = S

R: Yeah. I mean why did you do it? I mean, why did you decide to er, go all that way and come all that way back slowly? Why not just go for a two-week holiday to Barcelona or something?

S: Well I think, I think that the important thing is that you feel that you are free to, to go more or less where you want and to make your own decisions all the time. I think that is important but I, I noticed er, in fact just the, the other day looking at one of these wildlife magazines that there was a wonderful er, trip being offered down to southern Chile and Argentina which is always a place that's attracted me. And you know, you go on these boats into places that you couldn't possibly get to otherwise and there are all the experts on hand to tell you about the bird life and so on. And I thought much as I'd like to go there and it might be the only way to get there it wouldn't, I wouldn't really, quite apart from the fact that it costs a lot of money, I wouldn't really want to do it because I, it's very important that you can sort of make your own decisions, that's the exciting, exciting thing about it.

R: But that also has its own disadvantages, doesn't it, it? I mean... There must be some stress that you're going to get stuck in the middle of nowhere and not know where the hell you are and not know the language.

S: Yes, yes. That's, that's true. There is stress and I think you tend to forget, about that once it's completed successfully and you've survived and nothing...

R: You only remember the good bits.

S: ...happened, you tend, to, tend to remember the good bits.

R: But you also spent a long time, I mean eight months coming back from India.

S: Well, actually yes, and I felt it would have been quite easy to go on forever. Erm, and the only point at which I stopped feeling that was when I was actually getting hepatitis though I didn't realise it. And people talk about your being jaundiced, but I got the symptoms of being jaundiced, of suddenly not enjoying things any more, before I had. And once I had the disease then I got better very quickly, which is a much better way round because some people have it and for a year or more afterwards they feel depressed and that life isn't worth living so ... so that coloured me, but otherwise I felt that one could quite happily have gone on.

R: You must have had a lot of a lot of jabs and things, inoculations before you went out. I mean, because a lot of people don't, don't, I mean, wouldn't want to go somewhere like India or somewhere where they felt that the er, er I don't know the hygiene didn't reach particularly high standards and they were frightened of, frightened of getting diseases. That doesn't worry you?

S: Er, well it does a bit, but I mean, I suppose life involves certain risks and I mean they didn't seem to me to be excessive. In fact, I mean, I don't, some travellers seem to enjoy taking risks for the sake of it which I don't do at all. I mean I like to try to find out as much as I can about where I'm going and whether it is a genuinely dangerous place or not.

UNIT 10 LISTENING 2

Bernard = B Richard = R

B: Yes, going across Brazil was pretty extraordinary. I got erm, I was travelling with an Englishman and we, we got a lift on a giant lorry, a really huge lorry carrying tons of fish, tons, I think 40 tons of fish to make plastic in Sao Paolo and erm, the, the, er, lorry driver was a bit like a good Samaritan er, because whenever we came across vehicles that had got stuck in the, er, in potholes I mean, giant holes, erm, whenever these cars disappeared into a hole he would get out his cable and fix it onto the car and pull it out and then go on.

R: Potholes big enough to for a whole car to drive into? God!

B: Oh gi. . .gi. . . oh giant holes, you can't imagine. I mean, big enough to hide 20 people in. And erm, Dennis and I had one er, we had one doubtful moment because we saw this chap reaching up to put his maps er in the, oh in the roof or something, and his shirt pulled up above his belt and under the shirt we saw a pistol. And we thought: Ah! Gosh! We'd better be a bit careful with this guy. Erm, because he had said, he'd said, 'Well, look, for the night why don't you go to this. . .' erm, oh it was a lorry drivers' hotel. He said erm, 'you just get out and go somewhere' – I can't remember where he told us to go – and we left our rucksacks in the lorry and we were a bit worried that perhaps he was going to drive off with a rucksack but of course nothing like it . . . was just our typical suspicious mind. He was very friendly and we spent the night in this erm, lorry drivers' stop. And I think we continued the journey for three or four days just, just crossing the bottom of the Mata Grosso which. . .

R: Didn't you smell a bit riding on a lorry full of fish?

B: It stank! It was horrible!

R: You stank of fish for about the next three weeks?

B: Well, I expect we did, probably.

UNIT 11 LISTENING 1

Richard = B Amanda = A

R: Yeah I mean, as I was saying that erm, most people have heard of acupuncture. Could you could you tell us exactly what it is, apart from sticking needles in people? Er, why do you stick them in people perhaps might be the question?

A: The needles are stuck in people to affect their energy. Now energy is a very abstract term, isn't it? But if you think that when we catch a cold we don't generally die, when we cut ourselves we don't bleed to death, that's because our body is working all the time to maintain our health. And that energy which makes us alive and keeps us healthy is what acupuncture works with. And . . .

R: Right. So why do you stick needles in. . .?

A: Because the energy flows around the body rather like the circulation of the blood. In other words it follows pathways. And at certain points along the pathways there are places whereby inserting a needle you can affect the energy of that pathway.

R: How do you know that?

A: The Chinese discovered that thousands of years ago.

R: Right. But how did they know it? I mean. . . (It is. . .) For someone with a Western scientific background, I mean not much scientific background but. . . Where do you know this energy's coming from and where it's going? How can you actually measure these energy paths?

A: The, the changes brought about in a person's energy, when you've used an acupuncture needle is felt on the pulses. I should perhaps explain that when a Western doctor takes your pulse, he's counting your heart rate. When an acupuncturist takes your pulse, he or she is feeling 12 separate pulses which correspond to the 12 meridians or energy pathways. And after a needle's been inserted and the energy has been affected in that pathway, all of the pulses will change to reflect that, that change in the energy.

R: So there is actually some definite thing that you know is there. The energy is there, you can feel it. . .

A: There's no doubt that it's there. You can feel it and more importantly the person experiencing the acupuncture needle can definitely feel it. Because the acupuncture points – the places where you affect the person's energy – are themselves very tiny. And if you stick a needle into a person and you miss the acupuncture point all the person feels is a very very tiny pinprick and nothing more. Much less than a pinprick from pricking your finger when you're sewing. When you put an acupuncture needle into an acupuncture point you feel a tiny prickle as it goes through the skin and then a very definite strong sensation. So there's no mistake on the part of the, of the patient or the practitioner when you contact that energy and affect it.

R: So there there's no danger that this feeling of energy or whatever when you put the needle in is psychosomatic that in other words, you put the needle in and they think they're going to feel something and therefore they do.

A: I think that when you consider that acupuncture has been used on animals for a very, very, very long time and animals have no expectation, I think that really answers that, that question.

UNIT 11 LISTENING 2

Richard = R Ian = I

R: The thing is that I mean . . . modern medicine . . . Governments actually stick tons and tons of money into the damn thing and it doesn't do any good at all, really, does it?

I: What do you mean it hasn't done a lot of good? I mean . . .

R: Well, I mean, okay, modern medicine involves what? Er, oh heart surgery for example, which is won. . . heroic surgery. The patients die.

I: Well, yeah but. That might be true but I mean a lot of other things too, involved in, in modern medicine.

R: Such as?

I: Well you know, think of all the other things like X-Rays, body scans and you know there was that guy whose hand cut off and the surgeons put it back on. . . microsurgery.

R: Yeah but yeah, but he couldn't use his hand afterwards.

I: (Eh?)

R: He couldn't use his hand afterwards.

I: Well, I thought he could.

R: (It's just sort of stuck on.) No. He might bend it around but he can't use it as a hand.

I: Well I'm sure, you know, . . .

R: The thing is that most, most, I mean, okay. People live longer these days er, and are generally in a better state of health than they were, say a hundred, two hundred years ago, but the main reason for that is improvement in sanitation in, in drinking water, the fact that our drinking water, ha ha, is usually clean.

I: Well okay yeah that means people living a lot longer but you know I think in the future we can expect people to live without a lot, without a lot of diseases erm, kind of improvements in genetic knowledge, things like that.

R: Yeah, but you think of the number of diseases which are still around. All these wonderful advances that everyone goes on about in in modern medicine. And how many diseases there are still around. They can't even cure the common cold for heaven's sake!

I: (Yeah, but I can't rem. . .) Yeah, but I mean, I've had a a cold, you know, maybe have a cold once a year but nothing else. I haven't had a serious disease for a long time.

R: Yes but that as I was saying this is, this is because of improvements, for example in diet. People are so much more healthy. The more healthy we are then the better your chances are of fighting the disease and the disease not taking over.

I: Yeah but I've been to countries, you know when the diet's been pretty lousy and er, you know. Well I suppose you're right, aren't you? Yeah.

R: I mean, take for example, take the Third World. Medicine. Some of the problems that they have there in the Third World are are simply because they don't have the clean water, the diet that we, sitting in a comfortable position in the West, do.

I: Yeah, but how do you know, how do you know what cau. . . How do you know what causes improvements in health? How do you test it?

R: Well, I'm not a doctor, I don't know, I mean I, I haven't got the scientific background to, to. . .

I: So it could be modern science, couldn't it?

R: OK, name me a few, name me a few examples of, of diseases which doctors can successfully deal with these days which they couldn't a hundred years ago.

I: A hundred years ago. OK, well, smallpox, I suppose.

UNIT 11 SPEAKING

CHIROPRACTOR is a term applied to a person who practises chiropractic. This is a system of adjustment by hand of supposed minor displacements of the spinal column. These minor displacements, or subluxations of the spine, chiropractors contend, affect the associated or neighbouring nerves. The claim of chiropractic is that by manipulating the affected part of the spinal column the patient's complaint, whatever it may be – for example, backache – is relieved.

UNIT 12 LISTENING 1

Richard = R Amanda = A

R: Did you see Ben Jonson win it?

A: No.

R: No, neither did I. But it think it was fair in a way. I think people. . . He was a, he was a scapegoat really. That they they sort of used him. . . people pouring out all sorts of illogical feelings on poor old Ben Jonson. I felt quite sorry for him.

A: Well, yes and no. But don't you feel that in a way he deserved it?

R: No!

A: Why not?

R: Well, everybody else was using drugs. I mean, it was all fair in. . . love and war.

A: But were they? I don't think they were, really.

R: Well, probably not some of them. But I mean. . .

A: Don't you think it takes away from the element of fair sportsmanship, you know, sort of (Well if everybody. . .) the spirit of international co-operation and. . .

R: It could do, but if everybody's using them then, you know. It's still fair, isn't it?

A: Some people were using them certainly but I think in today's society less and less people are using them, what with the sort of. . .

R: Well, the, the thing is that, I mean, people go to enormous lengths to improve their performance. I mean, they go, they travel abroad; they train in high altitude; (Yep) they train in. . . If they're ill they take an aspirin. There are certain, you know, drugs like that which you're allowed to take. There's obviously a prescribed list but I mean what's the difference between all of that and just taking a drug? You do enormous things to improve your performance anyway, why not use. . .?

A: Yes, but that's all natural, isn't it? You know, if you train hard (I don't think. . .) you work hard. . .

R: Well, training for how-ever-many hours a day is hardly natural.

A: Ah, but you have techniques etcetera, etcetera, whereas for instance taking anabolic steroids for instance, is a sort of massive injection of testosterone which can oh, for a start we don't know, it could have untold consequences in years to come. We don't know what the long term effects are, necessarily.

R: Well that's their, that's their business though, isn't it? I mean if through the drugs that they, they use they choose to ruin their own bodies long term that's, that's their choice.

A: Yes, but is that fair on the other competitors who are entering perfectly, you know, in all innocence, having taken nothing like this? Don't you think that if somebody's going to use it then everybody should use it or nobody should use it?

R: Well, I think people should, everybody should have the choice to use it. And if they want to use it or not it's it's really up to them.

A: Well, I don't know.

UNIT 12 LISTENING 2

Richard = R Helen = H

R: Could you, could you explain what it is? 'Cause a lot of people. . .

H: Well, it's very similar to gymnastics in water. Similar to figure skating or ice skating. It has the same sort of components so that you are. . . You have two sections to. . . A figure section when you have to do gymnastic type movements and then you have a sequence section where you do routines to music and they are judged under two headings, and that's technical merit and the choreography side.

R: I can imagine a lot of people being rather cynical about it, about how this relates to what we normally think of as a sport which is as, running as fast as you can or trying to beat someone in, on a tennis court or on a football pitch or something, like that. Doing something to music.

H: Yes. Yes, I think this, the tendency is to, or was initially – it isn't as bad as you know it used to be – to ridicule it and it tends to be through lack of information and lack of knowledge of it, are the people who usually make these comments. So anyone who's ever tried in water just even to do a somersault would appreciate the tremendous skill involved, and having been involved myself with coaching the speed swimmers at the Olympics there is no comparison in the skill of a synchronised swimmer in comparison to a speed a speed swimmer. It's totally different concept. One is subjective and the other is objective.

R: Right. There's erm, what about the, I mean you talk about the skill but what about the, the physical fitness and stamina involved?

H: Oh I mean, if you're talking about a 5-minute routine erm, a great deal of the time is underwater so the power as well as the endurance and of course a tremendous flexibility you have to sort of experience it really yourself to realise how vital that is as a part of it. The, the event and the strength required in a solo routine – one activity when you, you enter the water could, you could be under the water for about a minute plus. And that is a great length of time. If you held your breath for a minute you'd appreciate . . .

R: I'm not going to try it!

H: No, and it's jolly difficult. So I think really that is the problem. It's total lack of information when people criticise it because they really don't understand the terrific skill involved which does involve endurance, strength, flexibility and endurance.

UNIT 13 LISTENING 1

I mean it's a bit difficult to comment on an article like this, because what the article actually fails to tell you is basically, you know, they're saying that he's, out of the blue, he's suddenly started exhibiting this behaviour. Erm, I suppose it's, my comment would be that I'd like to know a little bit more about the background there because there are a few things about his behaviour that I wouldn't say is exactly normal, but there are a few things about his behaviour that, that particularly a lot of the young people who we work with. . . I mean it's quite a common problem (yeah) i.e. kicking against authority is a typical, and it's recognised by virtually anyone who works with

juveniles as a normal part of growing up. Right? (Yeah) Also experimenting with drugs. I mean we're talking about cannabis here, aren't we? (Yeah I think so.) We're not talking about hardened drugs. I'm not saying it's acceptable; what I'm saying is that it, it's something that a lot of young people do actually try out and alcohol as well. Erm, and it's probably a fairly healthy age to be starting to experiment. In terms of running away that's not really, I mean, you start to get a few warning sort of signs there. I mean, is he running away because of pe. . . because of friends that he's met? Has he got in with a group of maybe older young people who are influencing him or is it the way that his parents are reacting to him that are making him want to run away? (Yeah. Yeah) Erm, so there are the. . . I guess I'd like to really interview this mum and this family and actually find out what the true situation is. (Yes) The other thing is in this, what I'd be saying is that er, she's saying her son needs a real dose of punishment. Is that because he's acting out, because he's smoking cannabis because he's actually seems to be going through a fairly. . . not normal sort of growing up process, but a lot of his behaviour is typical growing up behaviour.

UNIT 13 LISTENING 2

Bernard = B Mark =M Catriona = C

B: But do you sometimes find that it goes so far that. . . I mean, very occasionally that you really do sort of er, I don't mean hit them, particularly, but you you get really furious and you, you can't really control yourself? Do you, do you find yourself. . . Have you ever found yourself in that position?

M: Certainly. Now. . . I have actually struck them from time to time. Only half a dozen times.

B: Well me too. I mean I, I freely admit once or twice it's happened.

M: And it hurts me so much (Right) that it's so appalling that I've stopped doing that and what I'll do is I'll actually turn round and walk away. I feel as though I'm very weak in a sense doing that, and I don't, and I'm. . .

B: Well, I think that's a good, I think that's a good solution.

M: Well, I'm worried what effect it has on them. I don. . . I mean I don't know whether they perceive me as being weak or whether they. . . it actually gives them a chance hopefully to think about what they've done. (Yes) I think it may do that because things tend to blow over fairly quickly after that.

C: Me? I, I don't know. I mean, I have hit Emily and I felt so bad about it afterwards as you said that I swore never to do it again. So yes, I mean, yesterday for example we had this confrontation where she wanted to open the fridge door and get some milk. And she instead of saying, you know, 'Could I get the milk please?' – I was making a salad – she sort of whacked me and said, 'Hey move over, I want the milk,' or something and I was just in that sort of mood as you are in the evening. I felt this is, this is not polite behaviour so I'm going to say, 'Look Emily, I'm sorry, you don't do that. Will you please shut the fridge door, start again. And er, just say: Could I get the milk please?' And she just wouldn't. And she stamped her feet (I know) she. . . 'I want the milk!' and she screamed and I just would not let go and stood in front of the fridge, sort of blocked it and said, 'You're not getting the milk until you ask me politely,' and I didn't shout, I was very calm erm, and we had this awful discussion. At the same time my mother arrived for dinner, saw this going on sort of — she can let herself into the house — saw this going on and sort of left again, went round to the garden and we had, it was about three or four minutes with this stamping feet and in the end Jim, who was there, picked her up physically and took her up to her bedroom and said, 'You stay there,' erm, and we went on and started having dinner. And then she came down, with a huge teddy bear, very sort of calmly, came down and said, 'Oh, can I have some supper please?' (Yes) And she was so nice, sweet, she sort of stayed up there.

B: I think these things do tend to blow over pretty fast, don't they?

C: It, it, I was very glad I hadn't done anything myself though. I was glad that Jim took over.

B: It's very good to have a second party around who can, can er, defuse the situation.

UNIT 14 LISTENING 1

. . . on a lot of open executive programmes here we would have erm, a, a tutor working with a group to help them facilitate that process. (Right) So we are working with them to learn about themselves, the way they. . . their own strengths and weaknesses, their relationships with others, in within teams and the whole ideas of leadership and developing others to a common goal.

Do you get any feedback from companies that presumably send managers to you, er, feedback on such and such a person has improved, is now better at this, or she's better at that?

Yeah, that's a good question, isn't it? Somebody's been in here for a week's course or whatever. They've had (the, you know), the latest injection of knowledge, has this in fact in some way improved their job performance? If you were working in a training field you can sometimes do that. You can say 'well I taught this person this and now let's see if that person can demonstrate that'. This works very closely in a skills area where, where erm, manip. . . manipulative skills are important for example. (Where you. . .) What we are more concerned with here is not so much skills training as development work. So (we), Henley puts an input into a person's longer-term career development. In that sense it's not quite so easy to see a correlation between input of training experience and output of job performance. You can't quite measure it in that way. And I don't say that in a dismissive sense to er, trivialise or minimise the problem of dealing with that question because it is a question that we grapple with quite a bit here because if companies can't see an

improvement eventually then they will clearly stop sending their people to places like Henley or anywhere else. The issues that we are grappling with in that area are no different than the similar issues in er, parallel organisations.

UNIT 14 LISTENING 2

Richard = R John Eckersley = JE

R: You said to me the other day that you erm, you don't run it as a business. But we've been . . . How long's the school been going? Since 1955?

JE: It's been going since 1955. Yes.

R: And it's still going so. . .

JE: So it, it can't be too bad, yes.

R: So it mu. . . what do you mean, what do you mean it's, you don't run it as a business? It's. . .

JE: I think, I think what I meant by that an (and don't take it too seriously). . . Erm, because I don't think we're about to go bust. But er, I think what I meant by that is that erm, quite a lot of language schools are run often by erm, large organisations, er, with the object of maximising profits and that's their, that's the, the sole object of the, of the exercise is to get as much money coming in as possible. Erm, they er, this has never been the way we've looked at things, I mean, I this this is what I've done all my life and I think if you, if you don't actually enjoy doing what you're doing there's not much point in doing it anyway. Er, we've we, we get our satisfaction I think from providing a good course some, something that the students enjoy doing that we think they're going to get profit from, they'll tell their friends about — we get a lot of students coming who've er, been recommended by friends or relatives who've been to us before — er, also a place where, where people enjoy working. I think this is very important that the, the people who work here, not only the teachers but the secretaries and technician, all the other people who work in the school, should actually enjoy taking part in this exercise and of course that my wife and myself should as well. So in that sense it's not, it's not run purely from the point of view of the accountant saying: 'How can we maximise profits? How can we cut down our expenses?' er, you know, 'What's the most cost efficient way of doing this?' We tend to look at it the other way, 'What would we like to do?' er 'What sort of equipment should we buy? Should, should we . . . Would computers be useful to use in the school? Would it be useful to have a erm, video camera?' For example, then go and buy it rather rather than thinking, 'How cost effective will this be? What extra cash will this bring us?'

R: It's, I suppose it's a difficult thing to to prove, cost effectiveness on, I mean buying capital equipment like, like computers or video. They're not cost effective really in any tangible sense, I suppose, are they?

JE: Well, they could be.

Practice Section Key

UNIT 1

GRAMMAR

Complex sentences

1 a Last night I watched a film on TV.
  b *Co-ordinate clause:* and watched a film on TV
    Subordinate clause: Although I should have been doing some work last night,

2 a <u>who</u> <u>read</u> grammar <u>books</u> <u>for</u> <u>fun.</u>
  b <u>because</u> <u>it</u> <u>is</u> <u>full</u> <u>of</u> <u>long</u> <u>words</u> <u>like</u> *<u>co-ordinating</u> <u>conjunctions.</u>*
  c <u>that</u> <u>the</u> <u>phrase</u> *<u>linking</u> <u>words</u>* <u>is</u> <u>not</u> <u>always</u> <u>precise</u> <u>enough.</u>
  d <u>While</u> <u>it</u> <u>may</u> <u>look</u> <u>easier,</u>
  e <u>that</u> <u>they</u> <u>spend</u> <u>hours</u> <u>studying</u> <u>details.</u>
  f <u>unless</u> <u>we</u> <u>are</u> <u>careful.</u>
  g <u>until</u> <u>they</u> <u>study</u> <u>them.</u>
  h <u>If</u> <u>we</u> <u>can</u> <u>already</u> <u>speak</u> <u>the</u> <u>language</u> <u>well,</u>

3 1 b because it is full. . .
  2 a who read grammar books. . .
  3 f unless we are careful
    h If we can already . . .
  4 c that the phrase linking words. . .
  5 e such a lot that . . .
  6 g until they study them

Verb forms

a True: there are a number of future 'forms'
b True
c False: it is an invitation
d True
e True
f True
g False: it is an example of the present perfect
h True
i True
j False: the last sentence does not contain a passive

LEXIS

Strength of adjectives

The stronger adjectives are:
a hate
b in agony
c filthy
d disgusting
  (In all the above, the weaker adjective tends to sound more polite. In the following, there is no appreciable difference in register.)
e acclaim
f admire
g hilarious
h huge
i freezing

Vocabulary differentiation

1 a) collocation
2 b) collocation
3 c) meaning
4 a) collocation
5 b) meaning
6 c) collocation
7 a) collocation
8 c) collocation
9 a) collocation
10 b) collocation

Dictionary skills

1,2 and **3** Students' own answers. These will depend to some extent on the dictionary that is being used.

Collocation

achieve a result
tell a story
make time/changes/an apology/a promise
have a look/time/a break/a cold
break a promise
spend time
accept an apology
take a look/time/a break/a risk
run a risk
catch a cold

UNIT 2

LEXIS

Idioms and phrase using gesture

1 a greeting; finishing a deal; congratulating
  b warm greeting
  c parents leading children; couples showing affection
  d religious blessing
  e applauding
  f when you are upset
  g in class; at a large meeting to vote or show support for something
  h surrendering

2 a help
  b try, attempt
  c manual labourer
  d with long experience
  e come to the attention of people you don't want to know
  f get out of control
  g controlling, training

3 a when you need to pass on (secret) information
  b after an argument
  c when you want to show you don't care or can do nothing about something
  d when you are saying goodbye to someone who is a distance away from you, for example on a train
  e trying to say something to someone who can't hear you
  f when you find something surprising

4 Register

1 bloke = informal man = neither
2 exhort = formal encourage = neither
3 horrible = neither abhorrent = formal
4 lethargic = formal sleepy = informal
5 agree = neither comply = formal

Phrases with *give*

5 a give or take
  b gave rise to
  c give him hell
  d give my right arm
  e give way to
  f gives as good as she gets
  g give and take
  h Give me a ring
  i gave the game away
  j given (3 weeks) notice

6 1 c
  2 c
  3 d
  4 d
  5 d

GRAMMAR

The definite article

1 *Suggested answers:* the States, the Prime Minister, the equator, the centre of a circle

2 a morning paper - we don't know or it doesn't matter which one
the cinema/theatre - emphasis on the building rather than the activity of watching a film/play
the phone - in this sentence, the indefinite article would not normally be used
the train - it doesn't matter which: there is presumably a choice of several

3 They are examples of generic reference where a single example is used to stand for the whole class. i.e. the dog = dogs.

4 The *zero* article

Use of definite or indefinite articles usually indicates reference to the building or place of work. Use of zero article usually refers to the activity taking place in the buildings, or the function of the buildings.
e.g. 'going to prison' involves being a prisoner, 'going to the prison' involves visiting or working there.

5 Meals usually take zero article unless they become specific e.g. 'the lunch I had yesterday'. Occasionally they may take the indefinite article, usually when qualified by an adjective e.g. a light supper, a late lunch, a hearty breakfast.

6 *zero*: cancer, flu, diabetes, stomach ache
indefinite: a cold, a fever, a stomach ache, a headache, a temperature

7

1	a	10	a	19	-
2	-	11	a	20	a
3	-	12	the/a	21	the
4	the	13	-	22	a/the
5	the	14	a	23	the
6	a	15	the	24	the
7	the	16	the	25	the/-
8	the	17	a	26	the
9	the	18	the		

UNIT 3

LEXIS

Phrasal verbs: *on*

1 The following are approximate answers. Students should be aware of the difficulty of providing exact synonyms.
  a moved closer to
  b loved greatly to an extent which other people think is excessive
  c came to like after a period of time
  d betrayed (but the connotations are not as strong)
  e surreptitiously obtain information
  f quickly took and used (connotations of relief or glee)
  g return, the effects come back
  h provided generously
  i disapproved of (possible connotations of snobbery)
  j oblige me to eat
  k make you realise/emphasise

2 a make my dog attack
  b attacked (verbally) as a group
  c attack suddenly and without warning
  d attack from a crouching position

3 a They are all transitive.
  b 1h, j, k; 2a

4 a spurred on
  b going on
  c frowned on
  d catch on
  e carry on/soldier on
  f sew on

  – *spur on*, *rabbit on*, *soldier on* and *cotton on* are more colloquial than the alternatives

  – *sew on* is more specific than *put back on*

  – *look down on* perhaps suggests greater superiority than *frowned on*

Idioms with 'on'

  a on the house
  b on at me
  c on about
  d have (got) a lot on
  e on to a good thing
  f on and off
  g on the look out for
  h on to him

Collocation

  Suggested answers:
  a shoddy
  b odd
  c distinguished
  d cushy
  e backbreaking
  f promising
  g hopeless

Animal idioms

  1 a)
  2 b)
  3 b)
  4 c)
  5 c)
  6 b)
  7 c)
  8 b)
  9 b)
  10 b)

GRAMMAR

Participle and verbless clauses

1 *Suggested answers:*
  a Damp and dirty, the room smelt disgusting.
  b Having finished the chapter, I put the light out and sat in the dark, thinking.
  c Born in Maldon, he grew up in Oxfordshire.
  d Embarrassed, she offered an apology.
  e This book, disgusting and immoral, should be banned.
  f Being responsible for the damage, they should pay for the repairs.

  g Using a fine brush, the archaeologist brushed away earth from the skeleton.
  h By looking down on the blue-collar workers, the management creates tensions within the firm.

2 *Suggested answers* (many other possibilities exist):

> Dawn was breaking, ¹*cold and grey*, as I walked slowly and disconsolately home. ²*Thinking about it*, it had been a fruitless night's work: nothing had gone according to plan. ³*Tired and fed up*, I turned into my road, ⁴*not really looking where I was going*, and vowed never to make the same mistake again. If Jack had been more trustworthy things might have been better. But Jack, ⁵*never having done an honest day's work in his life*, was a worthless good-for-nothing, as I would have seen sooner if I'd kept my eyes open. ⁶*Arriving home*, I put my key in the lock. And then froze. ⁷*Faint but constant*, the sound of running water was coming from somewhere inside. I turned the key and burst in, ⁸*fearing the worst*. Water, ⁹*foul-smelling and filthy*, was everywhere and standing in the middle of the lake that used to be my living-room, ¹⁰*smilingly sheepishly*, was Jack.

3 c = a cleft sentence
  Suggested answers:
  a It was with Angela that I danced all night. (i.e. Not Ruth)
  b It was in Leeds that he went to university. (i.e. Not Cambridge)
  d It was to Glasgow that he walked all the way. (i.e. Not Edinburgh)
  e It was in 1978 that I left school. (i.e. Not 1977)
  f It was her pronunciation that I found the biggest barrier to communication. (i.e. Not her grammatical inaccuracy)

UNIT 4

GRAMMAR

Position of adjectives

1 a The following show the usual positions of the adjectives (some may be less commonly used in other positions).
   Adjectives before noun: eventual, cardiac, occasional, existing, adoring.
   Adjectives after link verb: aware, ready, reminiscent, content, alone, asleep, alive, ill, fond, glad, unable.

  b Students' own answers

2 Common collocations are:
   fall asleep, feel ill, be/feel alone, be/feel glad, be aware of, reminiscent of, existing arrangements, adoring wife/husband, be fond of, be/feel content.

3 *Suggested answers:*
  a I'm afraid it's bound to happen that way.
  b I'd be willing to do it for you if you like.

c I am loath to continue with this for much longer.
d The situation is liable to escalate out of control.
e I am inclined to agree with you.
f I think you should be prepared to be disappointed.

4 a They express moods or feelings.
  b aware *of*
     surprised *at/about + noun*
     anxious *about + noun*
            to + verb
     certain *of*
            to + verb
     upset *about*
     sure *of/about + noun*
            to + verb
     afraid *of + noun*
            to + verb
     worried *about*
     frightened *of + noun*
              to + verb
     sorry *about*
            to + verb
     sad *to + verb*
     confident *of*

LEXIS

Adjectives

1 a scant
  b knotty
  c searing
  d flagrant
  e belated
  f thankless
  g fleeting
  h paltry
  i chequered
  j commanding

2 a 3 labour-saving device
  b 11 far-reaching consequences
  c 5 low-cut dress
  d 13 long-standing agreement
  e 1 second-class citizen
  f 2 last-minute change of plan
  g 9 one-sided argument
  h 12 all-out attack
  i 10 deep-seated resentment
  j 6 interest-free credit
  k 8 face-saving formula
  l 7 odds-on favourite
  m 4 strong-arm tactics

3 *Suggested answers:*
prime minister designate – one who had been elected
but has not yet taken office
president elect – as above

evil incarnate – made real/in a living form
ice-cream galore – large quantities of something

4 Students own answers. (Learner Training question.)

GRAMMAR

As

1 a indicating simultaneity
  b indicating comparison
  c = *because*
  d = *though*, to indicate something is true but does not affect the truth of your main point
  e = *like*, in the same way
  f = *playing*. A standard expression possibly derived from the meaning of *like*
  g introduces a clause which describes similarity.

2 a as such
  b as if/as though
  c such as
  d as opposed to
  e as long as
  f as good as
  g so as to
  h As for

UNIT 5

GRAMMAR

Relative clauses

1 *Suggested answers:*

> It was on Sunday that my great aunt Edith, [1]*who(m) we hadn't seen for 5 years*, came to stay. She was a formidable lady [2]*who had been a teacher all her life* and terrified both my sister and me, [3]*who were only about seven or eight at the time*. Despite the fact that she was approaching her 90th birthday, [4]*which she intended to totally ignore*, she showed no sign of infirmity, either mental or physical. At eight o'clock in the evening, [5]*when we normally have our evening meal*, she announced that she was going for a walk down the lane [6]*which went past the back of the house*. My sister and I followed her, hiding behind the trees [7]*which lined either side of the lane*. Three quarters of an hour later, great aunt Edith, [8]*who showed no signs of tiredness*, finally returned and announced that she was hungry now.

2 a Sarah, whose birthday is in July, is my niece.
  b Her friends who/that remembered it bought her a present.
  c The boy you saw her with is her brother, Barry.
  d The only car I've ever had is a Rover.
  e Trams, which used to be in most English cities, are now found in very few.
  f I had a student who/that was a bus driver in Rome, where he lived.

3 a informal (that)
   b formal (for whom)
   c formal (in which)
   d informal (no relative pronoun, position of *in*)
   e formal (to whom)
   f informal (no relative pronoun, position of *to*)

4 a The road along which the man ran was long and straight.
   b The small town I was born in (in which I was born) has grown enormously.
   c The man I borrowed the book from has asked for it back.
   d There is no way in which this disease can be prevented from spreading.
   e This language is used by different cultures, which all use it differently.

LEXIS

I Phrasal verbs: 'Up'

   1 All deal with the concept of *approaching*. They do not fit easily into the categories.
   2 They all deal with the concept of *creating*. They may also be related to *increasing* in the idea of building up something from nothing.
   3 They deal with the concept of *separating*. The meaning is connected to completion. *'Up'* acts as an intensifier.
   4 They all deal with the concept of *appearing*. Metaphorically, they could be related to the literal meaning of *'up'*: if you turn a card up, you literally move its position so that the face lies upwards, not downwards. Its value therefore appears.

Adjectives and prepositions

2 resistant to   heedless of   mindful of
   conversant with   fraught with   lacking in
   riddled with   reminiscent of   similar to
   averse to   devoted to   susceptible to

3 Collocation

   a heedless of, fraught with, mindful of,
   b resistant to, susceptible to
   c riddled with
   d devoted to
   e lacking in
   f mindful of

4 Collocation: *Drive*

   a the main influence
   b windy conditions with very heavy rain
   c make one want to drink alcohol heavily
   d exasperates me
   e a tough negotiator
   f made the point emphatically
   g beaten in the argument
   h What is the point you are trying to make? (getting at?)

5 Verbs of movement

   skid, crawl, swerve, brake, draw up, cut in, hurtle, overtake, pull out, spin – used to describe the movement of a car
   soar – a bird flying high above
   freewheel – a cyclist coming down a hill
   gallop – a horse moving very quickly
   flow -- the movement of a river
   take off – an aeroplane leaving the ground
   plunge – something/someone diving in the water
   rush – a person moving quickly because they are in a hurry
   stroll – a person walking at a leisurely pace
   drift – something carried away by water
   glide – the movement of a plane with no engine
   spin – the movement of a wheel or something rotating

Unit 6

GRAMMAR

The passive

Suggested answers:

   a Traveller's Cheques (are) not accepted.
   b Children under 16 (are) not allowed in this bar.
   c She was sentenced to three years' detention.
   d It has been suggested that the Governor may be considering withdrawing from the Presidential race.
   e It has been claimed that Miss America is the victim of blackmail.
   f If the current economic decline continues it won't be long before Great Britain is overtaken by other European countries in terms of industrial output.
   g A teenage joyrider was being treated in hospital last night, after he crashed into four cars and injured four people.

LEXIS

Newspaper phrases

These answers are suggested only. Other possibilities may be equally valid.

   a The city council is supporting proposals to change constituency boundaries in the city.
   b Traffic/Street lights have again been requested following a fatal accident.
   c Tax demands have been reduced in order to meet a certain limit.
   d People living in Kidlington are likely to have to pay an extra 100% tax in order to prevent an economic crisis.
   e A Labour councillor has publicly requested more money for the police following recent attacks on old people.

f Companies are being strongly encouraged to find ways to improve their standards (of health and safety) as part of the European Year of Health and Safety.

g A man and a woman are demanding that the number of cars outside their house should be limited.

h Boat owners who moor their boats at a disputed place on the River Thames could be evicted because of an insurance problem.

i The Prime Minister promised yesterday to totally change public services in the 1990s.

j It was announced last night that a lord who ran away (from the police?) called Lord Moynihan secretly came back to Britain months before he died.

Reporting with nouns

a concessions
b stipulation
c notification
d allegations
e denial
f implications
g revelations
h objection(s)

News broadcast

(see transcript on page 171)

Collocation

1 gratefully *acknowledge*
   admit/concede defeat
   firmly *believe/deny/maintain*
   categorically *deny*
   stubbornly *maintain*
   violently *object*
   remark in passing
   clearly *state/stipulate*
   declare war
   strongly *deny/maintain/object*

2 a scathing *remark/report*
   to drop *a hint*
   to file *a report*
   an urgent *request/warning*
   an uncontrollable *urge*
   a casual *remark*

3 report/remark/insistence/declaration/comment

UNIT 7

GRAMMAR

Continuous aspect

State verbs

1 The following are not possible or extremely unlikely:
   e, h, i, j, k

2 a opened/saw/was standing/was crying/didn't seem/was starting

   b have often wondered/found/had been going on/noticed/had fallen/was starting

   c are doing/cried/looked/was trying/have been making/was trying

3 *Suggested answers:*
   a The speaker was interrupted when listening the first time. This could be an apologetic request for a repetition.

   b Polite intervention in a formal meeting. Depending on the tone adopted and the relative status of the two people, it could be made to sound respectful or patronising.

   c A fairly formal direct request for the opinions e.g. from a chairman of a meeting to a participant. 'I was wondering. . .' would soften the request and make it easier for the listener to make an excuse for not offering them.

   d A fairly strong invitation for the listener to admit that he/she didn't mean it. 'I was hoping . . .' suggests that the speaker has almost given up hope of the listener changing his/her mind.

4 Students' own answers.

LEXIS

1 Facial expressions

smirk = self-satisfaction, cruel amusement
frown = disagreement, puzzlement
grin = happiness
glare = anger
beam = extreme happiness
pout = sulking
grimace = distaste
scowl = displeasure
sneer = contempt

2 a Adjectives describing character

Positive:
genial chirpy irrepressible jovial considerate

Negative:
exasperating embittered frivolous gloomy sulky smug conceited

b and c Students' own answers

3 Collocation

a recall
b welcomed
c admitted, denied
d destroying
e retreat
f examined
g eliminate
h explained

4 *Wish, Hope and Want*

a hope
b hope
c wish
d wishes
e wish
f want

185

g hope

h wish

i want

j hope

k want

5 Sounds

Suggested answers:

a rattle: the wind rattles the shutters

hiss: a snake

rustle: leaves moving in the wind

peal: bells

b Students' own answers.

UNIT 8

LEXIS

1 Phrasal verbs: *Down*

a it indicates a lower position

b example: turn down, lie down, water down

2 Phrasal verbs: *Back*

a restraining, keeping in position

b example: draw back, sit back, put back

c returning to the original position: give back, get back, call back, spring back

returning a favour or action: phone back, write back, talk back

belonging to the past: look back, flash back

Dictionary work

3 irresolute

4 *Domineer* is stronger than *dominate*, with negative connotations.

Dictate is to give orders - it involves saying or telling. (It also has other meanings.)

Conquer is the act of putting yourself in the dominant position, usually through fighting.

Influence has the most positive connotations. You can influence people without having power over them.

5 Outraged (strongest), indignant, reproachful

6 *Zealous* is the strongest.

keen on

enthusiastic about

dedicated to

GRAMMAR

Conditional clauses

1 *Suggested answers:*

d *Situation:* Said to an exhausted person.

Meaning: If you take my advice. . . (UNREAL)

e *Situation:* Said to someone impatiently waiting for the results of a meeting.

Meaning: I don't know if they have finished but it's pointless asking because if they have they'll tell us soon. (REAL)

f *Situation:* Company director responding to complaints about department efficiency.

Meaning: You didn't tell me and it's too late now. (UNREAL)

g *Situation:* Teachers complaining about unruly pupils.

Meaning: They obviously aren't older. (UNREAL)

h *Situation:* Host to guest at a party.

Meaning: If you really are leaving, if you insist on it. . . (REAL)

i *Situation:* Complaining about noisy audience in the theatre.

Meaning: They did talk all the time. (UNREAL)

j *Situation:* Grumpy old lady on a crowded bus.

Meaning: You are inconsiderate. (UNREAL)

k *Situation:* Host at a party to guest who is wondering where her coat is.

Meaning: You are not leaving so don't worry about it: I'll get it for you when you need it and not before. (UNREAL)

l *Situation:* Person reminiscing about the teachers when she was at school.

Meaning: Sometimes they did talk all the time and when they did. . . (REAL)

m *Situation:* Passing a message on.

Meaning: It is possible you you will see her. (REAL)

2 1 a) and b)

2 a) and b)

3 b)

4 a) and b)

5 a)

6 a) and b)

7 a) and b)

8 a) and b)

9 b)

10 b)

UNIT 9

1 Advertising vocabulary

a product range

b market

c manipulation

d slogan

e Retailers

f Indoctrination

g consumers

h hoardings

2 Word formation

a hostility
b manipulating
c contemptible
d consumption
e statutory
f excessive

3 **a** to shed/cast light on = something which helps you understand

to see the light = to understand (especially in a religious sense)

something has come to light = something has been disclosed/discovered

She's a guiding light = somebody people follow as an influence

She wanted to see her name in lights = in theatre advertisements as an actress

b *Verbs:* get into, settle, rebut, break off, clinch, refute, *Adjectives:* heated, cogent, valid, irrefutable, convincing, compelling, bitter, spurious, tenuous, airtight, sound, rational

Link phrases

4 Students' own answers.

5 **a** It will be seen from this that. . . ; Thus. . .

b While conceding/admitting that. . .
It is also the case that. . .
It is nevertheless true that. . .
There is no question of. . .
It could be pointed out that. . .
It could be argued that. . .

c In defence of this/itself. . .
It should not be forgotten that. . .

6 Reference nouns

Suggested answers:

a allegation, claim, retort
b declaration, delusion, boast, claim
c explanation, pronouncement
d digression
e declaration, insight, vision, pronouncement
f viewpoint, declaration, contention, observation, remark
g boast
h viewpoint, view, assertion, contention, position
i pronouncement, revelation, declaration
j excuse, explanation, declaration

GRAMMAR

So, such, this, that, these, those

Suggested answers:

a this

b that
c This
d so
e So
f Such
g those
h these
i So
j These

Punctuation: Apostrophes

a It's a strange sort of advertisement. Its message seems somewhat obscure at first until you notice what's going on in the background of the picture.

b Several of the students' complaints centred on the timetable. Its complexities made it practically impossible to follow.

c Stephen Jones' mathematics tutor was also a leading novelist.

d Is that your bag or hers? Perhaps it's Anne's.

e One of the committee's resolutions was passed after the chairman's intervention.

Reflexive pronouns

Suggested answers:

d I'm not particularly fond of his music myself but I know a lot of people who are.

f She had done all the work herself.

g He insisted on giving the present to Carolyn himself and not leaving it for her to pick up.

UNIT 10

LEXIS

1 *Suggested answers:*

a deeply hurt
b seriously injured
c greatly exaggerated
d really/deeply sorry
e totally/radically redesigned
f completely/hopelessly lost
g eminently successful
h blindingly obvious

2 openly hostile
blissfully ignorant
virtually impossible
dimly lit
securely locked
highly successful
deeply religious
strikingly beautiful

3 Verb/noun collocation

Suggested answers:

a arrriving
b going at it
c move
d fall for something/someone
e accept (no)
f risk
g talk
h search
i go to

4 Synonymy

Students should use an English/English dictionary.

5 Idiomatic intensifiers

1 bone
2 freezing
3 dog
4 raving
5 dirt
6 crystal

6 1b) 2b) 3a) 4b) 5c) 6a)

GRAMMAR

Perfect aspect

1 a bought, have only listened
  b have just read, Have you heard
  c has been
  d has often been criticised
  e have always felt/always feel, have proved
  f have lost, started
  g fell, has remained
  h haven't been, gave
  i saw, have been interested
  j has worked, has made

2 The perfect continuous

a I've been writing a letter to the bank manager.

= Emphasis on the action. Uncertain whether the letter is finished.

I've written a letter to the bank manager.

= Completed action. Emphasis on the result.

b I'd been walking for nearly two hours when I finally reached the garage.

= Emphasis on the effort of walking as opposed to the arriving.

I'd walked for nearly two hours when I finally reached the garage.

= The arriving is more important than in the above example.

c The English team have been playing well this season.

= Emphasis on the continuity of the playing.

The English team has played well this season.

= Up to now. Emphasis on the result: they're well placed in the World Cup qualifying rounds.

d How have you been getting on?

= Recently. Emphasis on (continuous/repeated) action.

How have you got on? = in a specific, completed task.

e I've been living in Banbury for the last few months. = temporarily

I've lived in Banbury for the last few months. = I've got a house there.

f It's been snowing overnight.

= Emphasis on action of snowing.

It's snowed overnight.

= Emphasis on result: the ground is covered in snow.

g Sharon's been spending all her money on John again.

= Progressive suggests this is an often repeated action in the view of the speaker.

Sharon's spent all her money on John again.

= Emphasis on the result: she has no money left.

h What have you been doing?

= Interest in the activity. (You've got mud all over your face.)

What have you done?

= More interest in the result. (You're standing next to a dead body with a knife in your hand.)

i I've just been watching a rather strange programme.

= Emphasis on watching. The programme may not have finished.

I've just watched a rather strange programme.

= Completed action.

j Who's drunk my coffee?

= Completed action: the result is I have no coffee left.

Who's been drinking my coffee?

= Interest in the action. There may be some coffee left.

UNIT 11

LEXIS

1 Medical vocabulary

1 infection
2 virus
3 outbreaks
4 epidemics
5 antibodies
6 immunity
7 symptoms
8 chills
9 fatigue
10 brought on
11 illness
12 common cold
13 debilitating
14 cough
15 sore
16 subside
17 respiratory

2 Medical quiz

1 typhoid, cholera, small pox, hepatitis, malaria (by tablet)
2 anaesthetic
3 malaria
4 carcinogen
5 tuberculosis
6 The treatment of illness by sticking the ends of special needles into a person's body at particular pressure points.
7 German measles
8 cholera
9 physiotherapist
10 A person who treats illness by the manipulation of the spine and other areas.

3 Discourse markers

Students' own answers.

4 *Suggested answers:*

It is widely believed that medical science has been gradually and systematically reducing civilisation's diseases. People believe that ignorance and superstition combined to allow epidemics like the medieval plagues to take place. *However*, during the 19th and 20th centuries scientists finally managed to discover what caused infectious diseases and begin to cure them with drugs and immunisation. *Above all*, improved technology and advances in anaesthesia enabled surgeons to carry out sophisticated operations while penicillin and antibiotics helped complete the advance. *And yet* some people disagree. They point out that more credit ought to be given to social reformers who campaigned for purer water, better sewage disposal so as to improve living standards. The drugs and antibiotics merely speeded up the process. *Although* their contribution was valuable, it did not lower the level of disease in general. *On the contrary*, increasing numbers of people depend on drugs and doctors for meeting the ordinary problems of everyday life.

5 Students should refer to an English/English dictionary to check their answers.

GRAMMAR

Focus

1 *Suggested answers:*

a Rarely do I take the car into town.
It is rare that I take the car into town.
Taking the car into town is rare for me.

b What I find particularly annoying is the loud music from next door.
Particularly annoying, I find, is the loud music from next door.
The loud music from next door is what I find particularly annoying.

c Every weekend, Mark takes his children out.
Mark's children are taken out every weekend by him.
What Mark does every weekend is take his children out.

d What I want to do is fix the car before we go away next week.
Before we go away next week, I want to fix the car.
Fix the car before we go away next week is what I want to do.

2 *Suggested answers:*

a Progress continued throughout the century. By the end of it, the basics of human anatomy were established.

b Surgery remained at a very primitive level. Rather limited also, was pathology. Things didn't begin to improve until the discoveries of bacteriologists. (The original word order is also acceptable.)

c (The original word order is probably the best.)

d He was mean, cruel and selfish. His lack of hygiene I shall ignore.

e (The original word order is probably the best.)

f 'Now watch carefully. What I'm going to do is make a small incision here, avoiding any major blood vessels.' (The original word order is also acceptable, but students should note the frequency of cleft sentences when explaining procedures.)

UNIT 12

LEXIS

Dependent prepositions

1
a	on	f	to
b	to	g	to
c	from	h	to
d	in	i	to
e	into	j	to

2
a	for	f	from
b	of	g	on
c	on	h	with
d	from	i	to
e	on	j	in

3 hint at   contend with   care for/about   clamour for   refer to   yearn for   react to   spy on   long to/for   suffer from   shrink from   resort to   invest in   opt for   grapple with   listen to   wallow in   sympathise with

GRAMMAR

Modal Verbs

1 *Suggested answers:*

a I could have run very fast when I was young.
b I may have misunderstoood her point.
c You should have offered an immediate apology.
d Every morning I would go for a swim in the sea before breakfast.
e She wouldn't accept my offer without certain preconditions.

f   We couldn't leave the school grounds during morning break.

g   He couldn't have got there so soon.

h   It must have been my mother.

i   You should have told me.

j   He couldn't be an authoritarian figure.

2   *Suggested answers:*

b   Something must have happened.

c   She must have forgotten.

d   He must have been keeping it secret.

e   He must have gone on holiday.

f   They may have set off late.

g   They could not have been very busy.

h   They must have changed their mind.

i   I must have done something to offend her.

j   She must have gone to bed late.

3   *Suggested answers:*

a   there might have been an accident.

b   Somebody must have told her

c   he will have read it by now.

d   She would have driven off without the money

e   I would agree to go and give lectures

LEXIS

Phrases with *get*

1   *Suggested answers:*

a   *recovered:* less informal

b   *They married:* unusual, more formal

c   *beat me:* equally informal but is not strictly the same thing as it implies a definite conclusion to the argument

d   *grasp:* different connotation

e   *be dismissed/sacked:* as with b above, '*get*' + noun is more common than the verb form

f   *receive:* more formal

g   (no strictly accurate alternative)

h   *understand:* though the connotation is more to do with not seeing why the joke is funny

i   *annoys me:* a less informal alternative, though with some different connotations

j   *making progress:* less informal

k   *to cross the river:* similar to b and e above,

l   *go to, get to:* has connotations of actually arriving

m   *achieves what she wants:* a less idiomatic alternative

n   (no natural sounding alternative)

2   Students' own answers

Phrasal verbs: *away*

3 and 4   Students' own answers

5   *Suggested answers:*
(there may be some overlap between meanings a and b)

a   keep away, take away, break away, run away, give away, blow away

b   pack away, boil away, throw away, wash away, put away, die away, pine away

c   work away, talk away, blaze away

6   *Suggested answers:*

a   continuous activity

b   lessening or disappearance

c   lessening or disappearance

d   lessening or disappearance

e   distance or separation

f   distance or separation

UNIT 13

LEXIS

Discourse markers

A

1   a   *Suggested answers:*
oddly   interestingly   at least   strangely   true curiously   mercifully   incredibly etc.

b   Students' own answers

2   a   All the phrases qualify the statement by showing that you are not totally committed to the truth of it.

b   Students' own answers

B

1   *To change the subject:*
now then   by the way   well now   actually incidentally   anyhow

To emphasise:
at all   really   without exception   positively   actually to say the least   surely   whatsoever   indeed

Both: actually
Example:
Actually, that reminds me. I saw John today.
I know you don't believe me, but that's what happened, actually.

2   a   at all, whatsoever

b   Surely

c   *Suggested answers:*
now then, look

d   *Suggested answers:*
1   indeed
2   positively
3   really
4   By the way
5   at all

GRAMMAR
Complex sentences

Example answers:

a As the sun began to rise from behind the mountain peaks, *the* slightly built young *girl,* dressed in an extraordinary combination of men's trousers and peasant smock, *ran* pell mell down the road *away from* the *home* from which, even now, the first few flames were beginning to show.

b Although he died soon after she was born, all the reports suggest that *her father,* who had reached fatherhood unusually late in life, *was a taciturn* and even a bad tempered *man.*

c According to many authorities involved in the study of the extended family, *grandparents,* and indeed aunts, uncles, cousins, brothers, sisters and so on, *are* all *crucial* factors *in the upbringing of children.*

LEXIS

Slang and idioms

1 *Clever:* a, b, f, g, h, i
  Stupid: c, d, e, j, k, l

2 *Approval:* a, b, e
  Disapproval: c, d, f, g

3 a deal with the basics
  b go away
  c lose one's temper
  d be in a bad mood
  e teasing
  f very close friends
  g die
  h avoid
  i stop work
  j mad

UNIT 14

LEXIS

1 a assembly line
  b boom
  c by-product
  d merger
  e audit
  f brand name
  g overhead(s)
  h break even
  i consignment
  j parent company
  k backlog
  l unique selling point
  m fixed assets

2 a introductory offer
  b take-over bid
  c private enterprise
  d early retirement
  e share index
  f limited liability
  g cash flow
  h starting salary
  i retail chain
  j pretax profits

3 a Public limited company. Used at the end of a public limited company's name e.g. Swaseby Engineering plc. to indicate its legal status.
  b Corporation (U.S.), or Company (G.B.). Used at the end of a company's name.
  c carbon copies. Used at the end of a business letter to indicate that a copy is being sent to another person e.g. cc S. Jones.
  d enclosure(s). Used at the end of a business letter to list documents enclosed in the same envelope.
  e account. Used before a (bank) account number e.g. a/c 472987.
  f miscellaneous. Used mainly in lists.
  g per annum. Used especially when stating a salary or rent, e.g. £12,800 p.a. .
  h Managing Director
  i cost, insurance, freight. Used when listing costs of a product.
  j Public Relations
  k Private Limited Company (G.B.) or Incorporated (U.S.). Used at the end of a company's name to indicate its legal status.
  l received. Used to indicate receipt of goods.
  m id est (Latin) = that is. Commonly used to explain a point more fully: *This should be referred to the highest level i.e. the Managing Director.*
  n compare. Used to introduce a reference to something similar. Often used in footnotes to academic books.

GRAMMAR

Future forms

1 b)
2 b)
3 a)
4 a) (the other two are also possible though less likely)
5 c) (or b)
6 a)
7 a)
8 b)
9 a)
10 b)